Designing Team-Based Organizations

Susan Albers Mohrman
Susan G. Cohen
Allan M. Mohrman, Jr.

Designing
Team-Based
Organizations

. . . .

New Forms for Knowledge Work

Jossey-Bass Publishers
San Francisco

◆ ◆ ◆ ◆ ◆ ◆ ◆ ◆ ◆ ◆ ◆ ◆ ◆ ◆ ◆

Substantial discounts on bulk quantities of Jossey-Bass books are available to corporations, professional associations, and other organizations. For details and discount information, contact the special sales department at Jossey-Bass Inc., Publishers. (415) 433–1740; Fax (800) 605–2665.

For sales outside the United States, please contact your local Paramount Publishing International Office.

Library of Congress Cataloging-in-Publication Data

Mohrman, Susan Albers.
    Designing team-based organizations: new forms for knowledge work/Susan Albers Mohrman, Susan G. Cohen, Allan M. Mohrman, Jr.—1st ed.
      p. cm.—(The Jossey-Bass management series)
    "Reflects four years of research . . . conducted largely at the Center for Effective Organizations at the University of Southern California"—Pref.
    Includes bibliographical references (p.   ) and index.
    ISBN 0-7879-0080-X
    1. Work groups. 2. Organizational effectiveness. I. Cohen, Susan G. II. Mohrman, Allan M. III. University of Southern California. Center for Effective Organizations. IV. Series.
    HD66M653   1995   95-3732
    658.4'02—dc20

FIRST EDITION
HB Printing 10 9 8 7 6 5 4 3 2 1

The Jossey-Bass
Management Series

Contents

. . . .

List of Tables, Figures, and Exhibits

Tables

Figures

Exhibits

Preface

Designing Team-Based Organizations describes how to build a team-based organization: an organization in which teams are the performing units. We take an organizational design perspective and examine how to put together the components of this new organizational form. We argue that a team-based organization differs in fundamental ways from the traditional, bureaucratic model (with its lines and boxes, departments, individual jobs, and chains of command).

Creating a team-based organization differs from simply using teams; it requires the ultimate redesign of the entire organization. The transition entails multiple years of learning and iteration. The product is a dynamic, laterally oriented system in which teams and business units, in shifting configuration, enact an organizational strategy for succeeding in an increasingly demanding environment.

This book reflects four years of research examining teams in knowledge-work settings and many more years of research examining teams in general. The research was conducted largely at the Center for Effective Organizations at the University of Southern California and was made possible by the many organizations that sponsor that research center and find our products useful. This book itself is a response to a plea from the companies we studied to capture the emerging design model in a form that provides a useful guide for those making the difficult transition to a team-based organization.

Our research set out to see how teams in knowledge-work settings differ from those in production settings. Along the way, we discovered that work falls along a continuum from routine to nonroutine and that teams assume a variety of forms in all settings. Routine work is becoming automated; increasingly, all the work that remains is knowledge work. Our examination of knowledge-work settings (for example, research and development, sales and service, and new product development) made salient the fact that most organizations employing teams have a network of connected teams and that the effectiveness of teams cannot be understood apart from the organizational context in which they are embedded. This led us to look at the team-based organization as a system and to examine how the organization has to be designed if teams are its performing units.

This book is not primarily about teams. It is about team-based organizations. In a sense, it is a second-generation team book. It is not a persuasive book designed to extol the potential of teams and to convince managers that teams are the way to go. Rather, it is intended for managers whose organizations have gone the team route and who are struggling, having discovered that they are dealing with a complex transformation—managers who believe in the potential of the team-based organization and are staying the course. This book asks the reader to roll up his or her sleeves and grapple with what is required to create a team-based organization that works.

Our effort builds on a rich heritage. We are indebted to the work of sociotechnical theorists such as Eric Trist, William Pasmore, and Thomas Cummings. In addition, we rely extensively on the employee involvement framework articulated by Edward Lawler, and we were cognizant, in the design of our research, of the group effectiveness model of J. Richard Hackman. Primarily, however, we are indebted to our colleague Jay Galbraith. We borrowed liberally from his portrayal of organizations as designable entities and his fundamental concept of organizations as information-processing entities.

In stressing the *design* of team-based organizations, we may offend those who are more concerned with team dynamics. This book may seem overly rational to those readers. Although we take very seriously the human element of moving to a new way of doing business and the resistance that permeates all organizations embarked on this transition (and we allude to and occasionally discuss that human element), the book is fundamentally a design book. There are others who have dealt well with dynamics issues (such as leadership, resistance to change, team stages, and the psychodynamics of teams). We are indebted to them, because they help us know that design is not the only focus required of those attempting to effect a transition to team-based organizations.

We have taken a design perspective because of our belief that creating team-based organizations is not simply an issue of designating teams and teaching team-oriented behaviors. Teams violate the logic of the design of a bureaucratic, hierarchical, segmented organization. If the organization is not redesigned with a new logic, management can deal with dynamics and resistance to the point of utter exhaustion and cynicism and still not effect change in the way people behave. The traditional organization often chews up teams and spits them out.

We had the good fortune to deal with pioneering companies that were working through the difficult transition to teams and experiencing the demanding learning process. They had neither road map nor guide. This book is our attempt to document their learnings in a systematic design framework and to provide a useful road map for other organizations either immersed in this transition or about to embark on it.

Audience

Designing Team-Based Organizations is a practical design guide that embodies both theory and empirical research. It is not an introduction to teams, nor is it a book about how to make teams more effective. Our research suggests that teams are more effective if they are well designed and if the organization is designed to support them.

This is not an advocacy book; we do not believe that team-based organizations fit everywhere. This book is aimed at scholars, managers, and consultants who have an interest in organizational design—particularly in the design of organizations where teams conduct work. It can be used, for example, by design teams to guide the redesign of organizations that are implementing teams. It can be used by top management to understand the nature of the transition that is required. Consultants may find it useful in helping organizations get beyond the simplistic notion that establishing teams is enough to ensure collective, integrated task accomplishment. Finally, our hope is that *Designing Team-Based Organizations* extends the organizational design literature and that scholars will find it useful for this reason.

Overview of Contents

In *Designing Team-Based Organizations*, we present a research-based design model that systematically identifies the design choices that an organization needs to make to derive competitive advantages from being team based.

Part One addresses the challenges involved in organizing team-based settings—especially those settings that perform knowledge work. The book begins by describing how and why the use of teams and teaming mechanisms to integrate laterally has increased dramatically in recent years in response to competitive pressures.

Chapter One builds on the information-processing design framework to assert that teams are required for lateral integration and that the nature of knowledge work places particular demands on the design of teams. We introduce the research study of 203 teams in 11 companies that provides the foundation for this book, and we point out that team effectiveness depends on the design of the organizational context. In this chapter, we also present a change framework that an organization can use to design itself as a team-based organization, and we provide an overview of the learning that is required.

Chapter Two describes the broad contours of a team-based organization. We define teams as "groups of individuals who work together to develop products or deliver services for which they are mutually accountable," and we present a typology of teams. We depict a team-based organization in which teams are the performing units embedded in larger business units and make the point that authority in a team-based organization is not based on the level of position, as it is in a bureaucracy. The core team dynamic in knowledge-work settings revolves around the achievement of shared understanding within and across teams and levels. An effectiveness model is presented that will guide the unfolding of the design model in the book.

Part Two (Chapters Three through Seven) presents the organizational design model that is the core of the book.

Chapter Three provides a framework for identifying work teams based on process analysis (which examines the work itself), deliberations analysis (which looks at the key issues and trade-offs that need to be resolved), and task interdependence analysis. We apply this framework for the design of teams to three cases derived from our study: a defense program that designs navigational systems, a regional customer-service field organization that sells and services inventory control and security systems, and the consumer electronics division of a high-technology firm. In each case, the core work team is not able to contain all the work interdependencies; other integrating mechanisms are necessary.

Chapter Four presents the second step in the design model: devising additional integrating mechanisms that may be required to fully integrate work in complex knowledge-work settings. We describe a variety of mechanisms to integrate across interdependent teams and business units, including liaison roles, overlapping membership, cross-team teams (also called simply cross-teams), management teams, representative integrating teams, and individual integrating roles, and we show how these mechanisms are used in the three company cases.

Chapter Five describes the third step in the design framework:

the determination of appropriate management and leadership roles. We point out that formal managerial or team leader roles need to be established whenever the information-processing demands exceed the capacity of the team to handle them informally. We encourage organizations to put as many self-management functions as possible into the teams, to involve the teams in determining how various leadership tasks will be performed, to use lateral rather than hierarchical cross-team integration, and to create management roles to link work teams to the larger organization and make large-scope decisions. We describe the roles of team leaders, team managers, functional managers, and management teams in the new team-based setting.

Chapter Six provides the fourth step in the design framework: formulating the critical integration processes of direction setting, communication, and decision making. Direction setting must make clear the organization's priorities and criteria so that teams can make appropriate trade-offs; thus management must make sure that clear strategies are developed, communicated, and broadly understood and that goals are aligned at all levels. Information must be widely shared in the team-based organization, and channels of communication may need to be formalized to prevent information slippages from taking place. Timely and effective decision making depends upon clearly defined decision-making roles and responsibilities and the use of systematic decision-making processes.

Chapter Seven provides the fifth and final step: the design of performance management practices, which consist of a cycle of activities including defining the work, developing the contributors, reviewing performance, and rewarding performance. In a team-based organization, performance management is conducted with performing units at multiple systemic levels—the corporation, the business unit, and the team—and individual performance management takes place in a collective context. Performance management actively involves peers, customers, and managers, who are legitimate stakeholders in that performance, and it balances their competing perspectives and needs.

Part Three is concerned with the broader context of the change to the team-based organization. It synthesizes key themes that cut across the design chapters.

Chapter Eight provides an overview of the responsibilities of work teams and management teams in a team-based organization. The executive management team is responsible for the macrodesign of the team-based organization. Business-unit management oversees the configuration of teams and orchestrates the management of their performance. We make the point that management teams need to model open and participative behaviors in order for norms of multidirectional influence to be established. Team-based organizations often place demands on team members and managers that necessitate extensive skill development, and this development must be provided for.

Chapter Nine revisits the concept of empowerment. It contrasts our definition of empowerment—"the capability to make a difference in the attainment of individual, team, and organizational goals"—with the misconceptions that have emerged in many organizations. We make the point that developing an empowered team-based organization takes time, work, and learning.

Chapter Ten discusses the organizational and human resource systems that are needed to support the team-based organization. These systems enable common processes that integrate the organization and help it perform. We highlight the importance of the new information infrastructure for supporting team-based work. We enumerate the key issues to consider in using formal systems to drive processes, such as the dynamic nature of team environments and the tendency of systems to overly bureaucratize organizations. We make the point that, because the logic of many organizational systems is inconsistent with that of the team-based organization, temporary adaptations may need to be made while systems are being developed and changed. Cross-functional teams are advocated for the design and maintenance of the systems.

Chapter Eleven deals with implementation of team organizations. We emphasize that the transition to teams entails change that pervades all aspects of organizational functioning and involves fundamental changes in how people understand the organization and their role in it. We point out that not all organizational changes can be made simultaneously, and we propose a road map and a sequence. The implementation of a team-based organization is depicted as a learning process, and top-management leadership is stressed.

In Chapter Twelve, which concludes the book, we suggest that the changes people need to make to be successful in the team-based organization are fundamental, and we identify what needs to be learned in the future to create conditions for success. We point out that organizational practice is preceding theory and that new knowledge will be developed from the study of this emerging organizational form.

Acknowledgments

This book is the product of four years of collaboration by the three authors on this endeavor specifically and of many more years of collaboration with each other and many other colleagues at the Center for Effective Organizations (CEO). Edward Lawler deserves special mention not only because of his rich intellectual heritage and enriching collegiality but also because he has created the conditions at CEO for collaborative intellectual work. Gerald Ledford and Jay Galbraith have also been important in helping us develop our ideas over the years. Gerry's comments on an earlier draft of the book were quite helpful. Ann Feyerherm, a colleague during the first phase of the study, was a pleasure to work with and full of insight. The Graduate School of Business at the University of Southern California has provided a supportive environment for the kind of work we do.

The corporate sponsors of the Center for Effective Organizations make it possible to pursue the kinds of research that are reflected in this book. Our research model is one of collaboration with companies to explore mutually interesting issues. We are especially grateful and indebted to those companies that participated in this study:

Digital Equipment, General Mills, Hewlett-Packard, Honeywell, Hughes, IBM, Pacific Bell, Pfizer, Pratt & Whitney, Texas Instruments, and Xerox. In each of these companies, we had contact people who helped with the logistics of the study and many managers and employees who took the time to respond to interviews and fill out surveys. We owe special thanks to a number of individuals in these companies who were strong supporters and close colleagues in the research. Elaine Millam from Honeywell, Sue Freedman from Texas Instruments, and Stu Winby from Hewlett-Packard were terrific sounding boards, and they found ways for us to get ongoing feedback from members of their organizations. Andy Nix from Pratt & Whitney provided thoughtful feedback on our earlier draft and has been a rich source of understanding of the change dynamics underlying the creation of a team-based organization. Texas Instruments and Honeywell supported us in writing a first draft of this book. Without their support, our time-to-market would have slipped considerably.

The production of this book was a major challenge: the text went through multiple iterations. Liza Starr did the lion's share of the production work, with grace, good humor, diligence, and great proficiency. Thank you, Liza. Alice Mark and Anna ter Veer provided extensive project management support and data management and analysis services for a very complex project, meeting deadlines that human beings should not be asked to meet. Thank you, Alice and Anna. We also thank Annette Yakushi and Karen Mayo, who have provided friendship and support for this and many other projects over the years.

Finally, and perhaps somewhat nontraditionally, we would like to acknowledge each other. We were a knowledge-work team studying knowledge-work teams, and perhaps there's a book to be written on that topic. What a relief to have this finally go to press!

Los Angeles, California
February 1995

Susan Albers Mohrman
Susan G. Cohen
Allan M. Mohrman, Jr.

To Ed Lawler,
knowledge-team leader and good friend

The Authors

Susan Albers Mohrman is senior research scientist at the Center for Effective Organizations, Graduate School of Business, University of Southern California. She received her A.B. degree (1967) in psychology from Stanford University, her M.E.D. degree (1970) in education from the University of Cincinnati, and her Ph.D. degree (1978) in organizational behavior from Northwestern University. She has served on the faculty of the Organizational Behavior Department in the business school of the University of Southern California.

Mohrman's research and publications focus on innovations in human resource management, team-based organizations, high-involvement management, organizational learning and change, and organizational design processes. She has consulted with a variety of organizations, introducing employee involvement programs and labor-management cooperative projects, as well as with many organizations redesigning structures and systems.

She is the author of many books and articles. Her books include *Self-Designing Organizations: Learning How to Create High Performance* (1989, with T. G. Cummings), *Large-Scale Organizational Change* (1989, with associates), and *Employee Involvement and Total Quality Management: Practices and Results in Fortune 1000 Companies* (1992, with E. E. Lawler III and G. E. Ledford, Jr.). She is active in the Organizational Development and Change Division of the Academy of Management and serves on the review and editorial boards of several journals.

Susan G. Cohen is research scientist at the Center for Effective Organizations. She received her B.A. degree (1972) in psychology from the State University of New York, Buffalo, her M.A. degree (1977) in applied behavioral science from Whitworth College, and her M.Phil. and Ph.D. degrees (1984, 1988) in organizational behavior from Yale University.

Cohen has done research and consulted on a variety of approaches to improving organizational effectiveness, including group empowerment and effectiveness, employee involvement, organizational development and change, and participative management. She is particularly interested in the design and management of the team-based organization. She has been involved in a series of studies investigating team effectiveness in knowledge-work settings and self-managing teams in service settings.

She is the author of numerous articles and book chapters about employee involvement and empowerment, human resource strategies, and teams and teamwork; in addition, she is the author of several chapters about top-management and customer-service teams in *Groups That Work (and Those That Don't): Creating Conditions for Effective Teamwork* (1990, J. R. Hackman, ed.) and is currently working on *Teams and New Technology: Developing Information Systems for Collaborative Work* (with D. Mankin and T. K. Bikson). She serves on the executive committee for the Western Academy of Management and is active in the Academy of Management.

Allan M. Mohrman, Jr., is associate director of research and research scientist at the Center for Effective Organizations. He was formerly on the faculty of the College of Administrative Sciences at Ohio State University. He earned his B.S. degree (1967) in physics from Stanford University, his M.A. degree (1970) in secondary education from the University of Cincinnati, and his Ph.D. degree (1979) in organizational behavior from the Graduate School of Management, Northwestern University.

Mohrman's major interests are performance management, organizational change and design, the design of effective organizational systems for human resource management, and team-based organizations. He is currently involved in a number of research projects investigating these issues in organizations.

He is coauthor of *Doing Research That Is Useful for Theory and Practice* (1985, with associates), *Designing Performance Appraisal Systems: Aligning Appraisals and Organizational Realities* (1989, with S. M. Resnick-West and E. E. Lawler III), and *Large-Scale Organizational Change* (1989, with associates).

Designing Team-Based Organizations

Part I

. . . .

Organizations and Teams

The migration of teamwork designs from the factory floor to the administrative, technical, service, and managerial components of organizations has raised questions about the applicability of such designs in these new settings. Existing organizational design theory offers only general guidelines for team-based knowledge-work organizations. Organizations have struggled to implement team structures that, while offering great promise for helping to meet the heightened performance requirements of the new global economy, pose monumental design challenges and result in tumultuous change.

Chapters One and Two provide a context of theory and concepts for the team-based design model that forms the core of this book. We are not about the business of advocacy of teams. Rather, as Chapter One lays out, we believe that organizations should be reconfigured to perform work in teams when their strategy and the nature of their work call for such a design. This chapter grounds the book and the study on which it is based in the literature of organizational theory and design, and in the strategic changes that are requiring that organizations shift from the traditional hierarchical mode of organizing to one that is more lateral in nature. Lateral integration is built into the fabric of team-based organizations.

Chapter One also develops the notion that although effectiveness is a function of the way the team is designed, it depends to an even greater extent on whether the organizational context is designed to enable and encourage team functioning. We portray the transition from the traditional hierarchical, individually oriented organization design to a team-based design as a large-scale change process that challenges the assumptions and values that have become part of the culture of most established organizations. We outline the learning process that is entailed in such a transition. This book deals primarily with the stage of this transition during which the new organization is designed. Finally, Chapter One describes the two-phase, multiple-company study on which the book's design model and recommendations are based.

Chapter Two outlines the broad contours of the team-based knowledge-work organization, providing concepts, definitions, and frameworks that are essential background for the next sections of the book. Teams are defined as groups of individuals who work together to produce products or deliver services for which they are held mutually accountable. This chapter enumerates different dimensions along which teams can vary—including mission, structural foundation, and duration—that have implications for their design and management. Teams are quite varied phenomena, and designing team-based organizations requires an appreciation of their variety and an understanding of the applicability of different forms. Chapter Two portrays the team-based organization as a system of embedded and overlapping teams of various kinds, an image different from the traditional line and box, hierarchical organizational depiction.

The nature of knowledge work is treated in Part One. The work of knowledge-work teams is portrayed as the integration of different knowledge bases through processes that enable the expression and consideration of varied expertise and perspectives and the convergence of varied contributors on a shared understanding of the task, its goals, and the work methods. Empowering teams to effectively integrate laterally and accomplish their goals requires the articulation of clear direction and the development of the capability for effective performance. A research-based framework depicting the design features that lead to team effectiveness is presented. The design model developed in Part Two is based on this framework.

· ·

1

Designing Organizations
for Knowledge Work

The use of teams and teaming mechanisms to integrate organizations laterally has increased dramatically in recent years.
This is because many organizations, especially those that are
highly complex, have found that traditional hierarchical and functional approaches are inadequate to address their coordination
needs in a timely and cost-effective manner. During the past three
decades, an increasing number of production settings have found
that they could significantly improve their effectiveness by establishing teams that have responsibility for a "whole" part of the
work. These teams have been described as "empowered," because
in theory they do not have to seek hierarchical approval for many
of their decisions about how to do their work. They are also sometimes referred to as "self-managing," because they perform for
themselves many of the tasks that management used to perform,
such as scheduling and monitoring performance.

More recently, there has been an increase in the use of teams in
settings that house knowledge work. Settings that undertake new
product development, concurrent engineering, proposal writing,
technical sales, publishing, and system development, for example,
house knowledge work. Organizations have found it more difficult
to establish teams in settings such as these. In part, this is because
the highly interdependent and dynamic technology in these settings makes it more difficult to define, develop, and empower teams.

In addition, organizations generally apply models that were developed in production settings for routine work, and these team models do not always fit the new work settings. In fact, production settings themselves are automating many of the routine aspects of production; as a result, the work done by employees is increasingly nonroutine knowledge work.

This book presents a research-based model for systematically designing team-based knowledge-work settings—a model grounded in our two-phase study of teams engaged in knowledge work. We should not be interpreted as advocating teams for all situations, however. In fact, it is our belief that the first question an organization should address is whether it makes sense to establish a team organization. The organization should clarify its goals and articulate why it feels that teams will help accomplish them. It should decide whether the benefits to be derived from redesigning for teams outweigh the costs of the transition. It should determine where in the organization it makes sense to establish teams, and for what purposes. This book provides an overview of the magnitude of the redesign that will be required to establish a team-based organization, if a company decides to move in that direction.

Our argument is that organizations that intend to make substantial use of teams to do work, manage and integrate work, and improve work cannot simply establish teams, train them, and expect them to operate effectively. Rather, organizations must be designed (or redesigned) to support this new way of doing work. We refer to organizations in which teams are the core performing units as *team-based organizations*.

Why Teams?

During the past decade, the use of teams has increased dramatically in organizations, as we have noted. For the most part, this increase reflects the belief that teams are an appropriate structure for implementing strategies formulated to deal with performance demands and opportunities presented by the changing business environment. Increasingly, it is being recognized that the fit between strategy and organizational design is a competitive advantage (Galbraith, Lawler, and Associates, 1993; Nadler, Gerstein, Shaw, and Associates, 1992). Appropriate organizational design enables an organization to execute better, learn faster, and change more easily. Teams—one potential design element—should be adopted because they are the best way to enact the organization's strategy and because they fit with the nature of the work, not because other companies are using teams and claiming success.

The current increase in the use of teams reflects changes in the competitive environment of many organizations. Organizations are experiencing dramatically increased pressures for performance. They are being required to develop and deliver products and services at lower costs but with higher quality and increased speed. To meet this requirement, organizations must become good learning systems: they have to introduce improvements in their products and services, in the processes they use to deliver value to the customer, and in the ways they organize to carry out these processes. Organizations are having to formulate organizing strategies for dealing with these performance pressures.

A great deal of research and popular literature proffers teams of various sorts as an appropriate design in response to these pressures. Much of the literature on quality management recommends cross-functional teams to make improvements in organizational processes (for example, Deming, 1986; Juran, 1989). This recommendation is based on the understanding that organizational processes cut across organizational units (such as functions) and that a process cannot be optimized without examining it in its entirety. A similar logic has been employed by current proponents of reengineering (Hammer and Champy, 1993; Davenport, 1993), who recommend that cross-functional design teams radically reconceive the processes employed to deliver value to the customer and then redesign the organization around these processes. Cross-functional teams are a likely result, because many functions are required to enact each process in its entirety.

Teams are also a favorite design choice in the literature examining speed, cycle time, and time-to-market (Stalk and Hout, 1990; Wheelwright and Clark, 1992; Myer, 1993). Time can be compressed if activities that have traditionally been performed sequentially by different parts of the organization are performed concurrently. In concurrent engineering, for example, the requirements for manufacturing a new product are addressed simultaneously with the development of that product. Time can be saved because the activities are parallel rather than sequential. Even more time can be saved if the activities of those developing manufacturing processes and those developing the product design are integrated, so each participant is informing, influencing, and learning from the others. This integration optimizes manufacturability and prevents costly and time-consuming rework. Cross-functional teams are an ideal home for work of this kind.

Literature on the process of innovation and learning also points, if not specifically to the need for teams, at least to the need to establish linkages between the various perspectives in the organization. Innovation occurs when different perspectives and knowledge bases are joined, resulting in the reframing of problems and solutions that would not have been likely or possible from within one perspective (Kanter, 1983; Pinchot, 1985; Senge, 1990). Organizations excellent at learning have a rich constellation of teams and networks that span parts of the organization and connect knowledge and perspectives (Mohrman and Mohrman, 1993).

To respond to performance pressures for speed, cost, quality, and innovation, a flatter, more lateral organization has been predicted by a number of theorists. Galbraith (1993, 1994), for example, expects to see teams being used more and more at the managerial level to integrate the various parts of organizations, which in today's global, customer-driven economy are increasingly juggling concerns of product, customer, and geography. He predicts more decision making in teams or by managers whose job is to set up processes to integrate the various contributors required to carry out a project or meet the needs of a customer. Essentially, his argument is that performance pressures and the complexity of the environment being faced by organizations today have exceeded the capacity of the traditional, functional, hierarchical organization to effectively coordinate and integrate. Traditional approaches, which rely on hierarchically determined decisions, goals, rules, programs, and job descriptions, are insufficient in the dynamic, complex, and demanding world now faced by many companies.

Increased performance pressures carry with them a need for more efficient and effective processing of information by the organization. Galbraith has developed a basic design framework to help organizations develop ways to meet their growing information-processing needs. His framework posits that increasing complexity in organizational environments creates situations that outstrip the ability of traditional design components like hierarchy, rules, and goals to respond to. Additional integrating mechanisms like teams and various linking roles are needed to adequately process the needed information.

This framework is based in part on the groundbreaking research of Lawrence and Lorsch (1969), which found that in dynamic, complex, and uncertain environments, organizations have to elaborate and subdivide their parts to attend to all the relevant components of their environment. Companies that rely on rapid introduction of many new products with a complex customer set are examples of organizations that require high levels of differentiation. Lawrence and Lorsch found that high levels of differentiation present a concomitant requirement to develop more ways to integrate across the organization. Such integrative approaches go beyond reliance on the hierarchy and its bureaucratic trappings. Lawrence and Lorsch and Galbraith offer teams as one way to accomplish such integration. Liaison roles and managerial integrating roles are other examples. The current emphasis on teams stems in part from the fact that they can be a way to handle lateral integration without proliferating the management structure. They fit with the emphasis on the flattening of the organization.

While performance pressures are driving many organizations to a more lateral way of functioning, financial pressures are driving others: they can no longer afford the costs of the burgeoning hierarchy as a means of integrating increasingly complex work. These costs include not only expenses resulting from proliferation of managerial and control roles but also those resulting from the delays and lack of responsiveness and learning that are built into an organization that is horizontally and functionally segmented. But teams, a likely design component of the flat, laterally oriented organization, are not an inexpensive design feature either, as Galbraith points out; they involve the costs of coordination time among multiple people. For that reason, they should be used only where they are appropriate to both the task environment of the firm and the nature of the work to be done.

The key question to ask is whether a particular task is best accomplished by establishing teams to allow members to integrate their activities. The task may be the delivery of value to the customer in the form of products or services; it may be learning, innovating, and improving organizational functioning; it may be providing support to internal customers, who in turn deliver products and services to the external customer; it may be managing the organization or the business unit or integrating across parts of the organization that have to function in a coordinated way. These kinds of tasks are best performed in teams *if* they require on-line integration of highly interdependent performers. Teams should not be established simply because there is a need for speed, efficiency, quality, innovation, and customer responsiveness. They should be established because a team structure is the best way to achieve the integration required to accomplish these strategic goals.

One more factor should be mentioned to clarify why flat, lateral organizations are becoming more prevalent. Information technology can now widely distribute information that was once vertically aggregated to inform strategic and operational decision making in the managerial and executive ranks of the organization. This means that employees at the lowest levels of the organization now theoretically have access to information that would allow them to make informed decisions about matters that used to be dealt with higher in the organization. Thus multiple participants can bring varied perspectives and expertise and can use widely distributed information to make integrative decisions. In short, a team with the requisite expertise can function as a mini–general manager. Decisions no longer have to go up a hierarchy to get to someone with aggregated information and a broad understanding of the parts of the organization. Organizations that can capitalize on this technological capability by establishing the appropriate fit between their information technology architecture and their organizational design will achieve a competitive advantage in terms of time, cost, and responsiveness.

Challenges of Organizing for Knowledge Work

Organizational designs that were suitable for routine work in stable environments no longer fit most organizational settings. Increasingly, organizational success depends on making complex trade-offs, learning and implementing new approaches, and applying advanced knowledge.

The challenges of organizing team-based settings for knowledge work are illustrated by the experience of a commercial electronics division of a well-known Fortune 500 firm—one that we will refer to as Analytico. The firm had implemented cross-functional new product development teams one year before we came on the scene. The teams included full-time R&D, manufacturing, and marketing members and part-time finance, quality, and human resource members. Teams were still working unevenly, with the majority of members struggling to understand and implement this new way of operating. However, two teams were achieving significant improvements in development time,

manufacturing costs, and market responsiveness, so division management felt that this new approach was the right way to go. We were
involved in a diagnostic study of the teams.

The following comments were abstracted from two two-hour
group interviews with a representative cross section of managers and
employees:

> The basic problem with our teaming effort is that this is
> just such a complex place. We're trying to make a new
> generation of product, which by itself is a mammoth
> undertaking—about a four-year process—and at the
> same time dealing with a moving target. Marketing
> keeps bringing us new information about how our cus-
> tomers' organizations are changing and how they'll be
> using our product quite differently. It's a very fast-devel-
> oping area of technology, both in technological capabil-
> ity and in applications. Even as we're developing the
> product, the customers are redesigning their processes,
> and they now say they would like our product to have
> software internally that they used to provide in-house.
> It's a moving target.

> Last week our division manager came back from a group
> meeting with new information about where our product
> needs to fit in the greater constellation of group prod-
> ucts. It turns out that another division has developed a
> display capability that has greater functionality and can
> be produced at the same cost as our displays. Group mar-
> keting feels that our market share will be enhanced if
> there is consistency across our greater family of offerings.
> But that means rethinking connections in a very funda-
> mental way. Our team's work has come to a halt.

> Customers are telling us our company's interface with
> them is too fragmented. They want it to be easier to

understand the whole family of group products, and they don't like the fact that they're making choices across related and overlapping products being produced within different divisions. So suddenly we're having to try to coordinate and reduce redundancy between divisions, when in the past our strategy has always been to have parallel development efforts and let the market be the determiner of which products we continue. This brings into question the value of some of the development we've done so far, at least in my team.

Just when we're starting to get used to this team approach, and to feel like as a team we really do have the authority to make decisions and get on with it, we're told that a key group strategy is going to be leverage. We're going to have to use as much work that's being done in other teams and other divisions as possible. That has some very immediate implications for what we're doing, as there are at least three other teams in this division and elsewhere in the group that could use what we've developed and vice versa. Mind you, these other divisions don't even use the same software that we do, so communicating is going to be difficult, even if everyone is so inclined. The problem is that for any of us to redirect our development efforts at this point in time will mean a lot of rework, not to mention that we've really come to believe that our approach is the best, and we're kind of psyched to be able to carry our "baby" forward.

I like the team I'm on, and I feel that we've made great strides in coordinating our work. We've come up with some nifty approaches to working our hardware/software trade-offs, and believe it or not it was our manufacturing members who helped us figure out this approach. The problem lies in the other people in the division who are still in functional areas. Our manufacturing members are terrific, but they just found out yesterday that the assembly area (we share a common assembly area with five other products) has committed to some new technology that even our manufacturing people weren't aware of. This will have basic implications for our design and will result in some rework. I can see how in the long run, and perhaps even for our product, this change will make a big difference in manufacturing flexibility, but in the short term, our team goals are shot.

Everyone seems to be talking as if their teams are going hunky-dory. And I guess even I have to admit that talking to each other as we go along is better than not talking, which is what we used to do. But what I see is a bunch of people who are experts and basically take a "prove-it" attitude in dealing with each other. And the engineers in my team are continually going off in secret and doing their own thing, totally disregarding marketing's concerns. It's like they feel that they can come back to us and say, "See, I told you so." They just don't seem to get it. You've never seen such incredulous looks in your life as when we tell them that our customers aren't planning to have scientists use our equipment anymore; they're having more and more of their analysis work done by technicians. Even though we've taken R&D on field visits and they've heard the plans, they come back and say, "Nah, they'll change their minds. That won't work." A couple of our chemists used to work for our customers, and they're continually denying the data. They say, "I've been there, and that's not what they need."

Our finance representative serves on five teams. She's going all out to be a good team member and to make sure she's learning about the products and the business. But that means she's continually in meetings when you need her. We really don't need her all that often—only when we're making trade-offs—but it's pretty irritating not to be able to call her when we need her. Sometimes we have to make these trade-offs pretty quickly. We try not to be constrained by scheduled meetings since we're all right here. But these people with so many memberships aren't flexible enough for us.

The same problem afflicts our managers. There are so many things being juggled in this division right now, and across the group, that they're always in meetings. They're on a myriad of teams trying to integrate everything. We haven't successfully broken our business up into chunks, because the products and technology are so interrelated. Can you believe that our management team is now directing the work of twenty-three different teams? Getting thoughtful time from them is next to impossible. And it looks like now we're going to integrate across the whole group. That ought to provide total gridlock. I know we have teams so each of us can take more responsibility for our collective product, but right now I have to tell you that I'm glad I'm not responsible for this division.

Analytico is struggling with the challenges of organizing for nonroutine knowledge work in a complex environment. Believing that new products are best developed by cross-functional, empowered teams, it established them, trained them, and tried to give them significant authority. Its problems, both internal and external to the teams, are representative of those we have encountered in a good many of the companies we have examined, and they have to do with the nature of knowledge work, which will be described below.

Knowledge work entails the application of knowledge bases and the processing of information. It is frequently carried out by people with highly developed and often specialized knowledge sets: accountants, physicists, diagnosticians, aeronautical engineers, marketers, and so forth. Most have gone through extensive education and training, becoming steeped in the "thought-world" of their discipline (Dougherty, 1992). They have learned to attend to certain aspects of their environment, to value particular approaches to work and ways of thinking, to filter information to conform to their paradigms of understanding and action, and to value particular outcomes. Communication and integration across the thought-worlds of different specialties is not easy, as was demonstrated in the earlier quotes from Analytico's personnel. Integrated, collective action is also difficult. Many knowledge workers have come to think of themselves as professionals, and they expect a certain amount of autonomy based on their discipline expertise and the collegial determination of standards (Von Glinow, 1988).

Although some knowledge work (for example, certain accounting tasks) is routine and analyzable, much of it is nonroutine. In most organizations, the routine work is well understood and has been organized into effective programs or procedures. Where expertise is required is in carrying out the procedures. Nonroutine work, on the other hand, includes much variety and many exceptions to any programs that have been developed (each customer presenting a different combination of requirements, for example). It may also be characterized by an incomplete cause-effect understanding, which introduces uncertainty into the work. This is true, for example, of research and development that pushes the frontier of knowledge. The nonroutine nature of the work means that decision making requires judgment (Thompson and Tuden, 1959) and interpretation (Pava, 1983) by those who carry it out. In contrast, decisions in routine work can largely be made by applying programs and computation. The process of determining if the work is being carried out correctly is more objective.

Nonroutine knowledge-work settings tend to be characterized

by high degrees of interdependence, because there are multiple, concurrent conversion processes that influence each other (Pava, 1983). In a new product development project, for example, related processes include the development of hardware, software, marketing plans, and manufacturing processes. As was demonstrated in the case of Analytico, the interdependencies are not always constrained to a particular project or engagement. Pava referred to this as the "virtually saturated" nature of the work interdependence in knowledge-work settings, where "it seems as though everything totally depends on everything else" (1983, p. 51). In addition, much knowledge work exists in highly dynamic and complex environments, as is the case at Analytico. This introduces additional uncertainty into organizational decision making.

The list below summarizes the key differences between routine and nonroutine work:

Routine Work	Nonroutine Work
Programmed	Emergent
Repeated patterns	Varied, unique
Analyzable	Interdependent
Well understood	Uncertain
Static	Dynamic

Some knowledge work is routine. Most nonroutine work is knowledge work; that is, it is unprogrammed and requires the application or creation of knowledge. The distinction should not be interpreted as a simple delineation between production and nonproduction work. As mentioned earlier, many production settings have automated their routine work, leaving nonroutine work (such as improving processes and dealing with exceptions) to employees with a good deal of technical expertise. Conversely, some knowledge work entails routine application of knowledge. Processing insurance claims is an example. In reality, much knowledge work is a combination of routine and nonroutine work. For example, some engineering work involves straightforward application, while other engineering tasks are not yet programmed. Medical treatment is another example: although there is an effort to develop protocols for treating various diseases, reducing the amount of judgment that need be applied, human and disease variability leave judgment as an inevitable component. It is the nonroutine nature of the work that poses the most difficult design challenge for organizations.

Nonroutine knowledge work operates at the edge of what is known—and therefore what is programmable—and what has to be learned in order to complete the work (Mohrman, Mohrman, and Cohen, forthcoming). Thus it necessarily involves learning. The focus of that learning may be on the *content* of the work that is done, the *process* of the work, or the *organization* that is required to carry the work out:

• Learning that focuses on the content of the work that is done might entail the generation of new knowledge, as in the scientific exploration of the reaction between chemicals and the environment that enables the development of a new pesticide. It might entail the joining of different kinds of knowledge, as in the apprehending of the business model of a customer in order to develop an information system that meets business needs.

• Determining the best process for integrating the knowledge of multiple specialists and the customer in the development of customized information systems and making the trade-offs inherent in such development is an example of process learning. This task might include learning about what kinds of information are required from the customer and when that information is required, as well as methodologies for involving experts in applications, architecture, and service in making cost-benefit trade-offs. Another example of process learning is reassessing how various medical specialists, family members, and the patient are involved in the treatment of diabetes and reconfiguring the steps by which various interventions are

carried out. Both content and process learning can result in knowledge that leads to greater programmability of work.

• Examples of learning about organization include determining
how to organize to support the processes required to develop customized systems or to deliver efficient and effective medical care for
diabetics. Senge (1990) argues that organizing should be viewed as
a discipline and that organizational learning will occur when there
are processes in place to develop a deeper understanding and application of this discipline. This is highly relevant to the organization
of knowledge-work systems, for we have argued above that one of
the competitive challenges being faced in today's environment is
the need to learn more quickly than the competitors: learning in the
areas of content, process, and organization.

The major organizational challenge in nonroutine knowledge-
work settings is to integrate the work of the various contributors. In
these settings, teams are essentially established as forums in which
the various interdependent specialties can integrate their work to
accomplish collective goals. Teams are structural mechanisms
through which task interdependencies can be worked out, issues
involving trade-offs between various perspectives can be resolved,
and solutions and approaches that build upon the diversity of relevant expertise and perspectives can be determined. The design of
knowledge-work teams is tricky, however, given the high levels of
interdependence and the dynamic and uncertain environment in
which much knowledge work is performed.

Team Designs and Knowledge Work

The word *team* is used to refer to an interesting assortment of organizational structures. Among them are quality improvement teams, work
teams, management teams, and integrating teams. We will describe
these various kinds of teams in Chapter Two. Here, however, we draw
on past literature to describe the domain of knowledge-work teams

and to make a distinction between the use of teams as integrating mechanisms and teams as self-contained performing units. This distinction underpins much of the discussion in the book and helps clarify the design challenge of creating team-based organizations.

Teams have been identified by Galbraith (1973, 1994) and by Lawrence and Lorsch (1969) as an approach that can provide necessary integration across parts of the organization. In his organizational design model, Galbraith also describes the use of self-contained units, which could be teams and/or business units. The creation of self-contained units is an approach that *reduces* the need for information processing across the organization, because these units can operate relatively independently of the rest of the organization. Teams as integrating mechanisms, on the other hand, enable coordination and integration and thereby *increase* the amount of information that is handled across the organization.

The sociotechnical systems literature (Trist 1981; Cummings, 1978; Pasmore, 1988) has advocated a design process that often results in the creation of self-contained teams. These teams are referred to variously as self-managing teams, autonomous work teams, self-directing teams, and self-regulating teams. They are established to fully manage and execute a portion of the workflow. Through a technical analysis, the organization delineates portions of work that can be carried out by a team of people to foster effective technical performance and employee outcomes of satisfaction and motivation. Technical outcomes are fostered when the team is able to handle all aspects of the work, including any variances and exceptions that arise. Tasks that used to be performed by specialized support groups, such as maintenance and quality control, frequently become team responsibilities. Social outcomes are optimized when the team has responsibility for a "whole" task and enjoys autonomy, variety, and meaningfulness of work. Studies of the effectiveness of organizations designed using these sociotechnical systems principles generally show positive impact on productivity and financial performance (for example, Beekun, 1989; Macy, Bliese, and Norton, 1991;

and Goodman, Devadas, and Hughson, 1988). Pasmore points out that self-regulating teams are most suitable for work that is stable, containing routine tasks, and where members have relatively equal levels of skill, with skills that can be acquired from one another.

Pava (1983) has advocated a modification of the sociotechnical model to fit highly specialized, interdependent, and dynamic knowledge-work settings. The analysis focuses on the key deliberations that have to go on in the organization to resolve trade-offs, establish direction, and enable coordinated activity. Deliberations are carried out in forums established to bring relevant parties together to resolve contention. Savage (1990) also has an integrative notion of teams. He portrays an organization with loose, dynamic decision-making forums, coalitions, and project teams that pull relevant people together from across the organization to take advantage of opportunities or perform tasks. Neither Savage nor Pava depicts these forums as stable, lasting structures; the forums last only as long as the organization has a need for a cross-cutting group to perform the particular function for which they were convened.

Our experience with knowledge-work settings is that they often have a need for both kinds of teams: integrating teams, whose purpose is to coordinate the efforts of different parts of the organization, and teams that are to the extent possible self-contained and focused on the accomplishment of a particular segment of the work of the organization. In a functional organization, cross-functional project teams actually have both of these purposes. They are established to integrate the work of the different functions *and* to be as self-contained as possible in accomplishing their task. Given the extraordinary amounts of interdependence in many knowledge-work settings, however, it is often difficult to fully self-contain teams. The problems at Analytico stem in part from this dual nature of the teams that were established. The structural and process design challenges that result from the conflict between teams' efforts to cope with interdependence and their efforts to maximize self-containment are the focus of much of this book.

Organizational Effectiveness and the Importance of Context

Because knowledge work involves the application of expert knowledge bases in the performance of highly interdependent work, one performance challenge is to ensure that the various contributors do in fact integrate their work. Whether they do or not depends on their ability to carry out processes designed to take advantage of the various knowledge bases and resolve the contention that is inevitable when the work of various expert performers has implications for and shapes and constrains the work of others.

In the first phase of our research, which will be more fully described later in this chapter, we spent a great deal of time talking with members of both high-performing and low-performing teams. We found that less effective teams frequently run into one or both of two barriers. First, they are unable to effectively surface and utilize the knowledge of one or more of the interdependent specialties and consequently operate with a partial set of information and limited perspectives. This might be true, for example, of a team that does not have dedicated marketing resources during the product definition stage of a new product development process and consequently does not sufficiently take the customer perspective into account in defining the product. Another example is a sales and service team in which the service specialists are accorded lower status than the sales agents, service members are not taken seriously, and service issues are not taken into account in pricing a system for the customer.

The second problem that less effective teams tend to encounter is difficulty in arriving at a shared understanding about what the team is trying to accomplish, the methods and priorities that should guide the work, and team content issues. This may be because different specialties value different outcomes, as in the case of a team where engineering representatives are optimizing elegance of design and manufacturing representatives are optimizing efficiency of production. Alternatively, it may be because different specialties have different languages and worldviews; and although team members think they have come to agreements, these unravel when members start to execute them.

Either of these problems can occur because of issues internal or external to the team. For example, failure to take into account the knowledge of some specialties may reflect internal interaction patterns or it may reflect a bigger cultural issue. It may reflect a team design error or a resource allocation issue (if, for example, an important perspective was not included among the team's membership). Failure to achieve shared understanding of goals, methods, and priorities may likewise reflect either internal process breakdowns or externally imposed conflicting goals and priorities. The latter is likely to be true when a clear organizational strategy has not been articulated, for example.

As we pored over our interview data, it became apparent to us that we could not understand team effectiveness by looking solely at how the teams operate. Teams that have enthusiastic members and leaders, well-thought-out plans, and appropriate expertise can be derailed by events occurring elsewhere in the organization—in other teams, in other divisions, in other disciplines, or at higher management levels. Teams can fail to attain the necessary expertise or to fully engage their members; they sometimes carry out the wrong activities because of lack of support or direction from their managers. Thus teams have to be understood in their context. In fact, it became clear to us that an organization can achieve only limited impact on team effectiveness by focusing on the design and development of the team itself. *Improving knowledge work requires designing the organization to enable and foster lateral integration.* That design results in team-based knowledge organizations that are able to spawn, nurture, and manage the activities of teams as performing units; it results in organizations that are systems of multiple, dynamic, interdependent teams.

Other studies have also found the importance of context. Organizational context has been identified as a point of leverage for improving the effectiveness of groups (Hackman, 1987, 1990). Organizational reward systems, educational systems, and information systems need to meet the needs of groups in order to encourage effort, instill knowledge and skills, and lay the groundwork for task-appropriate performance strategies in the team. Project team effectiveness has been found to be tied to how the team relates to and manages its context (Ancona and Caldwell, 1992). Likewise, Donnellon (forthcoming) found that whether new product development teams establish the interaction patterns of "real teams" rather than "teams in name only" depends to a great extent on the messages they receive from the organizational context. Even something as clearly internal to the team as the language the team members use reflects the larger organizational culture and appears to be sensitive to goals, rewards, and roles in the larger organization. These studies have tended to focus on the team and what it requires to perform effectively. From an organizational design perspective, it is a small leap from these kinds of findings to the conclusion that a team-based organization requires more than making sure that contextual supports are in place and that teams are cognizant of the importance of setting up the right relationship with the context. It requires that the context be designed to facilitate doing work through teams.

Our research examined the organizational design issues involved in creating team-based knowledge-work organizations, as we have noted. The design challenge facing management is to create a context that makes it more likely that teams can make and carry out decisions, that the various perspectives will be taken into account in decision making and in the integration of work, and that various contributors will be able to come to agreement. Our research found that the more the teams in an organization involve multiple disciplines, and the more the people in each team have to work effectively with people beyond their team, the more important it is that management uses every tool available to create a shared understanding of what the organization is trying to accomplish and to point people in the same direction. In such situations, there are very strong forces pulling people apart and making it difficult for them to effectively relate to each other's knowledge base and come to shared understandings. Management cannot simply create a team and expect it to be able to resolve trade-offs. This is especially true if there is disagreement among top management and no clear framework within which to consider the trade-offs. Making sure there is a clear strategy and that people are aware of the strategy, goals, and priorities of the organization, making sure that the right forums are in place to resolve issues for the organization in a timely manner, setting goals, providing feedback, and rewarding team members for accomplishment of shared goals are examples of the kinds of tools available to management to create the context for effective knowledge work.

Underlying the design model that is presented in this book is the need to create an organization in which it is likely that individuals will take each other's expertise and viewpoints into account and that diverse individuals will be able to come to a shared understanding that can serve as the basis for integrated execution.

The Transition to a Team-Based Organization

We have made the case that the transition to a team-based organization entails redesigning the organization. One conceptualization of the design features of the organization—the star model, which comes from Galbraith (1994)—is illustrated in Figure 1.1. Any organizational system, regardless of the model by which it is conceptualized, includes more than simply the structure of performing units. It also includes the characteristics and competencies of the people; rewards; human resource processes and systems, such as career paths and employee hiring and development; performance management practices, including goal setting, performance appraisal, and feedback; other processes, such as decision making, information processing, and communication; and technologies employed to perform the tasks. Galbraith (1994) makes the point that an organization learning to effectively utilize lateral mechanisms has to align the

Figure 1.1. Star Model of an Organization.

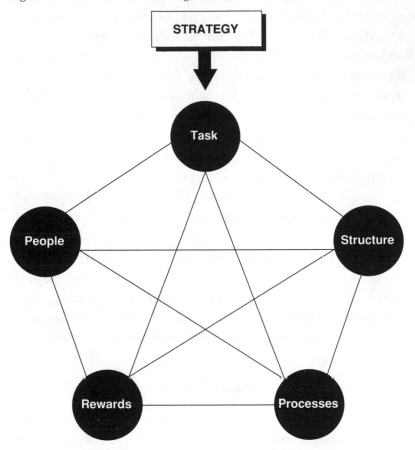

Source: Jay R. Galbraith, *Competing with Flexible Lateral Organizations*, *Second Edition* (pg. 4), © 1994 by Addison-Wesley Publishing Company, Inc. Reprinted by permission of the publisher.

different aspects of the organizational system to support that way of functioning, and we concur: in our research on knowledge-work organizations, we found that all these aspects of the organization do indeed need to change. The overall design depicted by the star model can only be successful if it successfully enacts the organization's strategy and allows it to compete in its environment (Galbraith and Kazanjian, 1986; Galbraith, 1994).

The transition to an organization that is able to design and redesign the dynamic configuration of teams required to carry out the organization's strategy and respond to performance challenges, to develop and support those teams, and to provide a context in which they can function effectively involves a significant technical and social change process. The technical issues entail the actual design of structures, processes, and systems; the social issues entail helping people in the organization undergo a fundamental change in their understanding of how the organization works and their new roles in it, as well as helping them gain the capabilities to operate effectively in that new environment and to enact their new roles. This transition challenges deeply held values and assumptions about what constitutes effective performance. In some cases, it works against preferences of managers and employees to perform as individuals and receive direction from supervisors. Because of the magnitude of the technical and social change required, creating an effective team-based organization is a multiyear process.

The data from our and others' studies provide strong evidence that if an organization intends to use teams as performing units, it cannot simply impose them on the existing traditional, hierarchical, individually oriented organizational design. The tendency of many managements is to create the teams and then, when teams run into problems, pour training and other support into them to help them learn to be more effective. These managements do not think of themselves as designing and implementing a team-based organization; they think of themselves as installing teams.

The design and implementation of a team-based organization is a learning process. Because the team design has to be tailored to the setting and the work that is done, the people in each setting have to first learn what is the best design. That learning is generally spearheaded by a design team; however, the design team works interactively with the rest of the organization to involve other members, take advantage of their perspectives, and educate the organization about what to expect. Figure 1.2 illustrates the nature of this self-design and learning process (from Mohrman and Cummings, 1989). Its three iterative stages will be discussed below.

Laying the Foundation for Change

The sequence starts with laying the foundation for change through activities that get people involved in developing a shared understanding of what the organization is trying to accomplish. This is the stage at which the organization determines a strategy for meeting its performance requirements, which may include the establishment of a team-based design. This stage also results in clarification of the criteria that will guide the design stage and be used to evaluate the new team design once it is up and running. The criteria are a product of the following three processes, which together lay the foundation for the design and implementation:

1. *Specifying the outcome and process values driving the redesign.* Say, for example, that a systems company has a strategy of providing full service with unparalleled customer responsiveness to capture and retain market share. It may plan to redesign its sales and service operation as a team organization in order to accomplish this. To achieve high levels of customer satisfaction, the organization may seek, in its design, to encourage "one integrated face to the customer" by pulling together the necessary and varied expertise to deliver complete services and by having all personnel share the goal of customer satisfaction. Given that goal, the criteria for the design of the organization would include the outcome of customer responsiveness and satisfaction as well as process indicators to determine whether all the various contributors do indeed share a common set of objectives pertaining to the customer.

2. *Learning as much as possible about organizational design features and approaches that promote the desired outcomes and processes.* This may include reading about successful cases and about organizational design theory. This book, for example, provides frameworks useful in determining how the organization might be redesigned. Learning activities may also include visiting successful organizations that foster the desired values or are known to have exemplary practices (and therefore model what is possible). The visiting organization

Figure 1.2. Self-Design Strategy for Team-Based Organizations.

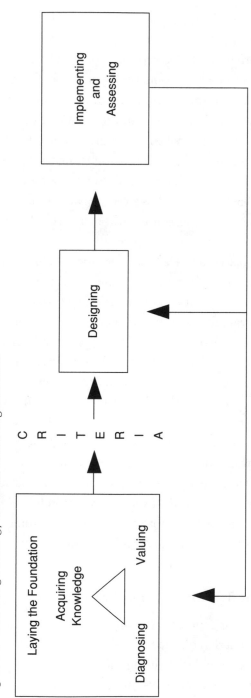

Source: Susan Albers Mohrman and Thomas G. Cummings, *Self-Designing Organizations: Learning How to Create High Performance* (p. 37), © 1989 by Addison-Wesley Publishing Company, Inc. Reprinted by permission of the publisher.

might learn, for example, that similar companies are able to generate changes in estimates of system costs in twenty-four hours through iterative simulation processes—a vast improvement on the organization's week-long sequential handling of change requests. Thus one criterion for the new organization might be that team members have simulation tools and that an integrated response to customer change requests be achievable in one day. Whatever the specific tools chosen, through reading, education, and visits, the organization will learn that there are several alternative structural approaches (each of which has strengths and weaknesses) to combining various contributors into customer-focused teams.

3. *Diagnosing the current organization to determine the extent to which it is characterized by the kinds of features that foster the desired values and the extent to which the desired outcomes are being accomplished.* The organization might explore whether the contributors feel that they share a common goal of customer satisfaction or whether they see themselves as working at cross-purposes, and why. If the organization discovers, for example, that the objectives of different contributors are not complementary, one criterion for the new organization might be that it have a goal-setting process that includes a check for complementarity of goals between different functional contributors. The organization might learn from its customers that they find it annoying to make multiple contacts with multiple contributors in different parts of the organization in order to get a problem resolved. If so, one criterion for the new design might be to create a single interface with the customer and to hold all contributors accountable for responding to customer problems identified by that interface.

Designing the Team-Based Organization

The design stage generates the broad outlines of the team-based organizational design on the basis of the criteria and the knowledge base that were formulated during the foundation stage. This is the stage at which creative thinking occurs (for example, thinking about the process in the work area) and design trade-offs occur (for example, trade-offs between functional and project or customer orientation). Design of a team-based organization also needs to be based on a careful analysis of the work that is done by the organization, and all the design features shown in Figure 1.1 need to be addressed. Part Two provides a design sequence, conceptual frameworks, and tools for addressing those features.

Given the magnitude of the organizational change required in the transition to teams, it is highly unlikely that the initial design (or redesign) will be complete or exactly right. It will have to be tailored and filled out as the organization implements it. The initial design may not include, for example, all the performance management practices; these may need to be added in a second set of implementation steps. The design that is generated in the first iteration should specify enough design features to begin the learning process, however.

Implementing and Assessing

The design process yields the broad outlines of the team-based organization. It specifies structures, processes, systems, people practices, and roles that differ from the status quo in fundamental ways. It implies new behaviors, skills, and ways of doing work and making decisions. It requires capabilities the organization has yet to develop. Change of this magnitude cannot be achieved by a one-shot implementation. It is best accomplished through an iterative implementation process that involves ongoing organizational learning.

The planning of the implementation process and sequence is an important transitional activity, distinct from the design process. In planning for implementation, the questions being answered are these: Given the nature of the design we are putting in place, what implementation sequence is best and what implementation activities are required? Given that all aspects of the design cannot be put in place at once, where should we start?

Successful implementation necessarily involves learning. The organization must learn more about the appropriate design and about what is required to effectively implement it. Organizations inevitably underestimate both the extent and the difficulty of the transition. The terms *team, teamwork,* and *coordination* sound as straightforward and natural as motherhood and apple pie. In reality, though, they are not. Teams can learn as they go, but only if the organization builds in both time and activities geared toward that learning. Ongoing assessment is the key learning activity.

Assessment and implementation proceed simultaneously in an iterative process carried out in an action-learning mode (see Figure 1.3). As action is taken to implement the design, data are regularly collected to determine progress: Is the design indeed being implemented as intended, and if not, what are the barriers? What additional design features are needed? Then plans are made to supplement the design and/or the implementation support in the organization. This iterative process continues as more and more features of the design become fleshed out. At some point, the assessment turns to outcomes: Are customers indeed more satisfied? If not, why not, and what needs to be modified to yield higher customer satisfaction?

Chapter Eleven discusses implementation and assessment in more detail. It describes both the social and technical aspects of the change process and the major transitional issues that were faced by the organizations we studied.

Earlier, we said that teams should be adopted because they are the best way to enact the organization's strategy and because they fit with the nature of the work. We add to that another factor: teams should be adopted only if the organization is prepared to embark on a transition that will ultimately affect all aspects of organizational functioning and all organizational members.

The Study

This book is an application of the results of four years of research. We set out to determine what factors influence the effectiveness of teams in knowledge-work settings. We wanted to determine

Figure 1.3. The Action-Learning Cycle.

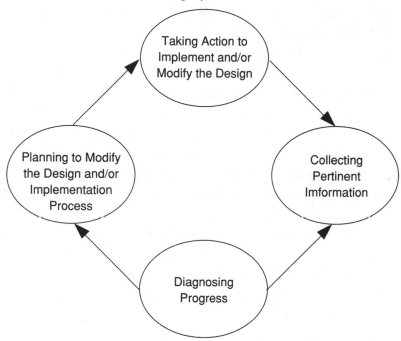

whether and how the team designs that work in more routine work settings have to be changed for dynamic, interdependent, nonroutine knowledge-work settings.

The first phase of our research involved an in-depth interview study with twenty-five knowledge-work teams in four companies. We spent four days per team interviewing members of the teams, managers of the teams, and other managers and internal customers in the business unit. Our sample included new product development teams in the areas of consumer electronics and consumer food products, corporate information system teams, human resource teams, technical services teams in the research labs of a large corporation that provided consulting services to the manufacturing plants and to the new product development teams, and customer-service teams in the field offices of a large electronics company. We were interested in the team model that was being employed, the extent to which it conformed to or differed from the self-contained, self-managing team that has been utilized in many production settings, the barriers and facilitators of team effectiveness, the various roles that were being played by team members and managers, team strategies, and team context. We used a grounded research methodology (Glaser and Strauss, 1967). Each site was studied by one researcher, who used a standard interview protocol but was free to probe and go beyond the protocol where it seemed appropriate. After each set of three team sites was completed (one site by each researcher), the research team met to share data, discuss patterns, and distill the variables that seemed to be making a difference in the performance of the teams. Based on an evolving model of team design and effectiveness in knowledge-work organizations, the protocol was enhanced and interim hypotheses were qualitatively examined in the next round of sites.

In this phase, we found that many knowledge-work teams were indeed quite different from the production teams we had studied in the past, primarily because of their embeddedness in a complex, interdependent context. Several of the knowledge-work teams that applied specialized knowledge in a routine manner were similar to the production model, indicating to us that the nature of the work is a key determinant of the form that the teams take. What intrigued us most was that, more often than not, the factors that prevented integrated, cross-discipline performance were factors external to any given team, such as a lack of consistent direction, changes occurring in another part of the organization with ramifications for the team, inconsistent functional goals, and shifting resource commitments. The team context appeared to be the overwhelming determinant of whether a team functioned effectively in accomplishing its goals.

In our later sites, we looked not only at teams but also at the business unit within which they were located. In this way, we systematically explored the contextual factors in operation. We became more and more convinced that to understand the effectiveness of knowledge teams, we had to look at the organizational system. Our final set of sites in the first phase consisted of teams in three different settings of a consumer food-products firm. By this time, our research team had generated a preliminary model of the organizational design features that influenced team and business-unit effectiveness in a team-based organization. We piloted a survey instrument in preparation for the second phase, when we planned to test the importance of these features in a broader sample of team organizations.

In the second phase, we studied twenty-six team-based business units in seven corporations. Product development programs, corporate staff departments, sales and service offices, product commercialization teams, and internal technology development teams composed our sample. With a few exceptions, these business units had been implementing their team designs for at least a year (and in two cases for more than two years). We spent two days interviewing members of each business unit to get an understanding of their team and business-unit design, the work they did, and the interdependencies in the unit. A survey was administered to all members of a sample of teams in the business unit (a total of 178 teams) and to managers and a sample of customers for each team. Managers and customers were asked about the effectiveness of the team and of the business unit as a whole along a number of performance dimensions that had been stressed by the team organizations we studied in the first phase. These data were pooled across organizations and analyzed to determine whether the design features that were measured were related to different levels of team effectiveness.

The team-organization effectiveness model that will be presented in the next chapter was developed in the first phase and refined in the second phase of our four-year study. This book is not a report of research results, however. Rather, it is an application of the findings of the study. Although we refer to our research and our research findings throughout—findings that are both qualitative and quantitative—the overall framework is a design model that is an application of these findings.

Using the large amount of qualitative information and quantitative survey analyses obtained in the two phases of our project, we developed our design model, which incorporates the relationship of design features to effectiveness and our qualitative understandings of the processes of design and transition that were faced by these organizations. Working with a number of business units, we have also had the opportunity to try these concepts in action and, in the Lewinian action-research tradition (Lewin, 1951), to learn about team-based design by working with and observing business units in the process of designing themselves.

One of the most concrete uses of our research in these pages is in the examples we offer to illustrate various points. We relate many of the design concepts to a number of cases based on business units that we studied—cases that we develop in detail. In one case, we have added several design features from a second business unit that we studied, in order not to have to proliferate the number of cases required to demonstrate different design choices. The cases are fictitiously labeled, in order to preserve the anonymity we promised to companies.

Key Issues

The key issues facing those who are considering the transition to a team-based organization are these:

1. In team-based organizations, teams are the core performing units.

2. Teams are a way to achieve integration and coordination through lateral processes.

3. Teams are also a way to achieve the strategic objectives of speed, cost, quality, learning, and innovation.

4. Establishing team-based organizations in knowledge-work settings entails designing the organization to support lateral integration between disciplines and across parts of the organization.

5. The change from a traditional, hierarchical organization to a team-based organization requires redesigning the organization.

6. The implementation of a team-based organization is an iterative process that entails social and technical learning. Assessment must be built into the implementation plan to ensure that learning occurs.

7. Companies should undertake the transition to a team-based organization only if that framework fits their strategy and the nature of their work and if they are prepared for the magnitude of the large-scale change that is required.

. . . .

2

Exploring the Contours
of a Team-Based Organization

I n a team-based organization, teams are integrated performing units. Their effectiveness depends on whether the business unit in which they are embedded has been designed to support integrated work. In knowledge settings that house nonroutine work, the key organizational challenge is to create structures and processes that foster the integration of the work of people with diverse knowledge bases and the work of a dynamic constellation of interdependent teams.

This chapter describes the broad contours of a team-based organization. It first provides a definition of teams and a typology of the different kinds of teams that are commonly established in organizations. It then provides a way to reconceptualize a company as a team-based organization—that is, an organization in which teams are the core performing units. It describes the integration processes that occur in teams and are closely related to team dynamics. It addresses the concept of "empowerment" and its relevance for teams. Finally, it provides the team effectiveness framework that guided and was confirmed by the research that underpins the design model developed in this book.

Definition and Dimensions of Teams

A team is a group of individuals who work together to produce products or deliver services for which they are mutually accountable.

Team members share goals and are mutually held accountable for meeting them, they are interdependent in their accomplishment, and they affect the results through their interactions with one another. Because the team is held collectively accountable, the work of integrating with one another is included among the responsibilities of each member.

Within this broad definition of teams, there are a number of different types that have been established and used effectively in organizations. These teams vary along a number of dimensions that have implications for how they are designed and managed. These dimensions—the team's mission, its relationship to the formal structure of the organization, and its duration—are discussed below.

The Team's Mission and Its Relationship to the Work Processes of the Organization

Organizations may establish teams for a number of different purposes. The purpose behind each team relates to the challenges of designing it and managing its performance. Many organizations are using a combination of the following kinds of teams:

• *Work teams* are established to perform the work that constitutes the core transformation processes of the organization (that is, the processes that result in the design and delivery of services, the design, manufacturing, and delivery of products, or the provision of services to those who design and deliver products or services). The production team is an example; it houses the contributors who carry out a component of the production process. Other examples are new product development teams, proposal teams, concurrent engineering teams, product commercialization teams, consulting teams, and industry sales and service teams. The outputs of work teams are the products or services that are delivered to internal or external customers, and their shared goals are phrased in terms of indicators of the effectiveness with which products and services are deliv-

ered—indicators dealing with such issues as quality, customer satisfaction, schedule, and cost.

• *Integrating teams* (sometimes called *process integrating teams*)
are established to make sure the work across various parts of the
organization fits together. These include teams that link together
the work of two or more interdependent teams, and teams that cut
across various parts of the organization that share a focus, perhaps
on a particular customer, product, technology, or geography. The
outputs of integrating teams are the direction they provide to the
units that are being integrated and the coordination that results.
Their goal is the coordination of efforts toward the shared focus.
The interdependence among the units being integrated often stems
from the fact that they are participants in a common organizational
process in which they play different but related parts.

• *Management teams* are a special example of integrating teams.
A management team is an integrating team whose power to influence the units that it is integrating comes at least in part from hierarchical position. It is responsible for coordinating the management
of a number of subunits (teams, work groups) that are interdependent in the accomplishment of a collective output, such as an entire
process or product. The outputs of the management team include
not only the direction it provides but also the management of the
overall design and performance of the unit for which it is responsible. Its shared goal is the overall performance of the unit. At the
top of the organization, the executive management team provides
overall strategic direction and manages the capabilities and performance of business units.

• *Improvement teams* are established not to perform the core
transformation processes of the organization but to make improvements in the capability of the organization to deliver its products
and services effectively. Process redesign teams, quality improvement teams, and other kinds of task teams and organizational
redesign teams are examples of improvement teams (Ledford,

Lawler, and Mohrman, 1988). The shared goal of these teams is improvements to the way in which the organization goes about doing its core work—improvements that make it possible for the organization to achieve better results. Their output may be the design of the improvements and/or the project management of their implementation.

Many organizations set up teams whose mission is the improvement of the processes of the organization, but this does not mean that improvement is the purview of improvement teams only. In fact, work teams and management teams retain responsibility for improving their own performance. One indicator of an effective team is its ability to continually improve its performance, through changes in the internal strategies it employs to do the work and the manner in which it relates to its customers and the other parts of the organization with which it is interdependent. However, much of the improvement potential in an organization lies in changing systems and processes that transcend particular teams, and change such as this requires a systemwide perspective. The literature dealing with both total quality management and reengineering advocates the use of cross-functional quality teams or redesign teams to conduct the problem-solving and organizational design processes that lead to significant improvements (Juran, 1989; Deming, 1986; Hammer and Champy, 1993).

The distinction between work teams, integrating teams (with the subcategory of management teams), and improvement teams is important, because each kind of team presents a different set of challenges to those managing the team. Work teams, which are accountable for a defined product or service, have a legitimacy that stems from their mission. They have responsibility for the strategies they employ in doing the piece of work for which they are accountable. Improvement teams, on the other hand, do work that sets the stage for *others* in the organization to change the way they do things. They can be successful only to the extent that others accept their ideas. Thus it is important that legitimacy be attributed to these teams by the groups who will be impacted (Mohrman and Ledford, 1985). Their mandate has to come from the formal leadership at the level at which the improvements are going to be made (for example, the business unit), and their authority in implementing the changes has to be conferred from that level. On the other hand, their efficacy in such implementation depends on their having addressed the issues of the units that will be affected. The same matter arises for integrating teams that are not management teams. Their authority to integrate the work of various performing units comes from their mandate from the formal leadership of the more inclusive unit, but their efficacy depends on addressing the needs of the various performing units and on the influence network they have developed (Galbraith, 1994).

The Team's Relationship to the Formal Organizational Structure

Teams can be formal units that appear on an organization chart and report as a unit to the next level of the organization, or they can be "overlay" structures that include individuals who are members of various formal units and who report various places. The difference is shown in Figures 2.1 and 2.2. These figures illustrate project teams, but they could just as easily illustrate customer teams or product teams. Figure 2.1 depicts an organization in which the project teams constitute the formal operational structure of the organization. Even though the members of each team represent different functions, they all report to a common manager. In this structure, the functions are not line but staff units whose responsibility is to maintain and enhance the functional capabilities of the organization. They may operate through overlay councils that link together functional experts from different projects.

In Figure 2.2, the formal structure of the organization is functional, and the projects are overlay teams. That is, they are composed of members who are formally located in different functional

Figure 2.1. Line Project Team Structure.

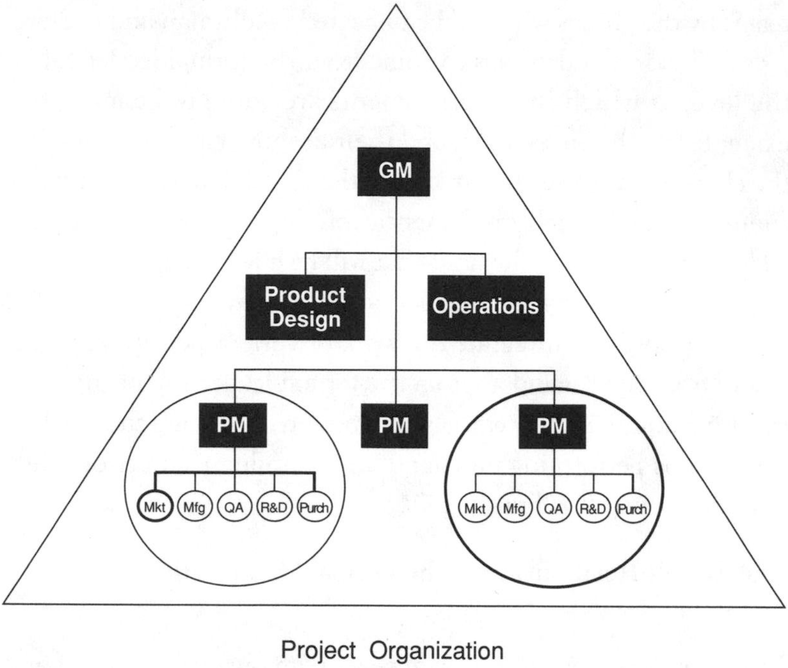

Project Organization

Key: GM = general manager; PM = program or project manager.

groups. One can conceive of the team structure as being "laid over" the formal organization structure. Members of the project team report to their different functional managers. Functional managers have responsibility for maintaining and enhancing functional capabilities, but they also have review and perhaps operational authority over functional contributors.

In a third type of organization—the matrix organization—project team members report to *both* their project and functional managers.

The differences between these three approaches are substantial. In the project organization, the challenge is to find ways for the functional perspective to be strong enough to ensure technical excellence and technical learning. The organization may want to create a technical council with responsibility for these issues. In the functional organization with overlay teams, on the other hand, the

Figure 2.2. Overlay Project Team Structure.

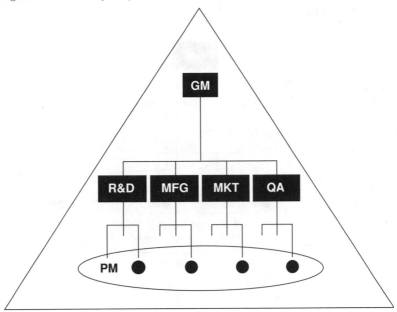

Functional Organization

Key: GM = general manager; PM = program or project manager.

challenge is to create sufficient focus on the given project despite the fact that members report to different bosses (who themselves may have conflicting priorities). Meeting this challenge may require a cross-functional management team to align the different functional bosses on the goals and priorities for the project.

Figure 2.3 illustrates the situation in which cross-functional project teams report to cross-functional management teams. The advantage of this design is that the management team is able to manage the various teams from a cross-functional perspective and is composed of managers who have functional management responsibility as well. If the management team is effective in providing integrated leadership, alignment can more easily be achieved between the priorities and expectations of each team and the functional requirements, even if individuals continue to report to their functional managers.

Figure 2.3. Cross-Functional Project Teams and Management Team in a Project Organization.

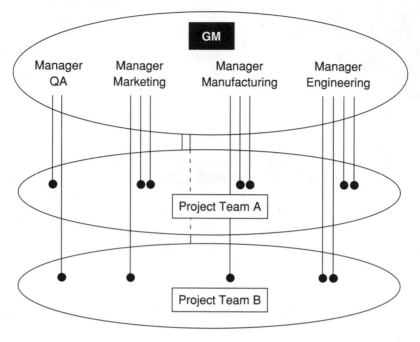

Improvement teams are often overlay teams. They draw from various organizational units in order to have the multiple perspectives required to deal with systemic problems and processes. They are often described as "parallel" structures, because they are envisioned as outside of and supplementing the organization's operating structure. The use of parallel structures has been advocated as a way to permit and stimulate creative and innovative approaches that might otherwise be snuffed out by the operating structure, with its preoccupation with operations (Stein and Kanter, 1980; Zand, 1974). Unfortunately, such structures are also sometimes treated as "extra"; as a result, their activities may be seen as low priority and the implementation of their recommendations may be considered burdensome or optional (Lawler and Mohrman, 1985, 1987). In this book, improvement teams will not be treated as parallel. They and other overlay teams will be treated as performing units that are part of the integrated system of teams that compose the organization.

The Team's Duration

Teams vary along a continuum from permanent (at least as permanent as any structure can be in today's world) to temporary. An industry-oriented customer-service team that is set up to service all hospital accounts through time would be viewed as an ongoing structure, designed to handle an ongoing flow of business. On the other hand, a proposal or bid team established for a particular opportunity might have an expected life span of only several months. In between these extremes are program teams or project teams that handle the life cycle of projects that could be several years in duration.

This distinction is important. Permanent structures can be managed within the normal periodic framework for goal setting, review, and reward. Temporary structures, on the other hand, often have a life cycle that is not congruent with the normal business and performance management cycle. Their projects may have milestones that reflect completion of a phase or step and that may not neatly fall into a calendar year. During the year, individuals may serve on a number of teams that are assigned a task, complete their task, and are sunsetted. Managers cannot rely on the normal performance management cycle to manage these teams; rather, they must develop performance management practices that fit with the life cycle of temporary teams and find ways to relate performance on a number of temporary teams to the consequences experienced by the individuals. If performance on temporary teams is to be considered a serious part of one's job, it must be formally recognized as part of one's performance.

An additional issue concerning time frame relates to the organization's investment in team development and self-management. It is very sensible to invest a substantial amount of time and energy in the development of permanent teams and those that have a limited but substantial duration. The organization will benefit greatly from the ability of these teams to manage themselves effectively. For teams with a short life—especially those with a technically complex task—it may not make sense to invest a great deal of time and energy in making them self-managing. Leadership, facilitation, and management may be needed to efficiently provide such teams with structure and to help team members develop strategies for task accomplishment. These supports may be just as important to long-term teams at the outset; but there the goal might be for the teams to gradually require less ongoing external or hierarchical support, eventually becoming self-sufficient. It will become easier for an organization to establish relatively self-managing short-duration teams as it becomes more proficient in the teaming process, because members will be experienced in self-management tasks. In the early stages of the transition to teams, however, short-duration teams may need more formal leadership.

The Organization as a System of Teams

Figure 2.4 illustrates a team-based organization—an organization in which teams are the core performing units. Rather than depicting the organization as a line-and-box diagram, we have chosen to depict it as a system with performing units nested within one another. This figure allows for all the types of teams that have been discussed above: the process teams depicted can be integrating or improvement teams, for example. By process teams we mean teams that are focused around a central business process, either to achieve the ongoing integration of its subprocesses and to make sure the business process is functioning as needed or to improve the business process by its redesign.

Figure 2.4 graphically illustrates several important features of the team-based organization. First, performing units are nested in each other; consequently, an individual who is part of a performing unit at one level (for example, a team) is also part of the larger per-

Figure 2.4. A Team-Based Organization.

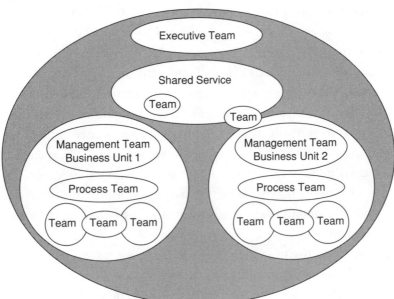

forming unit (for example, a business unit). The performance of the individual has to be judged in the context of the team of which he or she is a part. The performance of the team has to be judged in the context of the business unit of which it is a part. Performance out of context is of no value to the organization. For example, a team that does an excellent job of developing a price/performance product may have contributed little to a business unit whose strategy is to manufacture and sell commodities. Second, the figure implies the domain of authority of each performing unit. When a team is considering an issue that has implications beyond its bounds, the resolution of that issue must occur in a forum that has a broader scope than the team. That forum may be informal; that is, representatives of all affected groups may be informally convened to resolve a particular issue. On the other hand, there may be a formal structure, such as an integrating team or a management team, whose job it is to resolve recurring broader-scope issues.

An important issue for the team-based organization concerns the composition of management teams and integrating teams (such as process teams that cut across units). The scope of decisions that are in the purview of these teams is such that the teams need to be composed of individuals who can represent the perspectives of the various units that they are managing or integrating. A management team that is managing a number of cross-functional teams will be called on to give direction to and resolve issues concerning multiple functions. It must include people able to represent, speak for, and exert influence on those functions. Likewise, other integrating teams whose work will impact multiple performing units have to include individuals who can represent the perspectives of those performing units.

Depicting the organization as a team-based system enables the separation of scope of authority from our traditional notions of hierarchical levels or grades of jobs in a bureaucracy. For example, a process integrating team has authority to make decisions that result in the integration of the work of various teams. However, the members of the team do not necessarily have job grades and positions at a higher hierarchical level than the members of the teams they are integrating. In fact, the members of the process integrating team may be peer representatives from the teams that are being integrated. Nevertheless, in a systemic sense, the process integrating team has authority at a broader scope than the teams it is integrating. Continuing this line of thought, it is not necessary even for the members of a management team to be at higher hierarchical job levels than the members of other teams in the unit. It is necessary only that the team have authority to provide overall direction, to determine the overall design of the unit, and to carry out performance management responsibilities. Thus an organization can place individuals in those teams where their skills and knowledge can best be used, irrespective of what rung on a bureaucratic hierarchy they occupy. In fact, it becomes unnecessary to think of people as occupying a certain rung. *In essence, hierarchy is redefined in terms of the*

scope and domain of the decision-making authority of a team within the
system rather than in terms of a chain of individual reporting relations.

Work Dynamics in the Team-Based Organization

The structure of a team-based organization delineates how tasks and
the people who do them will be clustered into a network of teams
as performing units, each of which is held collectively accountable
for its performance. In Chapter One, we argued that the nature of
knowledge work creates certain organizational requirements that
must be addressed in designing the team-based organization. The
kinds of teams described in the preceding sections must be able to
operate effectively within these requirements.

Knowledge work involves multiple, specialized knowledge bases,
is frequently performed by specialists who expect professional autonomy (but are often embedded in highly interdependent work networks), is nonroutine, and requires judgment, interpretation, and
the creation of knowledge. Multiple, concurrent organizational
processes influence one another in organizations involved in knowledge work. For example, in a new product development process,
subprocesses may entail the development of software, hardware,
marketing plans, and manufacturing and testing procedures. Things
happening in quite different parts of the organization have implications for the work that is going on in many other locations. For
these subprocesses to be coordinated, individuals with different
worldviews have to integrate their work. Furthermore, the environment is dynamic, contributing an inherent uncertainty to decision making that already entails contention because of multiple
perspectives. The dynamics of teams in a knowledge-work setting
are affected by this uncertainty, contention, and complexity. In the
midst of all this, they must be able to establish sufficient shared
understanding to allow them to proceed with their work.

The nature of knowledge work establishes requirements that set
the stage for the within-team and cross-team dynamics that occur

in the organization. The essence of the collective work of a knowledge-work team is processing a complex array of information and
deciding on a course of action that guides the contributors in the
same direction so that their work fits together. Most knowledge-
work teams do not sit in a room and do all their work collectively.
They come together as a team or as subgroupings of members
to make sure their work fits and to consolidate their knowledge.
They make decisions that provide a context for each other's work.
For example, a drug commercialization team might meet to develop
a PERT chart showing the tasks that need to be completed prior to
the development of materials to support a new drug launch. The
team might meet again to make midcourse corrections to their
plans if team members find out from one of their regions that local
law has changed and that two forms of the drug will be required.
Meanwhile, multiple members of the same team might work interactively to produce a prerelease marketing brochure and, in the
course of doing so, combine perspectives and work out the contention between the marketers, who would like to be able to be very
optimistic in their descriptions of what the drug can do, and the
physicians, who promote caution. In all these cases, a number of
contributors come together to agree on a common approach, work
out common goals, join their perspectives and knowledge, or make
sure that the pieces that they are working on fit with each other.

Our study found that the activities associated with knowledge
work can be conceptualized as an iterative cycle that begins with a
number of players with divergent understandings and knowledge
and proceeds through processes by which the team converges on an
outcome (see Figure 2.5).

This *divergence/convergence cycle* occurs in phases, each of which
has a "product" that has to be agreed to by all parties. For example,
in a new product development team, the first phase may yield a concept that includes a high-level definition of product, market, and
manufacturing parameters. A later stage might yield a prototype. As
the project proceeds, the divergence/convergence cycle deals with

Figure 2.5. Basic Divergence/Convergence Cycle.

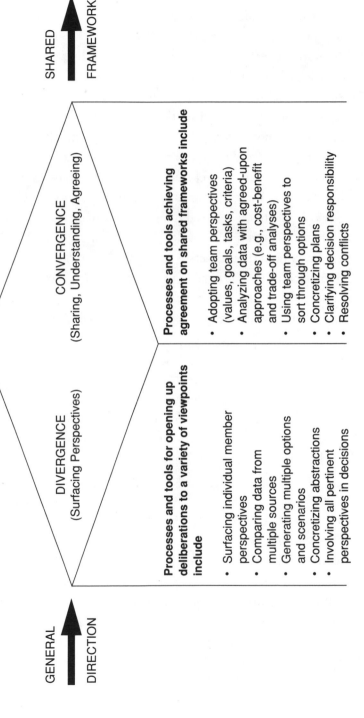

GENERAL
DIRECTION

SHARED
FRAMEWORK

DIVERGENCE
(Surfacing Perspectives)

CONVERGENCE
(Sharing, Understanding, Agreeing)

Processes and tools for opening up deliberations to a variety of viewpoints include

- Surfacing individual member perspectives
- Comparing data from multiple sources
- Generating multiple options and scenarios
- Concretizing abstractions
- Involving all pertinent perspectives in decisions

Processes and tools achieving agreement on shared frameworks include

- Adopting team perspectives (values, goals, tasks, criteria)
- Analyzing data with agreed-upon approaches (e.g., cost-benefit and trade-off analyses)
- Using team perspectives to sort through options
- Concretizing plans
- Clarifying decision responsibility
- Resolving conflicts

increasingly detailed and less global issues, since the earlier phases have provided a general framework for the later phases. At the beginning of each phase, contributors bring their own worldviews: knowledge bases, preferences, work and decision algorithms, and experience. Through a series of joint activities, the network of contributors carries out activities that contribute to the product; these activities also contribute to reducing the differences in the way contributors understand the new product development process and the product that is being developed. This is a process of "gaining alignment between the major lines of contention" (Pava, 1983, p. 71).

Much of what is referred to as group dynamics is shaped by the divergence/convergence cycle. Team members often have a hard time processing their diversity of viewpoints. They may be intolerant of each other and unable to see each others' points of view, or they may have conflicting self-interest. There may be a status hierarchy that prevents people from listening to each other. The right people may not be attending the meetings. Figure 2.5 lists processes and tools that can help teams go through the iterative divergence/convergence cycle. Effective teams are able to achieve a shared understanding by spending time working toward successful navigation of that cycle. Internal team processes that we found in our study to be related to the ability to arrive at a shared understanding include the following:

• *Adopting team perspectives*. Developing a viewpoint for the group as a whole. The process is one of shifting focus from individual views and issues to those of the team as a collective. The process of focusing on creating of a team performance value, a team goal, team criteria, team principles, or a team task can help members to see how their various individual values, goals, and tasks—while probably different—can still fit into those that they mutually agree to adopt for the team. This process is especially important because it results in team values and criteria that can be used in subsequent deliberations to sort through and make decisions about alternative options.

• *Analyzing data*. Using agreed-upon approaches and algorithms to sort through, analyze, and evaluate information. This can include cost-benefit analyses and various forms of trade-off analyses. Data should come from as many divergent sources as possible. The presence of data themselves can be a powerful source of convergence. (For instance, the availability of customer preferences often helps to easily cut through arguments about design choices and what services should be delivered.)

- *Evaluating options.* Using agreed-upon criteria and values to sort through multiple options or scenarios before making final choices.

- *Concretizing plans and actions.* Talking about tangible specifics instead of abstract concepts. Converting abstractions into reality. Firming up general, superficial agreements to make sure that there is true agreement. This process both reveals differences in how people operationalize ideas and gives people something tangible and concrete on which they can reach agreement and plan for action. Instead of just agreeing, for instance, that "customer responsiveness" is desirable, effective teams talk about and agree to specific examples (including, for instance, examples where customer responsiveness might work against other desired outcomes, such as cost) and make sure members are imaging similar boundaries to the concept.

- *Clarifying decision responsibility.* Making sure it is known which teams are responsible for which decision domains and assuring that those teams have the necessary breadth of membership. It is important to make sure there is agreement about where and how certain decisions will be made so that the various parts of the organization or members of the team do not each mistakenly believe that they have authority to make or veto certain decisions. This also includes being clear which decisions are team decisions and which lie in the bailiwick of particular members. (If a decision is primarily technical and independent of other considerations, for example, it may fall in the domain of one team member with highly specialized expertise. A team does not have to make all decisions collectively.)

- *Resolving conflict.* Applying various tools and techniques that allow the team to move from inevitable conflicts stemming from differing viewpoints by developing new shared viewpoints that reinterpret the conflicts in a resolvable way. This is perhaps the most important of all, since none of the above processes will yield common direction if the team does not work through the conflicting preferences and views of its multiple members. An effective team is not one that achieves common direction by fiat; it is one that deliberates where there are differing perspectives and finds mutually agreeable resolution.

The divergence/convergence cycle may not be satisfactorily navigated if teams lack adequate skills to apply information-surfacing, conflict resolution, and consensus-building processes or if they do not know of or have access to tools that are available to help groups process information and agree on direction. Both training and the involvement of skilled facilitators may help teams learn how to operate more effectively.

Lack of alignment can come from within the team, as when members begin with very different assumptions about and preferences for the project; or it can originate externally, as when other teams, higher management, customers, or even other divisions that have an interest in the project place competing demands on the work. The Analytico teams mentioned in Chapter One experienced considerable divergence from external sources. In dynamic, complex, and interdependent organizational settings, external factors are always going to impinge on team processes. Because the success of any organization depends on how well it handles the ever-present divergence—whatever its source—and encourages alignment, organizations need to structure themselves in ways that enhance the probability that contention will be effectively and efficiently resolved.

Team Empowerment and Self-Management

Popular discussions of teams frequently describe "empowered teams" or "self-managing teams" as the ideal, often with little definition of these terms and even less discussion of where they are appropriate.

The lack of clarity about these terms often leads to confusion during the implementation of teams: if management is unclear about whether and how it can influence teams, teams develop an unrealistic sense of their own autonomy.

The definition of empowerment that we have developed, based on our team studies, is this: "the capability to make a difference in the attainment of individual, team, and organizational goals." It has a directional element: teams are empowered to attain goals that fit with the overall strategy of the organization and conform to goals of the larger business units within which they are nested. Implicit in the directional element is the notion of reward: because individuals can best accomplish their own personal goals by contributing to team and organizational success, they are "rewarded" when they contribute to organizational success. Our definition also has a capability element: teams that are empowered have the knowledge, skills, information, resources, and power to perform in a manner that enables them to make a difference. Our treatment of this aspect of empowerment draws heavily on the high-involvement model of Lawler (1986, 1992). According to this perspective, people become involved in the success of the organization when they have access to empowering resources.

The depiction of the team-based organization in the preceding section sheds some light on the realistic limits of the power of a team. The team is defined by its scope, and it has the power to make decisions within that scope. Furthermore, it needs effective influence routes to teams that make broader-scope decisions affecting its ability to do its work effectively. *Power, according to this model, is both the authority to make decisions and the opportunity to influence decisions made elsewhere that impact one's work.*

Thus an empowered team is able to make a difference in the attainment of individual, team, and organizational goals, because it has clear direction and the knowledge, skills, information, and resources to do its job. In addition, it has power to make decisions within its scope and to influence decisions that are of a larger scope. Finally, team members experience positive outcomes when they perform effectively. Given this definition, it seems clear that a team will be more effective if the conditions for high involvement are created and the team is empowered. (Empowerment will be discussed in greater detail in Chapter Nine.)

The extent of team self-management is a more direct design decision. Self-management involves the movement into the team of management functions that traditionally reside with managers. It potentially places control over work processes and strategies, scheduling and coordination, resource utilization, performance management, and personnel decisions in the team. Substantial self-management has been attained in manufacturing settings where the technology is well understood and stable and the work of the team can be relatively self-contained (Pasmore, 1988). However, these conditions are not present in all work settings. The dynamic nature of many work settings and the interdependence necessary throughout many organizations make full self-management less attainable. Thus the determination of how much self-management to vest in a team needs to be an explicit part of the design process. (This issue will be discussed in more detail in Chapter Five.)

Team Effectiveness

Teams are established for a broad variety of purposes, and their effectiveness has to be judged in light of those purposes. In addition, however, teams have consequences for an organization that go beyond how effectively they, as performing units, accomplish their mission. For example, they have consequences for their own members and for their customers; and, to the extent that they are interdependent with the rest of the organization, they have consequences for other performing units. Thus a broad perspective is useful in judging team effectiveness.

Defining Team Effectiveness

Hackman has defined group effectiveness as consisting of three dimensions (1990, pp. 6–7). The first is the extent to which the group's "productive output (that is, its product, service, or decision) meets the standards of quantity, quality, and timeliness of the people who receive, review, and/or use that output." In this book, we refer to this dimension as *team performance*.

The second dimension is the degree to which, in the process of working together, the team "enhances the capability of members to work together interdependently in the future." In keeping with the continuous improvement focus that characterizes all of the companies we have studied, we focus on a closely related concept, the *learning and improvements* that the team has been able to achieve in its processes and in the way it organizes to do its work.

Hackman's third dimension addresses the development and need-satisfaction of the group's members—a dimension that is referred to in this book simply as *satisfaction*. This dimension was important to the companies we studied: they feared that, in the large-scale transition to a team organization, they would lose the commitment of their employees as a result of the demands and stresses of learning to perform effectively in teams and the uncertainty employees felt about how they would fare in a team organization.

As we have noted, team performance is not a straightforward matter of whether the team accomplishes its objectives, especially in knowledge-work settings. In our research, we encountered teams that were doing a good job of accomplishing team goals but were doing so at the expense of the performance of other teams with which they were interdependent. For example, we studied one technical support group that was meeting its throughput goals by avoiding complex and uncertain support projects that would have tied up resources and possibly interfered with delivery of more routine services to the majority of customers. A new product development team in another organization met its goals for cost, schedule, and quality, but it ignored the organization's need for the product to be developed in such a way that it could be optimized in the plant, which was introducing new manufacturing processes. Costs of rework and schedule delays were subsequently incurred by the plant.

We have come to think of team performance as occurring at two levels: the extent to which each team performs effectively in terms of its own productive output and the extent to which it contributes to the effectiveness of the larger business unit of which it is a part. Thus our criteria for the effectiveness of a team-based knowledge organization address the effectiveness of the teams that constitute it and the effectiveness of the business unit as a whole. Business-unit effectiveness is multifaceted: it depends not only on the effectiveness of each performing unit but also on how well the work of the performing units is integrated; it depends not only on the efficient application and effective utilization of resources within a team but also on whether there is efficient distribution of resources among teams.

In our study, we measured performance at both the team and the business-unit level along the following dimensions: cost effectiveness, quality, productivity, continuous improvement and innovation, customer satisfaction, speed, utilization of key skills, and member commitment. We also examined aspects of the organization that provided a shared way of operating, such as common processes, aligned goals, and a unifying strategy. The effectiveness of individual teams was also related to variables that permitted the teams to optimize their own operations, such as access to team-specific information and committed resources; while business-unit effectiveness was related more to variables that created focus on overall business-unit operation, such as unitwide information and a pay system based on organizational performance (in other words, factors that were not related to the performance of the teams themselves). The pattern of results substantiated our hypothesis that the effectiveness of team-based knowledge-work organizations is a function not only of the effectiveness of the teams but also of the extent to which overall integration is achieved. Looking ahead, then, designing team organizations requires attention to features that foster a dual focus on the team and on the larger system in which it is embedded.

In addition to measuring performance at two levels—the team and the business unit—we also measured it from a number of different perspectives. Teams and business units were rated by team members, managers, and customers on the same dimensions. Effectiveness ratings varied between the different raters, in a pattern indicative of the rater's perspective on and interest in the team. Team member ratings, for example, were highly related to the members' perceptions of the effectiveness of team processes. Managers and customers tended to heavily weight the various performance outcomes that were important to them, but their judgments of team effectiveness had little to do with the internal processes of the team.

Our interpretation of these different ratings of effectiveness is not that one or the other is correct; rather, different stakeholders have different perspectives, expectations, and needs regarding the team and the organization. Each perspective is legitimate, and overall effectiveness is measured in the extent to which the performing unit can meet the needs of its various legitimate stakeholders. This view underpins much of the discussion later in the book, which calls for considerable multidirectionality in the processes used in a team-based organization.

Our research has also underscored the importance of taking a broad perspective on effectiveness. We have found that, while performance may be of central importance in designing team settings, some design features can work against aspects of effectiveness that have long-term implications for performance and the viability of the organization. These additional effectiveness dimensions are improvement and learning, and satisfaction. As discussed earlier, improvement and learning are often major reasons for using teams in the first place. But the very design features that lead to improvement and learning can, in the short term, seem to work against performance. The introduction of such features requires intensive team processes that consume time and may be perceived by external stakeholders as deflecting the team's attention away from performance. Satisfaction, too, is necessary for the long-term viability of the human organization. Management must be careful not to make design choices that temporarily boost performance at the long-term expense of the relationship of employees to their organization.

An Effectiveness Framework for Team-Based Knowledge Organizations

Figure 2.6 presents the effectiveness framework for team-based knowledge organizations that was initially generated by our first-phase research, in which we contrasted struggling and effective teams. This model was then confirmed and refined in our work with a broader sample of team-based organizational units. We have focused on the organizational design features that contribute to effectiveness in these settings, rather than on the internal dynamics of teams. This is not to dismiss the importance of internal dynamics; however, we believe that the internal dynamics of teams are in great measure shaped by the design of the organization.

Figure 2.6 illustrates the fact that the success of teams depends upon their being used in environmental and strategic contexts where the nature of the task makes teams appropriate. It also illustrates the important design features of team-based organizations and shows how they can lead directly and indirectly to effectiveness.

Many organizations simply establish teams and expect teamwork to occur. Our research suggests that this does not always happen. Often when teams do not accomplish expected objectives, management simply arranges for more and more training, hoping that teamwork and integration of work will occur if people become more skilled. However, the organization is a system, and its components tend to complement one another and reinforce certain patterns of behavior. Thus the design components of an organization that traditionally fostered individual performance continue to reinforce that mode of performance. Establishing teams is not a big enough intervention to change behavior.

Certain behavioral conditions need to be in place in effective team organizations. We found that effective knowledge-work settings were characterized by high levels of integration and coordination. They were able to achieve timely decision making. Fur-

Figure 2.6. An Effectiveness Framework for Team-Based Knowledge Organizations.

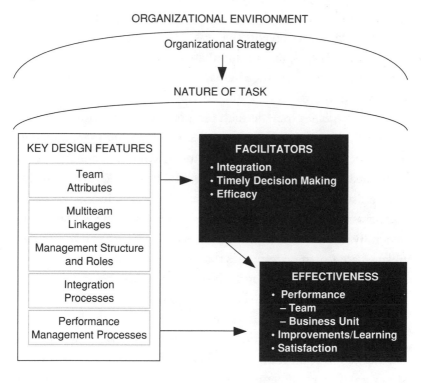

thermore, members had a high sense of confidence in their own efficacy—in their ability to accomplish their goals. These conditions, called *facilitators* in Figure 2.6, do not arise simply because teams are established, nor can managers direct, command, or will them to exist. In order for these conditions to exist, more than the structure of the organization needs to change. Many aspects of the organizational system have to be purposefully designed to support the new way of performing. Galbraith (1994), for example, stresses the development processes, planning and budgeting, and information and reward systems necessary to support lateral integration. Similarly, Hackman (1990) includes rewards, information, education and coaching, and facilitation.

Figure 2.6 also illustrates aspects of the organization that have to be designed to support effective performance in team-based orga-nizations. They promote conditions—integration, timely decision making, and efficacy—that enable teams to be effective, and they have a direct impact on effectiveness. They include team attributes, multiteam linkages, management structure and roles, integration processes, and performance management processes. Let us look at each in turn.

Team attributes include such factors as the composition of the team, whether contributors are dedicated, whether team members are co-located, the reporting relationships of team members, how often meetings are held, and the like. *Multiteam linkages* refer to the mechanisms established to handle interdependencies among teams and across the organization. In knowledge-work settings, teams are generally not self-contained. Both team attributes and multiteam linkages are structural responses that must fit with the task, and both contribute equally to performance facilitators and effectiveness.

Management structure and roles are also structural design elements. Here, however, the emphasis is on a redefinition of the hierarchical relationships and roles rather than on the lateral relationships emphasized in team attributes and multiteam linkages. All of these structural design elements contain important sets of implied skills and abilities that people must have in addition to those required to do the task.

Integration processes refer to the practices and actions by which the various structural elements, roles, people, and tasks are inte-grated. These include such things as communication processes, deci-sion-making processes, and direction-setting processes (for example, goal setting).

Performance management processes are especially important. These include the manner in which individuals, teams, and busi-ness units define what performance is to be, develop the processes and resources to achieve performance, review performance, and reward performers.

These various design features of the organization that support effective team performance are discussed in detail in later parts of this book and are the explicit basis for Part Two, where we go through the series of design choices that are required to create a team organization. These design choices include, but are not limited to, the structural features of the organization. They also include the design of organizational processes.

In general, our (and others') research has found that, although the internal processes that occur in a team are important to the team's performance, aspects of the organizational context in which the team exists are equally important. A team whose internal processes are excellent can still fail to accomplish its goals because of issues external to the team that influence its ability to perform. The organizational context includes human resource systems, managerial practices, decision-making and information-sharing processes, and the strategic and goal context in which the team operates. Thus managers in organizations that are transitioning to a team design must make sure that they shape a context that promotes effective team functioning.

Key Issues

Those designing a team-based organization need to keep in mind the following key issues:

1. There are a number of different kinds of teams, and they vary on three relevant dimensions: their mission (work teams, integrating teams, or improvement teams), their relationship to the formal structure of the organization (formal units or units overlaying the formal organization and pulling from different units), and their duration (temporary or long-lasting).

2. A team organization can be viewed as a network or system of teams in which teams are embedded in larger business units and have lateral relationships with other teams.

3. A team's authority is determined by the scope of its responsibility.

4. Empowerment of teams requires that they receive direction and have the capability to make a difference in the attainment of goals.

5. Effectiveness of a team-based knowledge organization is measured in the performance of teams, the teams' contribution to the performance of the business unit, the learning and improvements that employees attain, and the organization's satisfaction of employee needs.

6. The key organizational challenge in nonroutine knowledge work is to design structures and processes that foster the integration of the work of people with diverse knowledge bases.

Design Sequence for the Transition to Team-Based Organization.

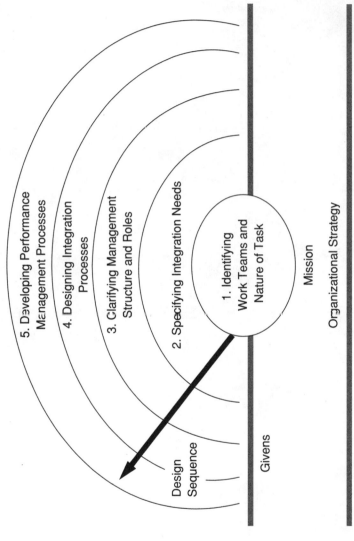

5. Developing Performance Management Processes

4. Designing Integration Processes

3. Clarifying Management Structure and Roles

2. Specifying Integration Needs

1. Identifying Work Teams and Nature of Task

Mission

Organizational Strategy

Environment

Givens

Design Sequence

Part II

· ·

The Design Sequence

The following five chapters—Chapters Three through Seven—are the core of this book. They sequentially address the five categories of design features first presented in Figure 2.6. The design sequence we present starts with the identification of the teams necessary to achieve the organizational mission. The figure to the left depicts this bottom-up sequence.

For the purposes of this design model, we assume that organizational strategy and mission have already been established and that the foundation for teams has been laid. Although the mission defines, in a very general way, the nature of the tasks to be performed, the tasks are also susceptible to design. In fact, it is impossible to identify work teams and determine their structure without simultaneously defining the tasks they are to perform. A particular team structure should be adopted only if it is the best way to perform and integrate the tasks required to deliver valued products and services to the customers. On the other hand, once that team structure has been deemed appropriate, tasks need to be configured in such a way that the teams have responsibility for an identifiable process or product.

We describe the identification of work teams (the first step in the design sequence) in Chapter Three. Chapters Four and Five address aspects of the structural context in which the team designs can exist. In Chapter Four, we describe the design issues involved in identifying the integration needs among teams and creating the linkages that set the stage for integration (the second step). Chapter Five presents the structural design options for management and leadership roles (the third step).

Chapters Six and Seven present the design issues underlying establishment of the processes necessary to make the structural designs work. In the companies we studied, changes in structure did not lead automatically to changes in such processes as communication. These processes need to be purposefully changed to fit with the new structural configuration and the changes in the way work will be done. In some cases, systems have to be redesigned to foster new processes. Chapter Six enumerates both hierarchical and lateral processes for achieving integration (the fourth step). Chapter Seven focuses on processes necessary to manage performance in team-based settings (the fifth step).

Three cases are presented as concrete examples of team-based organizations. These case organizations, whose team and integrating structures are explained in Chapters Three and Four, will be referred to throughout the book to illustrate the structural and process issues being developed.

The sequence presented in Part Two is a *design* sequence, not an implementation sequence. It is a guide to the second stage of the self-design model presented in Chapter One. It specifies a systematic way of thinking through the structures and processes that constitute a team-based organization. A complete design process addresses each of the design steps. We advocate that organizations moving to a team-based design think through all of the steps before implementing teams and arrive at least at a high-level preliminary conceptualization in each area. On the other hand, all design features may not be implemented simultaneously; and in some areas, such as communication, system development may precede complete implementation. Furthermore, the sequence of implementation may not follow the sequence of the design process. Implementation sequencing involves a different set of decisions, made with a vision of the ultimate design in mind.

Sometimes the distinction between design and implementation is unclear. The design represents the system of organizational elements that, when implemented, will create an effective team-based organization. As implementation occurs, the design that actually results can change for a number of reasons; organizations learn as they go through implementation and can refine and supplement the design they started out to implement.

Most of the organizations we studied did not initially consider the breadth of design issues that we will cover in Part Two. In most cases, they implemented teams and then discovered by trial and error that they needed changes in the design of the organization to enable the teams to operate effectively. Many made changes in the composition of the teams themselves, having discovered that the original team delineations did not fit the work or were unwieldy.

In part, this trial and error is an inevitable part of the design and implementation of fundamental change, as will be discussed in Chapter Eleven. On the other hand, this book is a product of what these companies learned and is intended to give other companies embarking on this journey a leg up. The companies we studied did not start out with a design guide such as this. Their learnings are incorporated into this design model, which we hope will be a useful tool for organizations as they lay the foundation for their team-based organization and design it.

Figure 3.1. Step One of the Design Sequence: Identifying Work Teams.

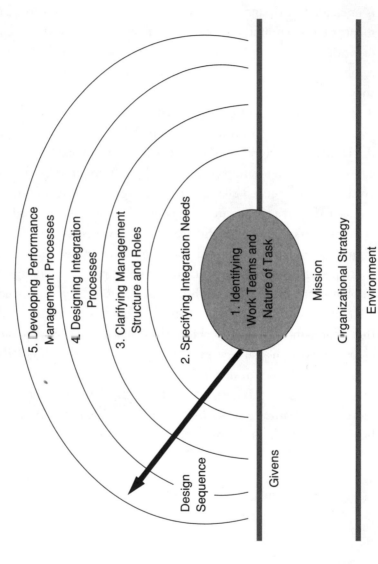

5. Developing Performance Management Processes

4. Designing Integration Processes

3. Clarifying Management Structure and Roles

2. Specifying Integration Needs

1. Identifying Work Teams and Nature of Task

Mission

Organizational Strategy

Environment

Design Sequence

Givens

Step One

Identifying Work Teams

The design sequence (see Figure 3.1), which works from the bottom up, begins with the identification of the core work teams, if any, that will be established to deliver a product or service or perform an identifiable part of a process. The transitioning organization initially explores this issue by examining the tasks—that is, the work to be done. Heuristic design approaches to help in this examination will be described below. Before turning to those, however, we will present a prototypical model of a work team and show applications in routine production and office work. We will then present three case examples that illustrate the application of the design heuristics to the determination of an appropriate work team design in non-routine knowledge-work settings. These three examples illustrate a variety of work team models. They will be used to illustrate concepts throughout the book.

The Prototypical Work Team

The prototypical work team has been fully described in the work of sociotechnical systems theorists (for example, Trist and Bamforth, 1951; Cummings, 1978; Pasmore, 1988). It has evolved primarily in relatively routine production settings and has two major characteristics that create the conditions for its effectiveness.

First, the prototypical work team is a relatively self-contained entity. It is collectively responsible for an identifiable and substantial part of the work of the organization. Because it houses all the tasks required for the accomplishment of its mission, it depends minimally on the task accomplishment of people outside its bounds. In its ideal form, the following attributes are in place:

- Support services are included in the team so that the team contains the key resources necessary to accomplish its goals.

- Individuals are cross-trained to facilitate flexibility of utilization of human resources and ease of coordination between members.

- Members are "dedicated" so that they do not have split priorities.

- The team reports as a unit to the organization so that members do not receive potentially conflicting direction from different managers.

Second, the team manages many aspects of its own functioning. Tasks traditionally performed by managers are moved into the team. These include the following:

- *Task management.* The determination of how to apply the team's resources in the accomplishment of its tasks, the determination of strategies to employ in completing the work, coordination of the integration of work between individuals, and responsibility for monitoring and improving the quality of the output.

- *Boundary management.* The management of the team's interfaces with the rest of the organization and with its internal and external customers. This includes ensuring that there are mutually agreed upon processes governing the interfaces and monitoring and improving interface effectiveness.

- *Performance management*. The management of the team's own performance as a collective entity and the performance of the members who compose it. This includes setting objectives, reviewing performance, finding ways to improve performance, and determining rewards.

Figure 3.2 depicts the prototypical work team in a routine production setting. As can be seen, this production team—a real team that works in a production plant—is self-contained: it houses all the tasks required to do its job. The operators in this team are cross-trained on machine operations, packaging, quality inspection, and preventive maintenance. The operators run the machinery that transforms the raw materials that come into their area. They also operate the machinery that packages the transformed raw material in plastic containers. They perform quality checks on both the transformed raw material and its packaging. Finally, they handle the routine maintenance so that the machinery is kept up and running. When they have a serious maintenance problem, they contact the maintenance technician assigned to their line. All the operators, including the team leader, report to the production supervisor. In addition to his job as an operator, the team leader has administrative responsibilities (such as keeping attendance records), and he facilitates team meetings. He also attends a weekly meeting with the other production team leaders and the production supervisor, at which they discuss common issues. The team meets weekly as well: team members review how well the team is performing by comparing its productivity and the quality of its output with its productivity and quality goals, and they discuss problems and suggest ideas for improvement. This structure has enabled the plant of which this team is a part to reduce the number of production supervisors. In the past, each production team had a supervisor; now there is a single production supervisor for the three production teams.

This type of work team is increasingly found in office settings as well. Figure 3.3 shows how one insurance company's operation has been organized into geographically based customer-service units. Each customer-service unit is divided into three work teams: a claims-processing team, an underwriting team, and a service team. The four claims-processing representatives in the unit highlighted in Figure 3.3 are fully cross-trained on life, disability, and health claims, and they do all the claims processing for California. The work is relatively routine, particularly since an information system has been installed to direct the representatives in the handling of most claims. The claims team reviews how it performs each week

Figure 3.2. Prototypical Work Team in a Production Setting.

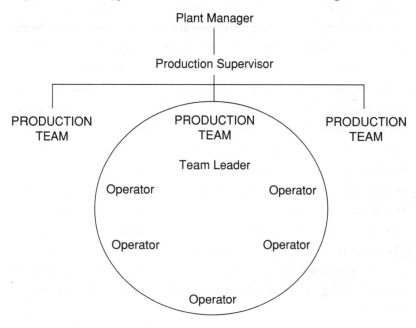

Figure 3.3. Customer-Service Units in an Insurance Company.

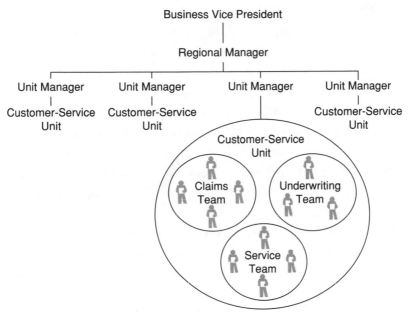

on the number of claims processed, the accuracy of the claims, and the speed of payment. The service team is responsible for correspondence, terminations, policy changes, and check writing, and service team representatives are fully cross-trained in these activities. They assess themselves daily against the standard of providing same-day service to all customer requests. Some service representatives have learned how to do claims processing, and they are available to help the claims team when there is an overload. Management is thinking about eventually combining the service team and the claims team and cross-training the members to increase flexibility. The underwriters are responsible for all underwriting in the state, and each underwriter is cross-trained on just two product lines. (The work is too complex for underwriters to be cross-trained on all product lines.) Each week, the underwriting team reviews its performance on the number of policies written and speed of response.

Although each of the work teams is relatively self-contained, sometimes coordination is required between claims and service or underwriting and claims. All the representatives know each other and coordinate on customer issues as required. They have access to the same computer systems, which expedites coordination. The customer-service unit manager has a monthly meeting with the entire customer-service unit, at which participants review their overall performance against targets, discuss any problems and issues that emerged over the month, and generate ideas for improvement. The unit manager has weekly meetings with each of the work teams, at which work team issues are discussed and ideas for improvement are generated. A customer-satisfaction survey is sent out biannually to the agents that sell insurance products and are serviced by the unit. Results are reviewed at the customer-service unit meetings and customer satisfaction continues to increase. Agents tend to visit with the teams when they are in the home office. This team structure has resulted in the elimination of three levels of management, cumulative productivity improvements of 40 percent, and a dramatic increase in agent satisfaction in this particular firm.

The nomenclature surrounding team-based organizations can be confusing. Notice the terminology in the above description of the insurance company, for example: all members of the customer-service *unit* meet together and address *unit*wide issues, and customer feedback is at the *unit* level. Some companies might think of the customer-service unit as a *team*, however, and of the three work teams as *subteams*. Our rationale for the labeling in this example is based on the fact that the claims, underwriting, and service teams are relatively self-contained and have collective accountability for team performance. In reality, though, what is called a *team* is arbitrary. (Some large teams may operate through a series of dynamic subteams, for example. That configuration is illustrated in the Netco case profiled later in this chapter.)

In both the production and office settings described above, the work is routine: it is well understood and can be programmed. In such an environment, it is a relatively straightforward process to delineate groups that can take full responsibility for a significant piece of work. To the extent that teams can be self-contained and manage themselves, the organization can derive the benefits of on-line coordination and diminished need for external support for and management of the teams. If the team tasks are well designed, the organization should also derive the motivational benefits that result from increased autonomy, variety, feedback, and significance of the work (Cohen, 1994; Hackman and Oldham, 1976, 1980).

Our research confirms that even in nonroutine knowledge-work organizations, the more closely the conditions of self-containment and self-management can be approached, the more effective the teams are. However, in nonroutine work settings, the interdependence network is often so complex that it is not possible to create self-contained teams, and managing the integration between teams is a major task. Consequently, the challenge is to design teams that can generate as much of the benefit of self-containment and self-management as possible while ensuring that there are integrating mechanisms that transcend the teams and effectively link their work. This means that the extent to which teams can manage themselves will vary; that determination needs to be made on a case-by-case basis.

Heuristics to Guide the Identification of Work Teams

Traditional *functional* organizations group people by common specialties and then break work down into functional packets that ultimately translate into individual assignments. Traditional *project* organizations often combine the different specialties required to perform the entire project but then break the work down for members of functional groups within the project. The underlying assumption of these approaches to organizing is that the most efficient way to manage work is to combine like specialties and have the manager manage technical performance and distribute and integrate the work. Formal cross-functional integration occurs higher in the organization, at the level that has general management responsibility. In a project organization, project managers may have management responsibility for contributors from all disciplines, serving as mini–general managers (Galbraith, 1994), but each discipline within the project may have a supervisor or lead who manages that discipline.

Moving to a team-based organization entails a shift away from the logic of a hierarchical breakdown to a logic of lateral distribution and integration of work. To ensure integration, the choice between whether teams should be functional or cross-functional should be based on an analysis of the work and its requirements and a determination of the level at which cross-functional coordination makes sense. Figures 3.4 and 3.5 illustrate two different organizational structures, one using functional and one using cross-functional work teams. In both cases, cross-functional coordination is accomplished.

Figure 3.4 illustrates core work teams that are functional, with the coordination being done by a cross-functional integrating team that can be either a management team or a representative team from the different functions. This organizational structure differs from the

Figure 3.4. Basic Model of Functional Core Work Teams.

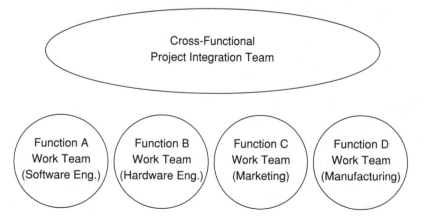

traditional functional organization primarily in that the functional contributors are organized into teams, presumably share a common set of deliverables, and manage how they go about using their resources to accomplish their goals. The assumption is that the team members need to work together to accomplish their objectives and that the organization will benefit by moving the within-function coordination into the team and having the team members integrate their own work rather than rely on managers. In addition, cross-functional integration occurs lower in this organization than it has historically in the functional organization. This model has been successfully applied in a number of companies that are using concurrent approaches to new product development and are moving away from the "over the wall" approaches of the past that moved the project sequentially from function to function.

Figure 3.5 illustrates cross-functional core work teams in an organization where the integration of multiple functions occurs within the core work teams and the work of different cross-functional teams is integrated by a larger-scope cross-functional team. Again, the larger-scope integrating team can be a team of managers or it can be a team of representatives from each core work team. The assumption here is that the contributors from the different functions need

Figure 3.5. Basic Model of Cross-Functional Core Work Teams.

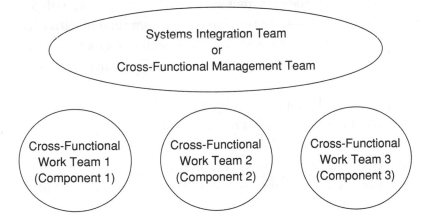

to work together to do their job and that the organization can benefit from establishing teams in which members of the different functions integrate their work themselves. This approach has been used in component design teams where the work of different disciplines is required in the design of each component and the components need to fit with one another. Boeing's design-build teams for each component of the 777 aircraft are an example of this configuration (Galbraith, 1994). Cross-functional second-tier teams integrate the work of component teams into aircraft subsystems.

Whether the core work teams should be functional or cross-functional depends on the key work processes, the nature of the work, and the level at which cross-functional coordination is needed. There are three heuristic approaches that are helpful in shaping the team design: process analysis, deliberations analysis, and task interdependence analysis. These will be briefly described below.

The first step in *process analysis* is to determine the essential work processes (Davenport, 1993)—the sets of activities that deliver value to the customer. The key question to ask is, What are the sets of activities that have to be conducted and integrated with each other to deliver value to the customer? For example, one field office that sells and delivers systems to customers defined two key processes for itself: (1) system definition and contracting and (2) system delivery, installation, and servicing. Within each of these processes are several tasks that are carried out by people with different specialties—tasks that have to be coordinated with each other. The organization needs to have a mechanism for integrating the work of these different specialties so that a customer experiences integrated services.

Figure 3.6 illustrates a high-level process map—a process analysis tool—for an actual new product development (NPD) project. On the left are the skill sets (in many disciplines) that have to be applied to various NPD tasks. The map itself portrays the manner in which the tasks relate to one another through time as the prod-

Figure 3.6. High-Level Process Map for New Product Development.

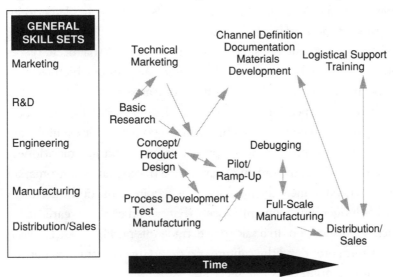

uct moves from concept to development, to manufacturing, and then to distribution. Over fifty people were involved in this NPD, some of whom were only partially dedicated. The company decided that it needed to create work teams within the project to integrate subprocesses. It applied the other two heuristic approaches (deliberations analysis and task interdependence analysis) to determine what work teams were required.

Deliberations analysis identifies dialogues that address ongoing issues that have to be resolved repeatedly in an organization in order to provide shared direction that enables people to complete their tasks (Pava, 1983). The key question in deliberations analysis is, What are the issues and trade-offs that often hold up work in the organization because of inability to arrive at a shared agreement about how to proceed or because conditions change and agreement falls apart? In a new product development organization, for example, trade-offs between schedule and functionality and between customer responsiveness and technical advances have to be resolved over and over again as products go through their development cycle. At another level, trade-offs might be made between putting a functionality in hardware or software.

Deliberations are not single-session conversations that decide issues once and for all. Rather, they are ongoing dialogues in which issues—those involving dynamic trade-offs among aspects of the business or competing perspectives, for example—keep resurfacing. Both customer responsiveness and technological evolution, for example, are key to the new product development organization just mentioned. At any one time, the organization may be trading off time-to-market and the need to meet the here-and-now requirements of the customer with a longer development process that would enable greater technical sophistication. In a sales office, trade-offs may be made between short-term profit and the capture of a new, large customer by cutting the profit margin on initial services.

Because disagreement over such issues holds up the work of the organization (or causes rework) if it goes unresolved, it is important for the organization to establish forums in which deliberations can occur. These forums need to include the various parties with information and knowledge pertinent to the issue. Work teams may be designed in such a way as to include the various parties to key deliberations. For example, a work team charged with handling the system definition process for a particular customer may include the technical people and the sales and service people key to deliberations about whether pricing should be based on actual costs and desired margin or the need to capture and maintain the customer. A new product development team may include members who can resolve the hardware/software trade-offs.

Task interdependence analysis examines where and to what extent individual contributors and teams are interdependent. A work team is a group of people who are interdependent in performing a relatively whole product or service. Only if a given team houses the main interdependencies of its work can it be held fully accountable for its performance. To the extent that members of the team depend on those outside of the team to accomplish the team tasks effectively, team performance is not fully under the control of the team and thus reflects the performance of the larger system, not just of the team.

Simple interdependencies can be routinized: that is, they can be handled by specifications, change-order procedures, and so forth; they do not require on-line deliberation and resolution. These routine interdependencies can span different work teams. Complex and reciprocal interdependencies, on the other hand—those where affected parties need to have access to one another—demand on-line resolution between the contributors (Thompson, 1967). Placing contributors in a team with collective responsibility for a whole service or product provides informal and formal forums for ongoing technical integration. (Team meetings, for example, are a formal forum.) In delineating teams, the key question having to do with task interdependence is, Where does the work that is done by different individuals require the greatest amount of on-line technical coordination in order to fit together?

This question is not independent of the process analysis and deliberations analysis questions discussed above. A team deliverable may be the completion of a process or a portion of a process. For example, a team may be established to define and price systems for customers. In this case, the team provides the integrating mechanism for the various interdependent components of the process. The product of this team is contracts to deliver systems to customers. To be fully independent in accomplishing that, the team has to house the parties able to carry out the deliberations that have to occur to define and price each system.

Figure 3.7 shows a rough breakdown of the three project work teams that the new product development organization (discussed above) identified after conducting deliberations analysis and task interdependence analysis. Figure 3.8 shows that organization's specific team configuration.

Analysis showed that key deliberations and work interdependencies were included in three clusters of activities that constituted

Figure 3.7. Clustered Components of New Product Development Process.

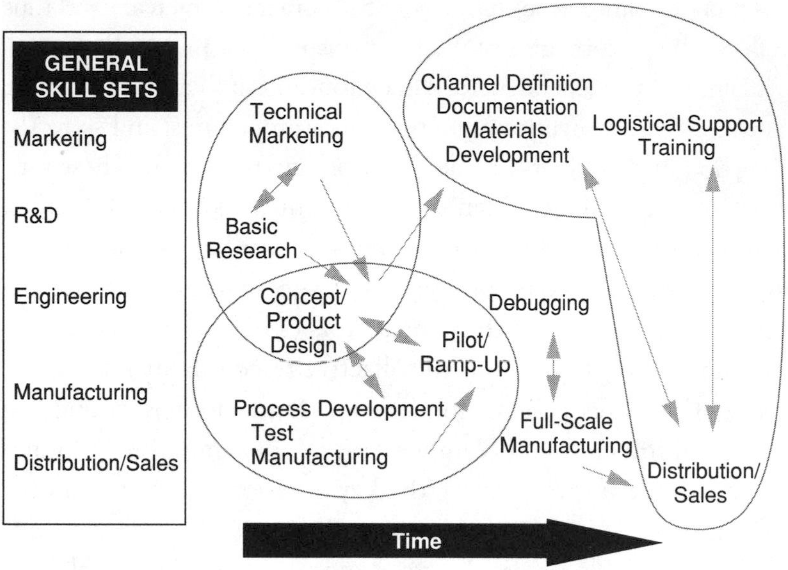

subprocesses. These were the design subprocess, the manufacturing process development subprocess, and the sales, distribution, and logistics subprocess. The project manager created two cross-functional teams. The design team included technical marketers, members of the research lab that had performed the basic technical research, design engineers, and a manufacturing process engineer (to provide the manufacturing perspective). The manufacturing process development team, which included two design engineers as well as manufacturing process engineers and product engineers from the factory, was charged with piloting the manufacturing process and managing the ramp-up process. All members of these two work teams were fully dedicated to the project, but several were members of both work teams, to provide cross-team integration.

It was determined that the marketers involved with channels, documentation, and logistical support and the representatives from distribution and sales were interdependent with one another and

Figure 3.8. Team Configuration for New Product Development Project.

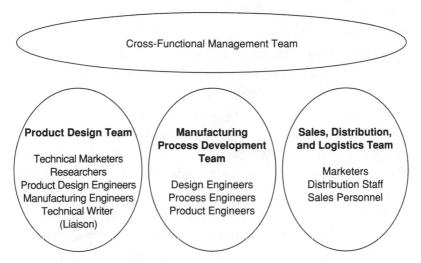

carried out key deliberations about how to get the product ready for the field. Therefore, they were constituted into a logistics team; and as such, they also serviced other NPD projects. Because their relationship to the design and manufacturing processes could be well specified, they were not members of those teams (although a technical writer served as a liaison to them in order to get up-to-date product data). In addition, the project had a cross-functional management team that provided overall project direction.

Having established some guidelines for the delineation of appropriate work teams in the first half of the chapter, we now turn to our three case examples.

Case Examples: Tronic Systems' Alpha Program, Netco's Field Offices, and Analytico's Consumer Electronics Division

In nonroutine work settings, it is often impossible to create fully self-contained work teams. Interdependencies go well beyond most teams; teams are interdependent with one another, and team members are interdependent with a broad range of contributors external to the team. The determination of core work teams involves thinking through a number of design options and determining which one results in the creation of teams that are as self-contained as possible, house the activities required to deliver value to the customer, and house as many deliberations as possible (so that the team is not continually dependent on decisions and deliberations conducted elsewhere in the organization). Once the appropriate core work teams are determined, designers must then determine how to embed them in the larger business unit. In other words, the context must also be designed.

In this section, three cases are introduced. We examine the design of the core work teams in each, illustrating the application of the three heuristic approaches introduced above—process analysis, deliberations analysis, and task interdependence analysis—and extract a number of design principles. The purpose is not to provide a complete specification of these heuristics but to show how the concepts get embodied in design. Each of these companies faces a different set of design issues in determining how to create work teams to deliver value to the customer. Because most knowledge-work settings house quite a complex array of activities, we have decided not to greatly simplify the design issues that have to be addressed in each of these cases. The essence of the design task is a series of iterative trade-offs that result in a system that has mechanisms to deal with the task performance and integration needs of the business unit. This series of trade-offs cannot be captured by a simple linear design map. For this reason, we have chosen to give the reader a sense of the process through example rather than prescriptive steps.

These three cases will be further developed in the next chapter, which deals with the design of mechanisms for integrating beyond and across core work teams to constitute a team-based business unit. They will also be used to illustrate the design features discussed in Chapters Five, Six, and Seven, which deal with management structures and roles and with integration processes and performance management.

Tronic Systems: The Alpha Program

Tronic Systems is a defense contractor. It designs state-of-the-art navigational systems that fit into air, naval, and ground systems. These technically complex systems integrate multiple technologies and involve both design and discovery. Like other defense contractors, Tronic Systems is facing extreme performance pressures, both for cost containment and for shorter development cycles, but the company does not want to sacrifice the high quality that has been its acknowledged strength. It recently decided that it could no longer afford the financial or time costs of the three- and four-level technical hierarchies that have traditionally been embedded in each of its programs responsible for a single navigational system.

A typical program at Tronic Systems, under the traditional structure, entailed a program manager and functional managers at the program level; in addition, each discipline (software, electrical, mechanical, structural, and systems engineering) had a supervisory and sometimes an additional technical lead structure within the program to provide direction, perform technical supervision, and integrate the work of individual contributors. Due to a shrinking market, the company had undergone downsizing, and its remaining workforce was mature and talented. This change provided management with an opportunity to rethink its hierarchical structure, and it decided to move to a flatter organization, with integration performed laterally and authority moved into teams.

Tronic Systems' Alpha Program is responsible for developing an electronic system that consists of three integrated "boxes," two of which are composed of integrated software and hardware subsystems. Traditionally, the organization broke work down into discipline-specific work groups (see Figure 3.9). In these work groups, unlike work *teams,* a manager and the supervisor and/or leads of each work group broke the work down into individual assignments and took responsibility for

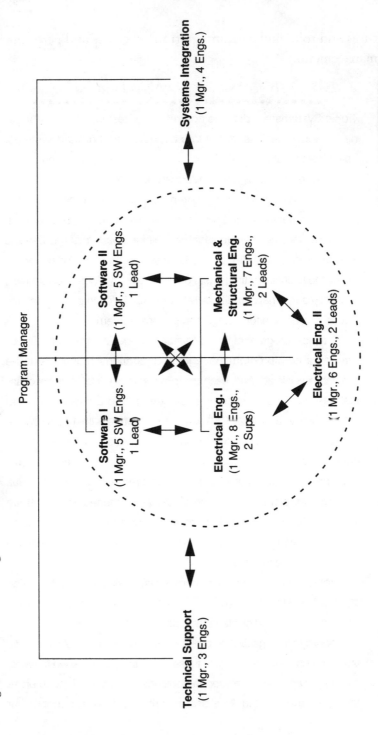

Figure 3.9. Traditional Program Structure at Tronic Systems.

integrating the total; individual contributors were held individually responsible for their assigned work.

The Alpha Program, prior to its reorganization, had fifty-six members, including a program manager, a discipline-based manager of each work group, and supervisory or lead positions in each discipline. Each of the disciplines required to develop the electronic navigational system that is the responsibility of this program were represented by one or more work groups. Each of the two software work groups developed the software for one of the two boxes that has integrated software. The two electrical engineering groups and the structural and mechanical/engineering group were functional and had responsibilities related to all three boxes. A technical support work group provided specialized quality and testing support for the entire project, and a systems integration work group monitored and directed the technical integration across the subsystems.

The double-sided arrows in Figure 3.9 indicate the reciprocal interdependence between the groups—that is, the places where work between the groups had to be coordinated on-line because what members of one group designed had repercussions for the work of members of the other group (and vice versa). The work groups were far from self-contained, as the many arrows suggest; these groups did not house all the tasks and skills required to produce a whole product. Nor could they be given complete authority over task-related decision making, because decisions made within one work group had repercussions for all other groups. For example, a design decision made in an electrical engineering group may have had implications for the work of the software groups, the other electrical engineering group, and the mechanical and structural engineers. In fact, a technical analysis conducted by Tronic Systems indicated that the people in these work groups had many more technical transactions with people outside their work group than with people within. The technical support and systems integration groups, furthermore, provided services for every work group. Each of these services cut across teams and had to be integrated for the entire set of teams.

This traditional design relied upon informal, person-to-person coordination between contributors in different work groups to address issues of technical interface. However, the managers and supervisors also played a key role in this integration, both within the work group and across work groups; in addition, they provided technical supervision and managed the performance of the work-group members. An advantage of this traditional design is that each work group was composed of one specialty and could be managed by a technical expert in that discipline. However, because of the huge number of cross-group transactions, the managers ended up being central to the boundary management process. Individuals and even work groups lacked the broader perspective required to make systemwide trade-offs. Many cross-boundary decisions ended up getting made by various assortments of managers, who thought through the trade-offs involved in the potential courses of action, or by the program manager. In turn, each work group was continually affected by these decisions made externally.

Tronic Systems' decision to move to work teams required a technical analysis of each program to determine the configuration of teams that most closely approximated self-containment, in order to be able to move as many decisions and task interdependencies as possible within teams and to decrease the number of decisions requiring cross-group and hierarchical decision making.

The task facing the Alpha Program was to determine which transactions could be handled in a routine fashion (for example, by specifications or change orders) and which required on-line deliberation. As many as possible of the latter needed to be located within teams; the former could be handled by formal procedures that efficiently integrated across teams. Alpha found no solution that provided complete self-containment, although two different designs were seriously considered.

Figure 3.10 illustrates the first design—one that combined hardware and software for the two component boxes where their integration was required and assigned a third team to design the hardware for the third box. The assumption underpinning this design

Figure 3.10. Proposed Alpha Program Team Structure A.

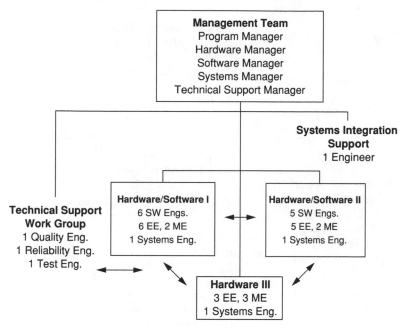

was that the key deliberations and task interdependencies had to do with the fit and the functional trade-offs between hardware and software. This design raised a new challenge for the organization, however, because one manager could not be a technical expert in the work of all team members in the teams that were composed of multiple specialties.

Figure 3.11 illustrates an alternate design for Alpha that combined all software into one team and created three hardware teams, each of which designed one of the component boxes. Multiple disciplines were housed within each of the three hardware teams. This design self-contained the creation of all software and the hardware for each box. The assumption underlying this design was that key technical deliberations and task interdependencies were within the development of the overall software subsystem and between the different disciplines designing the hardware for each box.

Figure 3.11. Proposed Alpha Program Team Structure B.

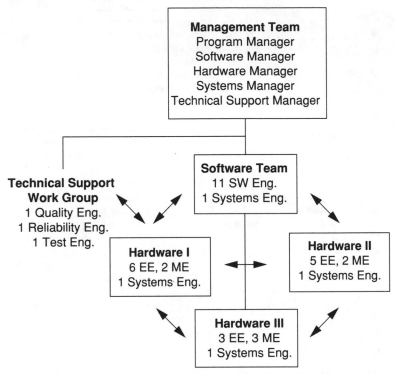

In both designs, the systems integration group was dispersed into the teams so that a team member would be responsible for working with fellow team members and representing the team in deliberations concerning the integration of the overall navigational system. The technical support group, on the other hand, was maintained separately, largely because that group's work involved as many cross-team as within-team transactions and because the group consisted of three individuals with three different technical specialties (meaning that, had they been assigned to other teams, each of the three would have had to belong to all the teams). The three members were not an interdependent team in accomplishing a shared performance, so each would be managed as an individual contributor.

As can be seen from the double-headed arrows, self-containment was not fully achieved in either design; each retained some reciprocal interdependence between teams. In addition, Structure A would require a cross-team software team to integrate the software, and both designs would require the organization to create an overlay team of the systems integrators from each team to address overall systems integration issues.

Despite the difficulty of technical supervision posed by the inclusion of software and hardware in the same teams in Structure A, Alpha chose that solution. The technical analysis indicated that the relationship between the software subsystems across the two boxes could be largely handled by specifications and one-on-one meetings to address specific issues. The problems that had in the past held up development of similar systems had to do with the integration of hardware and software. The analysis indicated that Structure A required the least cross-boundary decision making. It also allowed each team to be responsible for an identifiable product.

Table 3.1 summarizes the conclusions that members of the Alpha design team made about their processes, deliberations, and interdependencies. They concluded that the value added by this program consisted of the development of the integrated three-box system that would meet technical quality requirements and would be able to be efficiently manufactured. Subprocesses were the development of each of the three boxes. The design team saw key deliberations as involving trade-offs between cost, time, and functionality, between cost of manufacturing and cost of engineering, and between software and hardware functionality. The bulk of the on-line interdependencies were technical and required on-line resolution between designers working on each box. All these considerations led them to Structure A, which grouped contributors on each box into a team rather than grouping software and hardware separately.

The Alpha Program's team design deviates in several ways from the prototypical work team described earlier in this chapter. For example, there was no way for the Alpha Program to create self-contained teams that would make a "whole" product and would not be highly interdependent. In a sense, the natural team was the program itself. It would be possible to think of the program as the team and

Table 3.1. Primary Considerations in the Alpha Program Team Design.

Process Analysis:	The main process is the development of an integrated three-box system that meets design for manufacturing criteria and testing and quality requirements; subprocesses are development of each of three boxes.
Deliberations Analysis:	Cost of engineering versus cost of manufacturing Software versus hardware functionality Cost versus time versus functionality
Task Interdependence Analysis:	Significant on-line technical interdependence between designers working on each box Interdependence between boxes that can be handled by specification, face-to-face inter-action, and special systems integration roles

the others as subteams, of course, but this would not resolve the integration issues; it would simply move them to the subteams. Thus the best the Alpha designers could do was to maximize the self-containment of deliberations and task interdependencies and find ways to address deliberations and interdependencies that cut across the resultant work teams.

Another feature of the work at Tronic Systems that made it difficult to duplicate the prototypical self-contained team was the high degree of specialization. Because key deliberations and task interdependencies cross disciplines at Tronic, multidiscipline teams (which offer the advantage of increased familiarity across disciplines) were indicated; however, substantial cross-training within teams was not a serious option because of the large amount of formal education underpinning each discipline. Thus the Alpha teams provided increased ease of integration, but they offered less flexibility in resource utilization than would have been provided by cross-trained or functional teams. Software engineers and hardware engineers may come to work better with each other as they gain familiarity with each other's perspective, but they will most likely not receive the training that would be required for them to trade off tasks.

The Alpha designers decided not to place a quality, reliability, and test engineer within each team. Because these technical specialties exist in small numbers, Tronic Systems decided that it would be most cost-effective to share them across a number of organizational units. Consequently, the teams and these contributors will have to deal with their conflicting priorities. A test engineer servicing four teams, for example, would have to juggle the priorities of all four. Making these engineers full members of each team and tying them up in many potentially irrelevant meetings might have exacerbated the problem by reducing time spent providing services, however. Thus Alpha decided to view them as suppliers of a service (and to have clear service contracts and team evaluation of service levels) instead of making them team members.

Some specialties may house work that inherently is performed across units. Quality, for instance, may largely be an issue of fit across the whole system. This sort of work may not be best performed within a team that is designing a subsystem. Although such specialists perform tasks that have profound implications for the work of each team, they might best be included on an as-needed basis in team meetings rather than as dedicated members who are co-located with the team. One design challenge facing Tronic Systems was to create both a service ethic in the quality group (so that group members would see the teams as their customers) and an assessment process that would measure, among other things, how well the group met the needs of the teams for responsiveness. Assessment would then demand a systematic contracting process to clarify service commitments.

The Alpha Program illustrates the following issues in designing a team organization:

1. Organizational analyses often yield several possible ways to configure teams. Design team members will have to make trade-offs. In doing so, they should pick the design that best self-contains complete processes, key deliberations, and interdependencies that require on-line adjustment of work.

2. There are often reciprocal interdependencies between work teams that require further integrating mechanisms.

3. Not everyone has to be a team member. Some contributors might continue to be managed as individual contributors if their specialty is scarce and they would have to be members of so many teams that they would be unable to meet team commitments or if their technical task transcends multiple teams.

4. When services are provided to teams by nonmembers, a clear service contract is required, and the teams should provide an assessment of whether the services are meeting their requirements.

Netco Field Offices

Netco provides networked inventory control and security systems for a broad variety of commercial and industrial clients. Its environment has changed: customers are demanding much higher levels of service, and they are shopping for business solutions at a lower cost over the life of the system. The redesign Netco recently undertook was aimed at three objectives: getting better input from service early in the system definition and pricing stage, increasing the flexibility of response to the idiosyncratic needs of customers, and developing industry-specific solutions and deeper penetration of particularly lucrative industries.

As part of this overall effort, Netco redesigned its regional field offices in order to provide customer-focused, integrated service. Traditionally, the field offices were organized into discipline-specific work groups, most of which had two levels of management (see Figure 3.12). In the past, a sales agent would "drum up business," work with an appointed engineer to "spec" the system, price it, pass the

Figure 3.12. Netco's Traditional Field Office Structure.

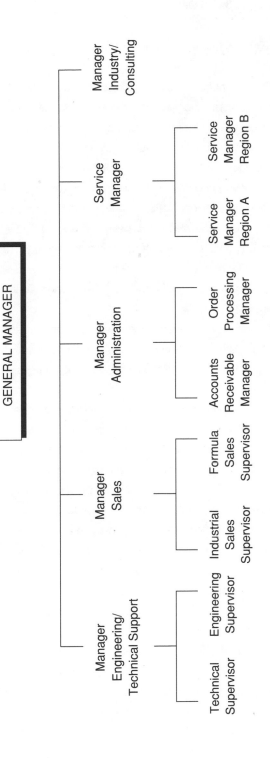

paperwork on to administration, and then turn the installation process over to the engineering/technical support group. Service technicians might be called upon to support the installation process; and after the installation was complete, service technicians would be assigned to the client on an ongoing basis. The up-front system definition and contracting phase would be loosely coordinated by the sales agent; the back-end installation and service transition would be loosely coordinated by an engineer who was the engagement leader. In addition, Netco recently added industry consultants who were able to analyze the business needs in particular industries and help customers define the system they needed. The industry consultants worked with sales and technical personnel at the system definition stage, although their role had not yet been integrated or accepted.

Netco identified two major processes that occur in its field offices. One is the system definition and contracting process and the other is the system delivery, installation, and servicing process. The design team determined that there was a need for service personnel to become involved in the deliberations regarding the system definition and contracting process, because the definition of systems affected later service costs and because there had been a tendency to undervalue the cost of service in the pricing of systems. Netco also wanted to create a group of people who had explicit responsibility for the development of industry business, developed expertise in that industry, and integrated all disciplines to provide highly coordinated value.

There were a number of key deliberations surrounding the two major processes identified by Netco. These included how much to tailor systems for industries and customers rather than utilizing formula systems; how much to emphasize generating revenue and market share by cutting margins rather than by offering superior custom designs and superior service; ongoing issues of cost versus schedule; and the question of which industries to invest in for growth.

During the system definition and contracting process, the consultant's knowledge of the industry and the engineer's knowledge of technical systems capability have to be combined and integrated to generate any given system definition. The service costs of various system designs have to be taken into account in designing a system and in costing it. Knowledge of the organization's growth strategy is also required to determine costing. Thus the industry consultants, engineers, and technical, sales, and service personnel are all interdependent at this stage. Furthermore, the information and experience gleaned from each system definition are needed by those who generate the industry growth strategy and the technical development strategy for the company. Netco saw rapid corporate learning stemming from various engagements as important to developing and maintaining product leadership because of the predominance of small, niche corporations that could become experts in certain industries.

During the system delivery, installation, and servicing stage, there is external interdependence with the warehouse, which is handled by the administration group. Engineers, technicians, and service personnel are interdependent in debugging the system and providing the necessary learning and familiarity among the service technicians for subsequent ongoing servicing of the system. The learnings that occur during this phase provide information that has implications for the company's system development strategy. (For a summary of issues related to Netco's various interdependencies, as well as process and deliberations analyses, see Table 3.2.)

Figure 3.13 illustrates the field office team structure that Netco put in place. Netco created two kinds of business teams. The first kind— the formula business team—contains all the skills needed to perform both the system definition process and the system delivery process for the company's "formula customers"—those who are not in a targeted industry and who receive relatively standard versions of the systems the company sells. The systems delivered to these customers require relatively minor customizing. The sales agents are responsible for convening and facilitating the integration of the work of the right assortment of contributors to fit with the nature of the opportunity. These engagement "teams"—subgroupings of the formula business

Table 3.2. Primary Considerations in Netco's Field Office Team Design.

Process Analysis:	There are two major processes: (1) system definition and contracting and (2) system delivery, installation, and servicing.
Deliberations Analysis:	Tailoring systems to meet industry-specific needs versus utilizing standard systems
	Generating revenue and market share by cutting margins (especially service) rather than by tailoring service and customizing design
	Investing for growth (industry versus industry, industry versus "formula")
	Weighing cost against schedule
Task Interdependence Analysis:	System definition and contracting:
	The influence of consultant's knowledge of business issues on system definition
	The influence of technical definition on installation and servicing needs
	The influence of industry growth strategy on costing strategy (sales)
	The influence of system definition issues on industry growth and technical strategies
	System delivery, installation, and servicing:
	External interdependence with warehouse (administration)
	On-site troubleshooting during installation (technical and service)
	The influence of service and technical learning on system development strategy

Figure 3.13. Netco's New Team-Based Field Office Structure.

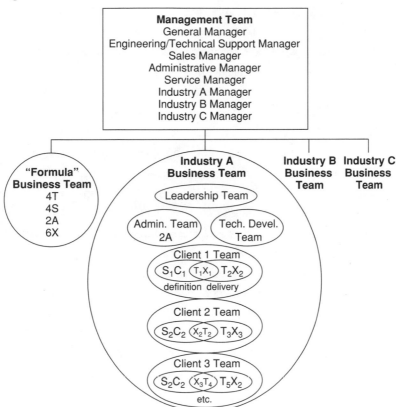

Key: C = industry consultant, T = engineering/technical support personnel,
S = sales representative, A = administrator, X = service personnel.

team—are temporary and dynamic, and a person might serve on as many as fifteen to twenty each year (and three or four at once). To encourage greater attention to service issues during the system definition phase, the formula business team is rewarded for the profitability of its service activities as well as for revenue and overall profit.

The second kind of business team in the field office is the industry-specific team, which includes industry consultants and the sales, service, technical, and administrative contributors. The several industry-specific teams, established to build Netco's business in each industry, concentrate on being full-service system providers for large industry clients. Within these teams, subteams deal with the whole life cycle of services for particular clients. Each client team is further divided into two subteams, which deal with the processes of system definition and system delivery. The consultant and sales agent on each client team are members of the system definition team, along with an engineer and a service technician who are also members of the system delivery team. These client teams were set up for continuing and new business with particular clients, so they are envisioned as permanent teams. However, individuals generally serve on more than one client team, because of the difference in size of the client engagements and the ebb and flow of activities during the life of a client relationship. Within each industry team is an administrative team that consists of two or more administrative specialists. They are viewed as service units, and their service is shared across the different client teams; the administrative specialists do not belong to the client teams, however, because of the unevenness of the administrative workflow through the life cycle of the client relationship and the fact that their interface with the various groups can be easily routinized. The real economies are to be found in their ability to divide up and prioritize the work between them. Each industry-specific team also includes a technical development team that cuts across the client teams and includes engineers and the industry consultants. Its role is to make and share minor technical enhancements to the core systems to meet industry needs and to communicate more advanced technical needs to the corporation's technical center.

Through its restructuring, Netco has created teams that are responsible for little businesses—developing business in an industry and delivering the full set of services for that industry. The full set of processes required to deliver value to the customers is included in each industry team, and there are no technical task interdependencies that transcend the team. In arriving at this team structure, Netco faced two major deliberations involving cross-team issues. The first was the determination of the relative investment of resources in the different business teams. The second was the determination of the areas of technical development that should "grow" the overall business. (In this latter arena, the field organization served as one stakeholder in the larger corporate deliberation that resulted in the priorities for the corporate technical center.) These cross-team issues were deliberated in the management team, where the different business units and functions were represented.

Netco was concerned that the new design would make it more difficult to manage for technical excellence. To address that issue, the functional managers were given responsibility for setting up representative overlay councils that planned development activities for each function, identified system and process improvement requirements, and created forums for sharing technical improvements across businesses. These functionally oriented activities had "teeth": functional plans as well as cross-functional team plans were agreed to by the cross-functional management team that allocated resources in the business unit.

Netco's field offices were able to create relatively self-contained teams by conceptualizing each team as a mini–business unit that serves a segment of the market. Within the industry teams, the client teams are not fully independent, largely because they have overlapping membership, they share administrative services, and they rely on a collective learning process. However, the work interdependencies and the key deliberations about client engagement are largely contained within the client subteam.

The Netco case illustrates the following issues in designing a team organization:

1. An organizational unit's work teams do not all have to have similar designs. Each design should be optimized to the task at hand.

2. A team that has overall responsibility for the delivery of a certain kind of service or for meeting the needs of a certain set of clients may operate through a series of dynamic subteams.

3. One way to integrate the work of two teams is to have overlapping membership.

4. If cross-functional teams perform the work, there may need to be functional mechanisms, such as councils, to identify development needs and spearhead the development of technical competencies and systems.

Analytico Consumer Electronics Division

Chapter One described the situation facing the commercial electronics division of Analytico as it moved to a team design. A consumer electronics division of Analytico is also in the midst of the transition to teams. It is redesigning to adapt to a more competitive marketplace. Historically a high-cost, high-quality manufacturer, Analytico has had to watch the erosion of this division's strong position in its market.

The consumer electronics division generates three to five new products per year and manufactures as many as twelve to fifteen products in all. The division's strategy to compete in an increasingly cost- and time-sensitive market is to move to low-cost production and to share components across products where possible (to reduce both design and manufacturing costs). It has moved to the concept of families of products and technologically related product lines. The products within a family are generally related along a dimension of low to high sophistication of technology and functionality in performing the same kind of task.

The consumer electronics division is part of an Analytico group, and both sales and manufacturing occur at the group level. The division conducts its own marketing, however, including some advertising and promotion. Its manufacturing function is responsible for working with the group-level factory to develop manufacturing processes and for the transition of the product from design to the plant.

The key processes for which the organization had to design were product family strategy and definition and product development. Product development included two subprocesses: product design and process development. The deliberations in these processes and subprocesses demanded multifunctional perspectives. Product family definition involved deliberations between marketing and R&D concerning trade-offs between technology development and family coverage. Product development required trade-offs between time-to-market, technological sophistication, and low-cost manufacturing (necessitating perspectives from all three functions). Thus the deliberations analysis indicated the need for cross-functional, product-oriented work teams.

The strategic emphasis on achieving commonality of parts and processes created and emphasized the importance of within-function technical interdependencies for R&D and manufacturing across products. On the other hand, the time-to-market pressure led to a concurrent engineering strategy that increased on-line interdependence between R&D and manufacturing within a product. Consequently, the design challenges faced by this organization seemed to pull it in different directions.

Figure 3.14 illustrates the work teams that were set up in this division to support the strategy. The core work teams house particular subprocesses: product design, process development, and product-line marketing. Marketing is conducted for each product line; consequently, all the marketing skills are included in each product-line marketing team. A cross-functional design team for each product is housed in R&D, and a cross-functional process development team for each product is housed in manufacturing. The division chose to locate core work teams within functions (and thus to facilitate the ease of coordination within R&D and within manufacturing to achieve commonality of parts and processes across products). A "mirror organization" (Galbraith, 1993) was created in manufacturing and R&D. Each of the two functions has a team to deal with each product, making it easier to integrate between the design and development processes for a particular product. The product-line marketing team, on the other hand, is aligned with sets of design and process teams that deal with all the products in a product line. (See Table 3.3 for a summary of issues faced by this division related to process analysis, deliberations analysis, and task interdependence analysis.)

Because of the large number of interdependencies in the organization, and the number of dimensions that have to be taken into

Figure 3.14. Analytico's Consumer Electronics Division Team Design.

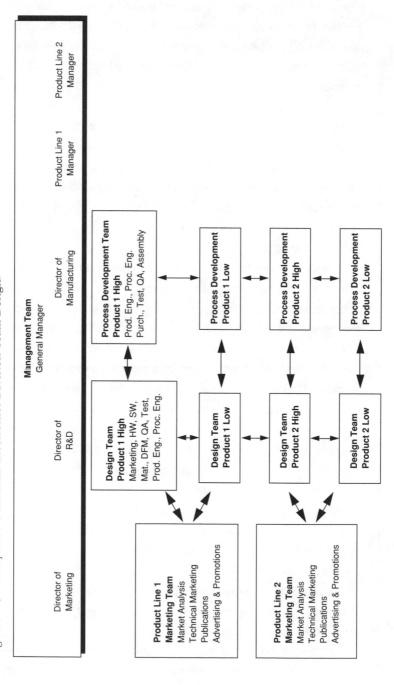

Table 3.3. Primary Considerations in Analytico's Consumer Electronics Division Team Design.

Process Analysis:	There are two major processes: (1) product family strategy and definition and (2) product development (including product design and process development).
Deliberations Analysis:	Optimizing product versus product line
	Technological sophistication versus low-cost manufacturing
	Advancing technology versus filling in a family of products
	Leverage versus optimized design
	Relative investment in the various product lines
Task Interdependence Analysis:	Interdependence between marketing and R&D re: product development
	Interdependence between R&D and manufacturing re: product development (design/process concurrency)
	Interdependence within R&D and within manufacturing across products (leverage)
	Interdependence within marketing across products in product line

account simultaneously in determining direction and in making decisions, these teams are insufficient integrating devices. The double-headed arrows in Figure 3.14 illustrate the on-line task interdependencies that still exist. Additional integrating mechanisms are needed to deal with these interdependencies across the organizational subprocesses. These will be discussed in the next chapter.

The Analytico consumer electronics division case illustrates the following issues in designing a team organization:

1. Cross-functional teams can be located within a function if the key interdependencies of the team are within the function.

2. An organizational unit may require a combination of functional and cross-functional teams.

Unfinished Business

While all three of these cases reorganized their core work into teams, the core work teams were not sufficient integrating mechanisms in any of the organizations. Reciprocal interdependence extended beyond team bounds. Consequently, all three organizations needed to set up additional integrating mechanisms. These mechanisms are the focus of the next chapter.

Key Issues

The list below summarizes general key issues facing those attempting to delineate appropriate work teams. These frame the more specific issues listed after each of the case examples.

1. There are a number of ways to configure teams, and team design should be based on careful analysis aimed at creating teams that do as much as possible to self-contain complete processes, key deliberations, and interdependencies required to carry out a work process.

2. Core work teams may be functional or cross-functional, depending on whether the complete tasks that require integration of effort between team members are functional or cross-functional in nature.

3. Increasingly, cross-functional teams are being utilized so that those doing the work can perform the integration of that work with other disciplines and can make trade-offs that require a multidisciplinary perspective.

4. If the core work teams are functional, cross-functional integrating teams may need to be established to achieve cross-disciplinary integration.

Figure 4.1. Step Two of the Design Sequence: Specifying Integration Needs.

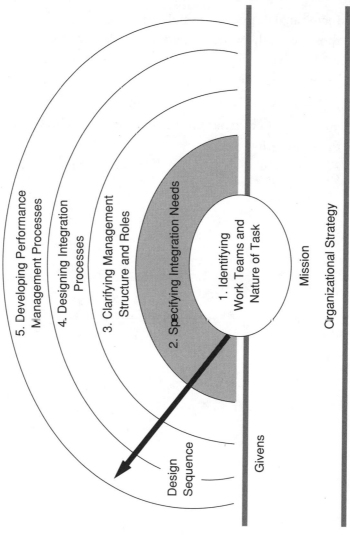

4

Step Two

Specifying Integration Needs

Delineating the work teams, discussed in Chapter Three, is the first of several steps in designing the structure of the team-based organization. This chapter addresses the additional integrating mechanisms that may be required to fully integrate work in a complex knowledge-work setting. The identification and design of these mechanisms is the second step in the design sequence (see Figure 4.1). In this chapter, we describe mechanisms for coordinating between individual teams and across all the teams that constitute a business unit and provide examples of such mechanisms from the three organizations profiled in Chapter Three.

Core work teams cannot handle all the interdependencies that exist in an organization or conduct all of its deliberations. Many interdependencies transcend teams and even business units, and many deliberations involve issues where the trade-offs are at a broader organizational scope than a particular team. There may be trade-offs across product lines, for example—an issue Analytico faces. Key business processes may be conducted by a constellation of teams, as is the case in the Alpha Program. Subprocesses may occur external to the business unit, if there are compelling economic or technical reasons to contract for those subprocesses or to set up a separate unit to handle them. Work teams have the authority to deal with only those issues that fall within their scope. For issues that cut across teams or are of broader scope, interteam or broader-scope mechanisms need to be established. *Whether or not an organization organizes its central transformation processes—those processes by which inputs are turned into products or services of value to the customer—into core work teams, it will probably need to set up lateral integrating mechanisms to deal with key organizational deliberations and to integrate technical and business processes.*

A caveat is in order here. The least costly forms of integration include the informal interaction that occurs between individuals in the course of performing their work and the specification of procedures (Galbraith, 1973) that enable work to be integrated without the cost of face-to-face coordination. However, in complex, dynamic organizations, it is often impossible to prespecify programs to guide integration, and the organizational design may not allow informal integration to occur reliably or quickly enough to meet the performance demands of the organization. Competitive requirements and/or corporate strategy may make it necessary for an organization to perform very quickly or to integrate across multiple complex dimensions, such as products, customers, or countries (Galbraith, 1994). Analytico, for example, seeks to optimize cost while delivering new products with rapid time-to-market. Decisions that achieve leverage across products at Analytico have to be made in a timely fashion so that each product can meet stringent time-to-market demands. Because of the number of perspectives that have to be integrated, individually initiated informal integration would be neither adequate nor efficient. In such situations, the organization needs to specify formal integrating mechanisms responsible for coordinating the different pieces of the process or deliberating complex trade-offs (Galbraith, 1994).

Work teams such as those described in Chapter Three encourage individuals to coordinate by increasing the ease of integration and the motivation to integrate. Individuals on teams are accessible to one another and are held mutually accountable for the overall outcomes. However, the creation of teams does not address two kinds of additional integration. First, in complex settings involving nonroutine work, it is highly unlikely that all of the technical interdependencies will be housed within one team. In the Alpha Program, for example, two interdisciplinary teams producing components are responsible for the development of software that has to fit with the hardware for each component. In addition, however, the software of both teams needs to fit together to form a technical subsystem across components, so there has to be a way to integrate the work of the software engineers in the two component teams. Second, strategic integration may be required across several or all of the teams that constitute the business unit. Strategy provides direction regarding priorities and criteria so that decisions involving trade-offs that cut across functions, disciplines, and teams can be resolved. For example, total cost targets for a product may be achieved by dynamically managing cost overruns and underruns across multiple teams: a client team with a potential large, long-term client may sell an initial system with a lower margin while another client team is in a cash-cow stage because of high-margin follow-up business. An integrating team may create common direction and facilitate such trade-offs across the work teams.

This chapter will first deal with mechanisms to integrate *among* teams—that is, mechanisms that enable teams whose work is interdependent to integrate with one another. Then it will deal with mechanisms to integrate across a business unit that involves many different performing units whose work has to achieve common purpose and be conducted within a common direction. Finally, it will provide an illustration of the full system of teams in each of the three case examples.

Integration Across Teams That Are Interdependent

There are different kinds of interdependencies between teams. In some cases, the work of individuals in multiple teams has to technically fit with the work of others. In these cases, the individuals can establish an informal connection, integrating as needed. If an engineer in one team is designing a device that has to fit into an environment being designed by an engineer in another team, for example, these two engineers can coordinate through specifications and through mutual problem solving.

In other cases, because the work of an entire team is affected by work that is going on in another team, the ongoing work of the two teams has to fit together. In these cases, there are several ways in which the work can be integrated:

- *Liaison roles.* It may be sufficient to appoint a member of a team to be a liaison with another team—the integrating mechanism chosen by the Analytico consumer electronics division for dealing with interdependencies between its functional teams (as shown in Figure 4.2). At Analytico, the relationship between each product-line marketing team and the corresponding product design teams is handled through a liaison from marketing (L1H) to the product design teams. That individual attends product design team meetings with the purpose of sharing marketing information that would be useful in the design process and gleaning information about the emerging design to inform the development of marketing materials. The liaison is a member of the marketing team, not the design team, but deals with design team members extensively and informally.

- *Overlapping membership.* Figure 4.2 also illustrates another kind of linkage between teams: overlapping membership. The technical interdependencies between the design team and the process development team at Analytico are substantial. Because of the concurrent engineering emphasis, driven by time-to-market considerations, it is important that the work of the design engineers be conducted in a manner that takes into account the needs of low-cost manufacturing. It is also important that on-line information be available to the design engineers concerning the constraints of the manufacturing processes in the factory and the manufacturing processes being developed by the process design team. The process design team needs immediate access to any

Figure 4.2. Integration Among Interdependent Teams in Analytico's Consumer Electronics Division.

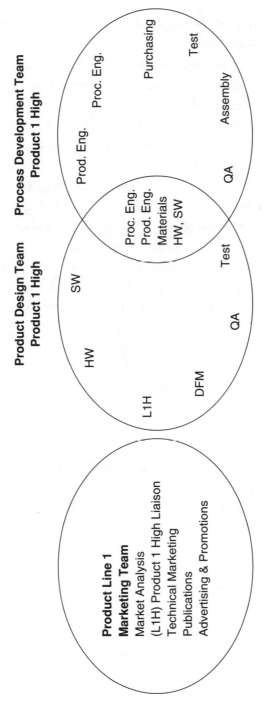

knowledge about the emerging design that has implications for the processes it is developing.

Overlapping membership was chosen by Analytico as a mechanism for achieving that close alignment. A product engineer, a process engineer, and a materials engineer from manufacturing are members of both the design team and the process development team. They sit with the design team during the design stage and have as a major responsibility the sharing of their manufacturing perspective and expertise. As soon as the process development team was convened, very early in the design phase, these individuals were also charged with bringing to it needed information about the progress of the design and keeping the design team abreast of progress and information about the process development team's work.

In addition, the R&D function identified a hardware engineer and software engineer to sit on both the design team and the process development team; their job is to represent the perspective of R&D in the process development team and to begin to work directly with the manufacturing engineers in the prototyping and pilot manufacturing process. All members of the process development team move into the factory and work with factory engineers and assemblers when the process is debugged. Overlapping membership is also used between the factory and the process development team. Assemblers and factory product and plant process designers are included as members of the process development teams. If possible, they are physically located in the division until the ramp-up process begins, at which time the whole process development team moves into the factory.

• *Cross-team integrating teams.* Figure 4.3 illustrates another mechanism for integrating between teams that are interdependent: the cross-team integrating team (also called a cross-team). Portions of the development of the overall software subsystem in the Alpha Program are located in each of two component teams. These software systems have to be able to work compatibly with one another. Although most of the interdependencies can be handled by speci-

Figure 4.3. Cross-Team Integrating Team in the Alpha Program.

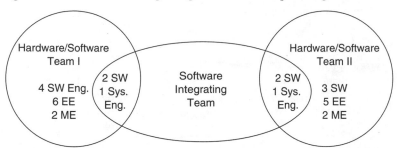

fication, there are likely to be changes in one component that have implications for the other. Simple technical adjustments can be handled by change orders; however, changes in more fundamental aspects of the system, such as its architecture, cannot. Furthermore, the decision to make such changes involves trade-offs between the two components and consequently cannot be made unilaterally.

Alpha set up a cross-team software integrating team, which consists of software representatives and the systems engineers from both work teams. This team deals with the systemic decisions and trade-offs that emerge and takes responsibility for making sure that changes are documented and communicated between teams in a timely manner.

Cross-teams are also useful when there are subcontractors or partners who are delivering components to an existing team or business unit. Figure 4.4 illustrates how such cross-company teams might operate if a subcontractor were delivering an additional software subsystem that had to be integrated with the software that was being developed in-house. It shows a cross-organizational team that includes representative software engineers and systems engineers from each of the two component work teams in the primary organization, as well as representatives from the software team in the contracting organization delivering the subsystem. Its function is to deal with interdependencies that arise because specifications and change-order procedures are insufficient to anticipate the changes

Figure 4.4. Cross-Team Integrating Team in an Electronics Program with an External Contractor.

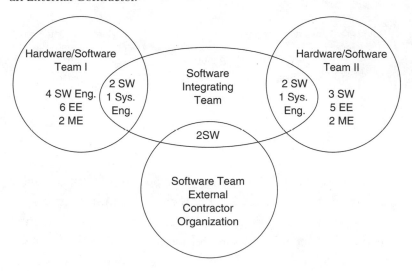

and technical learnings that result in more fundamental reconceptualizations of how the work fits together. It exists also to ensure that information is being documented and communicated in a timely manner between the two organizations. Although the Alpha Program does not require such a cross-company team, a number of the companies we studied did use this approach successfully.

Integration Across Multiple Teams and Components of a Business Unit

Liaison roles, overlapping membership, and cross-teams are ways of integrating the operational interdependencies between work teams. Other mechanisms are necessary to perform integration that transcends particular teams and to deal with deliberations or perform technical tasks at a broader scope—deliberations and tasks that create the context in which the teams operate.

These integrating mechanisms—management teams, representative integrating teams, individual integrating roles, and improvement teams—address broader-scope issues in the system than the work teams do. Consequently, in a systems sense, they are at a higher hierarchical level. But that does not mean that the individuals who compose them are at a higher hierarchical rank in the organization. It merely means that larger-scope teams or individuals have the authority to make decisions within which smaller-scope teams must operate. (The exception is management teams. Members of these may be at a higher rank in the organization and have position power that comes from rank as well as decision power that comes from scope of authority.) We will describe and illustrate these different integrating mechanisms below, again using our three case companies as examples.

• *Management teams.* The Alpha Program, Netco, and Analytico each created cross-functional management teams to manage the business unit. In the Alpha Program, the work teams report as collective units to a cross-functional management team that forges strategy and direction for the constellation of teams in the business unit, makes resource trade-offs between the different teams based on the strategy and the needs of the teams, and manages the performance of the various teams that report to them.

Each Netco business team has a manager who has membership in two teams: the management team for the field office and the business team's leadership team. The business team's leadership team consists of the manager of the business team and a service, sales, and technical coordinator, each of whom is responsible for allocation of resources across the dynamic constellation of client teams and for technical assistance and mentoring where needed. Thus the business team's leadership team handles the operational issues faced within the business team. The field office management team manages the overall strategy and the performance of the business teams.

Figure 4.5 illustrates the expanded team structure for Analytico's consumer electronics division. Its division management team is

Figure 4.5. Expanded Team Structure in Analytico's Consumer Electronics Division.

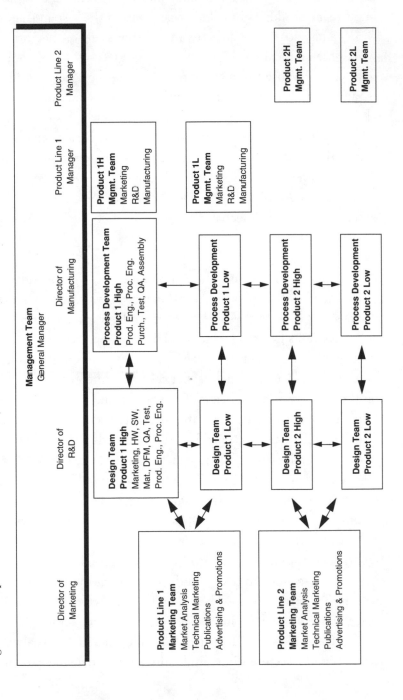

composed of functional directors and product-line managers. The various work teams are operationally managed by a functional manager, who reports to the functional director, who sits on the division management team. In some cases, the functional manager has responsibility for two teams. There are also intervening management teams: each product has a management team consisting of the R&D manager of the design team, the manufacturing manager of the process development team, and the product-line marketing manager. It is in the product management team that high-level cross-functional trade-offs are made for the product. These trade-offs stem largely from the fact that the division is pursuing a strategy that simultaneously pushes cross-functional integration in the development of new products (for speed and market responsiveness) and optimization of manufacturing and R&D processes across products. The product-line manager, who serves on the division management team, is responsible for integration across the different product management teams for the product line and the product-line marketing team and for ensuring that the goals of the product line are met. If issues that involve trade-offs between functional and product needs are not resolvable within the product line, the division management team provides the escalation path for resolution.

• *Representative integrating teams*. Many organizations use a variety of nonmanagement integrating teams to further integrate the work teams and to deal with other tasks and deliberations that have to occur in the organization. Although these mechanisms are representative in nature, they have authority for issues at a broader scope in the organization.

The Alpha Program created work teams that house the majority of interdependencies within team bounds. Each of these teams was formed to create some part of a final product, which is an integrated system composed of hardware and software subsystems. Members of each team address integration issues informally with members of other teams with whom they are interdependent. In addition to "local" integration issues that can be handled by individuals and the teams, however, there are also systemwide issues to be addressed and trade-offs to be made. To handle these, Alpha created a system integration team, which is led by a system engineer who is not located within a component team but is a peer of the other system engineers. The three system engineers from the component teams are part of that system integration team. The leader is responsible for keeping abreast of the system integration needs that occur across teams and for convening the team when appropriate. Since the team generally deals with technical issues that affect the work of the design engineers, the system engineers invite others to their meetings on an as-needed basis. In this manner, each involved work team is able to influence system integration decisions. The decisions that come out of this team, even though made by organizational peers, are binding for the three work teams. Figure 4.6 shows Alpha's full organizational network of teams.

Figure 4.6. System of Teams: Alpha Program.

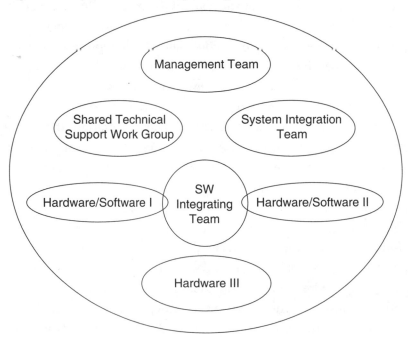

Netco's field offices are divided into business teams that are almost completely self-contained so that, beyond the management team, a minimum of integrating mechanisms are required. Within the business team serving each industry is a technical development team, composed of representatives from service and the technical/ engineering function, whose job is to share and disseminate new practices and learnings that emerge in different client engagements and to communicate to the corporate technical center the areas in which technical development would help grow the business. Also within each industry business team is an integrating team, referred to by Netco as a leadership team, which ensures that resources are allocated correctly across client teams. With the exception of the industry business manager, the other members are coordinators who are not hierarchically ranked above the others on the team.

There are two other integrating devices in each field office. Netco was concerned that the strong focus on business and client teams might result in the organization's losing its technical acumen, since functional managers would have little day-to-day operational responsibility. One way that Netco dealt with this was to give the coordinators in the business teams responsibility for some technical mentoring. However, the press in the business-unit teams is for service delivery, not for development. Consequently, two councils were set up to provide ongoing development for the service agents and for the technicians and engineers. The councils are chaired by the functional manager but composed of representatives from each business team, who together determine training and development needs and plan for their execution. Figure 4.7 shows the network of teams in each field office.

A number of integrating mechanisms are required to handle the complex integration requirements at Analytico. To coordinate the leveraging of manufacturing processes and design components across products, and to initiate process improvement efforts, several councils—a manufacturing council, an R&D council, and a coordinating council for each product line—were established (see Figure 4.8).

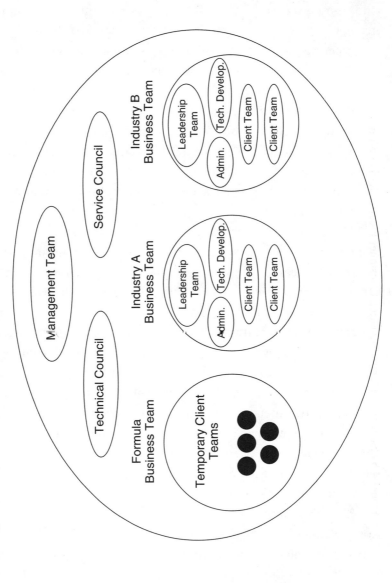

Figure 4.7. System of Teams: Netco Field Offices.

Figure 4.8. System of Teams: Analytico Consumer Electronics Division.

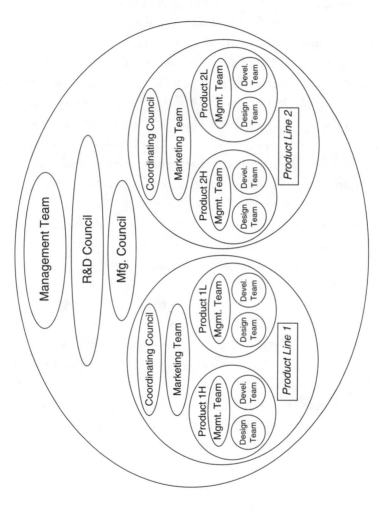

The manufacturing council consists of representatives from the process development teams of each new product that is being developed, as well as factory representatives. The director of manufacturing for the division is the champion for the team. The R&D council consists of representatives from each product's design team and is championed by the director of R&D. These councils have similar charters—that is, to identify where processes, components, and code can be reused across products and to initiate design and manufacturing process improvement efforts. The coordinating council for each product line consists of the product management teams for all the products in the product line, convened periodically by the product-line manager. Its function is to assess the health of the product line, identify areas that need attention and initiate improvement efforts, and formulate a product-line strategy as input to the division management team.

This division also uses one more type of integrating mechanism: individual integrating roles. These will be described next.

• *Individual integrating roles.* Often a large number of contributors representing a number of teams and cutting across several organizational units need to be integrated. Because integration needs may be emergent and involve various combinations of contributors, a team may not be the best integrating mechanism; the integration may instead require an individual, who can more flexibly adapt to the situation at hand.

At Netco (Figure 4.7), for example, the formula business team placed the integrative role with the sales agents, who are charged with assembling the right cast of contributors to deliver the needed services to the client. The sales agents do not have hierarchical power over fellow team members whom they are integrating. Rather, they work through informal processes.

In the Analytico consumer products division, the product-line manager also has such a role. This person is charged with integrating the work of a number of product management teams and the product-line marketing team (although only the product-line marketing team reports to the product-line manager) and chairs the coordinating council for the product line. One of the chief roles of this person is to identify areas where functional strategies and product-line needs are in conflict and to try to get resolution, either by working with the product-line teams and functional managers or by escalating the issue for consideration to the division management team. In addition, this person champions the product line as a member of the division management team and pulls together the various stakeholders to develop a product-line strategy and product-line goals and initiatives. (Figure 4.8 illustrates the network of teams in this division.)

• *Improvement teams.* Improvement teams, including quality improvement teams and process improvement teams, are a special kind of integrating team. They do not integrate *operations*; rather, their purpose is to initiate change in how the various parts of the business unit go about doing their work so that the performance of the unit is improved. These teams can exist at multiple levels in the organization, depending on the scope of their focus.

Often improvement teams are unable to get organizational cooperation in implementing the improvements that they design. This may be because they are mandated or spring up within the organizational system that they are trying to improve without commitment from the various parts of the organization that will be affected. Improvement teams must have legitimacy based on authority that is conferred from the same level of the organization that their efforts are focused on. For example, if a team has been charged with improving the administrative processes that are used throughout field offices, it must report to the field office management team and get its mandate from that level. On the other hand, an industry business team could initiate an improvement team to improve the initial client-needs assessment process in its industry. That team would have legitimacy to affect the client teams in that industry business team only if it received its mandate from the leadership team at that level.

Improvement teams have tended historically to be managed differently than work teams. Work on these teams has tended to be perceived as an extra assignment, and the teams' priority is often unclear. Their schedule, goals, and resources are often not specified, and their work is not always seen as authoritative in the organization. It is often unclear how, if at all, people's work on these teams fits with their "real" jobs and whether it affects how their performance is perceived or rewarded.

In most organizations today, time is a very scarce resource. The time spent by members of improvement teams is time *not* spent on the production of products or services. Added to that is the considerable time devoted by organizational members to introducing the changes that these teams generate. Thus improvement teams should be chartered only if the management team believes their efforts will pay off in terms of the future capabilities of the organization and if management is willing to invest time in their success.

Our research findings indicate that improvement teams must be treated like any other organizational project. In other words, they derive authority because they report to the proper location, they have goals and deliverables for which they are held accountable, and the work they accomplish is treated as part of members' core jobs. The authority to introduce changes and the commitment of management for the cooperation of the various parts of the organization affected will not happen automatically just because the team generated a good product. Rather, improvement teams have to be carefully designed and managed for success.

Key Issues

The key issues related to integrating mechanisms in a team organization are these:

1. Where the interdependencies cut across the whole business unit, work teams may not be sufficient integrating mecha-

nisms. In that case, additional integrating mechanisms are required to integrate across teams and to address businesswide issues.

2. Mechanisms that can be used to integrate across the interdependent teams include liaison roles, overlapping membership, and cross-teams.

3. Integration across a business unit can be achieved by management teams, representative integrating teams, and individual integrating roles.

4. Improvement teams are a special kind of integrating team. They exist to design new processes to better conduct and integrate the work of the organization. They must be managed as official projects, with goals, management support, reviews, and assigned resources.

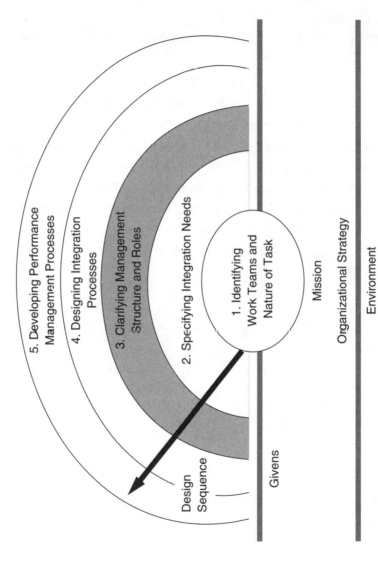

Figure 5.1. Step Three of the Design Process: Clarifying Management Structure and Roles.

5

. . . .

Step Three

Clarifying Management Structure and Roles

Interest in the management and leadership of teams has grown along with the use of teams. Several books have been written about what managers and leaders can do to help teams be effective (see, for example, Fisher, 1993; Manz and Sims, 1989). These focus on the processes and behaviors required to manage and lead teams and to help teams become more self-managing. They tend to highlight the role of the team leader or first-level supervisor, although some discuss leadership roles throughout an organization. This work has been very useful in helping managers begin to understand the behaviors required to manage effectively in a team-based organization—especially one that is trying to encourage self-management.

What is missing from this growing body of literature is an organizational design perspective. Determining the appropriate management and leadership roles for a team organization is a *design* choice. (The placement of this step in the design sequence is highlighted in Figure 5.1.) Key design questions include the following: What management functions should the members of work teams or integrating teams perform, and what functions should people in managerial roles perform? How much self-management should be vested in teams? What leadership roles should be established in teams? Under what conditions should people without hierarchical authority (for example, team leaders) perform leadership functions? This chapter addresses these questions. It compares traditional managerial roles to roles in the new team-based settings. It provides design guidelines for determining how much self-management should be vested in teams and addresses the conditions under which formal roles for managers or team leaders should be designated. It then describes the roles and functions of team leaders, team managers, functional managers, and management teams. It concludes by discussing the implications of the changes in reporting relationships in team-based organizations.

Traditional Managerial Roles

In a traditional organization, managers of work groups are responsible for task management, which includes breaking work down into individual assignments; determining work methods, processes, schedules, and resource allocation; monitoring progress; and ensuring that work among members is integrated. Managers also have a boundary management function: they make sure that work is integrated across work groups and is responsive to the requirements of internal and external customers. Managers are responsible for technical and discipline leadership as well. they make sure that the work of subordinates meets technical standards, that technical knowledge and skills continue to be updated, that work opportunities and career paths offer technical development opportunities, and that new employees are selected for their technical know-how. Managers also have a performance management role, defining, reviewing, and recommending improvements to performance for the individuals they manage.

Managers of business units have a strategic leadership role. They are responsible for setting the direction for the business unit and making sure that functional strategies are reconciled and integrated with the requirements of the business unit. They deal with hard-to-resolve exceptions and are the final escalation point for resolving cross-functional conflicts. In addition, they are responsible for making resource allocation decisions and determining trade-offs that support the business objectives.

The traditional program structure described in our discussion of the Alpha Program (and summarized in Figure 3.9) relied on traditional managerial roles. Prior to the redesign of that program, each work-group manager had task management responsibilities. Each manager broke down the work, gave individual assignments to the engineers, adjusted workloads as needed, monitored individual progress and effectiveness, and recommended improvements. Although individual engineers attempted to coordinate their work technically with others across disciplines, the managers performed key integrating roles. For example, if the electrical and mechanical engineers developing a component found it impossible to reach agreement on trade-offs required for integration, they would escalate concerns to their respective managers. These managers would then weigh their discipline-based objectives and determine criteria for integration. They often needed to escalate issues to the program manager because they lacked sufficient expertise about the other disciplines and knowledge of the broader system.

Each work-group manager in the old Alpha structure was in charge of a discipline and supervised people from that discipline. These managers had begun their careers in these disciplines and been promoted to their managerial positions. Thus they were able to provide technical supervision and mentoring. Some of them became directly involved in the technical problems of their group and recommended solutions.

The program manager was the only manager who viewed his responsibilities in terms of the development of the electronic system consisting of three integrated electronic boxes. He had the strategic perspective for this system. He spent considerable time in the beginning developing program objectives (with input from the discipline-based managers). Many issues were escalated to him, because the discipline-based managers did not fully understand the requirements of the integrated system, and he spent considerable time adjudicating cross-discipline conflicts. The program manager was also responsible for allocating resources among the various work groups and dealing with cost and time overruns.

The new organization of Alpha as a team-based program with three work teams, each responsible for the configuration of one of the electronic boxes, came as a response to the number of cross-boundary transactions, the managerial bottlenecks, and the resulting slowness in development time. This new organization, however, created new management challenges. Each of the functions previously performed by managers in the traditional approach now has to be accomplished in a manner compatible with teams.

Management and Self-Management in a Team-Based Organization

In a team-based organization, design choices need to be made about what task management, boundary management, technical leadership, and performance management functions should be placed in work teams. Prototypical work teams perform many, if not most, of the management functions themselves. They perform task management activities, including task assignments, work scheduling, coordination among members, and facilitation of team meetings. Team members also may be responsible for certain boundary management functions, including linking with other teams, suppliers, and key customers. Team members may be responsible for the technical mentoring, coaching, and cross-training of other members. Finally, teams may share responsibility for performance management, including the development of team and individual goals, the evaluation of team and individual effectiveness, and the recommendation of improvements.

This considerable amount of team self-management is especially suitable when the work of the team is relatively routine, can be substantially self-contained, and is conducted in a relatively stable environment. In such settings, the team manages itself in executing a programmable piece of the business, handling the problems that arise, making decisions, and finding the best way to meet its goals. Because members are cross-trained, each has a common understanding of the team domain—a fact that facilitates team-work. Even in these settings, however, a design decision needs to be made about what leadership and management roles are required to make sure that all management tasks get performed effectively so that none falls through the cracks.

We argued in Chapter Three that conditions in knowledge-work settings moderate the extent of self-management that is possible or desirable. Environmental turbulence—changes in the environment—may necessitate changes in the teams' work. The high levels of interdependence among teams and among those making unitwide decisions may also necessitate adjustment processes that cut across team boundaries. The need to adjust the way that work is done constrains self-management. In addition, knowledge teams are likely to contain members with different knowledge bases and with only superficial understanding of the whole domain. This means that the process of teamwork is itself more complex and conflict-prone. Managing the team's processes requires considerable process expertise and may best be done by individuals with a broad understanding of the work and extensive skills in process leadership.

Self-management functions may be vested in all team members, or they may be the responsibility of particular team members in designated leadership or integrating roles. Other management functions may be vested in managers with hierarchical authority. The extent to which teams assume management responsibilities and the extent to which special leadership or management roles are required depends upon the complexity of the work and the environment. There is not one right choice that fits all situations. Instead, the nature of the work needs to be considered and trade-offs evaluated before design decisions can be made. Thus team design needs to be done locally, not globally, with a specific work situation in mind.

Design decisions about how to accomplish the management and self-management of teams are contingent on the amount of information that has to be processed during task execution. Uncertainty, complexity, and interdependence all contribute to the amount of information that must be processed as work is done (Galbraith, 1973). If these factors are very high, resulting in significant information-processing requirements, managers and/or team members placed in designated team leadership roles will be needed to perform formal coordinating and integrating functions.

This need to designate special roles to perform management and leadership tasks may exist despite the fact that the team itself was created as an integrating device to enable members to have more ready access to one another and to more easily integrate their work. Informal emergent processes for integration will be facilitated by establishing a team, but these may be inadequate to meet the integration needs in many environments. Formal integrating roles are often required to supplement the informal integration processes (Galbraith, 1994; Lawrence and Lorsch, 1969).

Managerial or designated team leader roles should be established where the information-processing demands exceed the capacity of the team to handle them informally. These roles increase the capacity of the team to process information by helping it coordinate and integrate internally and/or externally. Managers/leaders to whom unresolved conflicts are escalated for resolution increase the capacity of a team to make decisions. Managers/leaders who perform technical mentoring help members develop greater task expertise, thereby reducing the information gap between what team members need to know and what they do know. These integrating functions supplement the on-line coordination directly done by team members.

The companies we studied struggled with how to manage the teams, whether to have team leaders (and if so how to choose them), whether to eliminate supervisors, and so on. Several findings from our study are relevant here.

We found that team effectiveness is positively related to the extent to which teams do their own internal task management, including planning, goal setting, performance review, and improvement of methods and approaches. It is negatively related to the amount of external integration team members need to do. (In the organizations we studied, members of knowledge-work teams did a lot of external, lateral integration: on average, they spent 20 percent of their time working with people beyond their team's boundaries. Most of them also had team leaders to help accomplish efficient integration.) Finally, we found that effective teams spend a minimum of time meeting, freeing up more time to do the individual tasks that contribute to the team's goals. The picture of an effective knowledge-work team shows a team that is actively involved in managing its own performance and tasks and that has found efficient ways to integrate both internally and externally.

Teams in our study depended on management primarily to link them to the strategy, decisions, and performance needs of the larger organization—to provide direction and timely information. In general, teams depend on management to take their needs into account in determining priorities and allocating resources. They may also depend on management to bring authority to the resolution of issues that cannot be resolved laterally either within or across teams because resolution demands trade-offs that take a broader scope into account. For example, the teams in the Analytico division described in earlier chapters needed direction from management about whether to hold up development in order to integrate components with another division or whether to pursue time-to-market at the expense of the new business strategy of leveraging across divisions.

The important role that managers play in linking the team to the larger organization is demonstrated in our findings regarding performance management. Manager roles in reviewing the performance of a team are positively related to team performance. Managers focus on whether the team is accomplishing what the business unit needs from it. This approach complements the team's own focus on its internal processes and on how to go about improving performance. For that reason, even teams that are relatively self-contained and do substantial self-management cannot be left floating without connection to management. So what are the appropriate formal management roles?

Most organizations moving to a team-based design are trying to flatten and simplify their structures, reduce costs, and streamline decision making. Creating formal integrating roles may seem to work against this objective, particularly if the roles are hierarchical. On the other hand, decisions do need to be made at broader scopes than the team, and teams do need to be linked to a collective purpose. The design challenge is to define appropriate hierarchical roles to deal with businesswide issues while moving as much authority as possible into the teams. Eliminating supervision while creating a nonhierarchical team leader role can require sleight of hand. The dangers are that management will have the same expectations of a team leader that it had of supervisors in the past, that the team leader will enact the team leader role in a hierarchical manner, and that the team leader will be perceived by other team members as a "supervisor in sheep's clothing." To escape those dangers, management must craft appropriate within-team leadership roles in a manner that preserves the ability of the team to collectively address performance issues.

Several design principles can be used to guide decisions regarding leadership and management roles. First, put as much self-management responsibility as possible into the teams. Second, involve team members in determining how the various leadership tasks will be performed (and by whom) so that team leadership is collectively owned. Third, when possible, use lateral mechanisms for cross-team and organization-wide integration so that teams participate in this integration. Fourth, create management roles where necessary to link teams effectively to the larger organization and its environment and to make large-scope decisions that affect strategy, priorities, organizational capabilities, and resource allocation.

Factors Influencing Management and Leadership Needs

The very design of teams and the attempt to self-contain within the team all the resources to perform a task help to reduce information-processing complexity (Galbraith, 1973). Even under the circumstances in which self-containment is reasonably complete, however, the complexity of a given task may overwhelm the capacity of members to effectively integrate. The factors that increase task complexity and information-processing requirements are the key contingencies that determine whether managers or designated team leaders in integrating roles need to supplement the on-line coordination done by members of the team in the process of doing their tasks. These factors are listed below and then discussed in turn:

Amount of interdependence

Size of team

Functional/discipline diversity of members

Degree of team self-containment

Amount of change

Technical experience and skills

Life span of team

• *Amount of interdependence.* The amount of reciprocal interdependence among members of a team can vary greatly. If it is particularly high, no individual on the team can make technical design decisions without involving several other team members. For example, one of the Alpha component teams has six software engineers, six electrical engineers, two mechanical engineers, and one systems engineer responsible for designing a highly integrated electronic component. Suppose that one electrical engineer's design influences the activities of three other electrical engineers, four software engineers, and the systems engineer. One software engineer's work influences the activities of one electrical engineer and the five other software engineers. The other people's tasks on the team are similarly interrelated in ways that cannot be completely prespecified. Discussions involving design decisions in which all or several members are involved take place in team or subgroup meetings. In cases such as this, a designated team leader can help ensure ongoing coordination and integration by keeping track of open issues, facilitating meetings, making sure that the right people are involved in key decisions, and so forth. The systems integrators in the Alpha component teams have such a role, in addition to contributing technical input to the integration decisions. In contrast, if interdependence is weak and diffuse, team members can handle their own coordination informally.

• *Size of team.* Similarly, the number of people on a team impacts information-processing requirements. It is far simpler for three people to coordinate their activities and decisions with one another than it is for twenty people. The extent of interactions, decisions to be made, points of view to consider, and planning to be done increases with the size of the team. Thus smaller teams, with their lower transaction costs, are less likely to need people in team leadership roles than larger teams. The two hardware/software component teams in the Alpha Program, for example, have fifteen and thirteen members, and the hardware team has seven. Considering numbers of members alone, each hardware/software team is more likely to need a designated team leader than the hardware team.

• *Functional/discipline diversity of members.* The greater the number of disciplines on the team, the more points of view will need to be considered. As we have noted, people from different functions or disciplines often inhabit distinct thought-worlds, based on different bodies of knowledge, different identification of critical issues, and different criteria for evaluating uncertainty (Dougherty, 1992). For example, the Alpha hardware/software component teams have members from four disciplines: electrical engineering, mechanical engineering, systems engineering, and software engineering. Integration between members of these disciplines is complex and may require "translators"—individuals with a broad-based background as leaders (Galbraith, 1994).

• *Degree of team self-containment.* The extent to which a team is self-contained has a critical impact on the information processing required (Galbraith, 1973). If the team has all the resources it needs to perform its task, then coordination and decision making are internal team processes. If a team cannot be self-contained—that is, if its work is reciprocally interdependent with other teams and contributors—then information-processing complexity dramatically increases. The transaction costs are boggling, for example, if thirteen team members from one Alpha component team need to coordinate their activities with several members each from the other two teams. Decision making is extremely cumbersome if the decision-making forums have to regularly involve, say, twenty-nine people. In the case of the software engineers at Alpha, a cross-team integrating team addresses overall cross-team integration. Another possible approach is for managers, liaisons, or team leaders to be assigned such boundary management functions.

• *Amount of change.* The amount of change that a team has to deal with impacts the complexity of the information processing it requires (Galbraith, 1994). Unanticipated technical difficulties or successes, changes in strategies and resource allocation, and competitive surprises can alter the mission and task execution strategies of teams. Particularly in the area of new product development, management's capacity to buffer the team from unnecessary external change allows progress to be made. This buffering may be facilitated by a team manager. The greater the turbulence, the more that a team may be overwhelmed by the decisions it needs to make. In turbulent situations, having a person in a leadership or managerial role to bring the information quickly to the attention of the team and facilitate a team response can expedite the team's capability to respond quickly and appropriately to change.

• *Technical experience and skills.* Whether or not discipline or functional mentoring can be done by members of a team depends upon their experience and skill sets. Clearly, more experienced and proficient electrical engineers can mentor a new electrical engineer. The more experienced personnel may also have some responsibility for training, coaching, and even cross-training the less experienced.

Special technical lead or mentor roles may be established in the team, and the people in these roles may be able to monitor the work of their less experienced peers, helping to ensure that it meets the standards of their discipline. Some teams may lack seasoned experts who can train and mentor other members, however. In addition, peers may lack the knowledge and perspective to guide each other developmentally and to provide career-planning advice. For some purposes, such as to uphold business technical standards, authority may be needed to fully perform a technical leadership role. If a project team manager is from a different discipline than some team members, he or she will not be able to provide technical leadership, and it will need to come from another source. These particular functions may fall to a functional manager or to a team structure (such as a council or standards board).

• *Life span of team.* When an organization is just beginning its transition to teams, the expected longevity of teams is an important consideration in determining how much self-management should be vested in the teams. It may not make sense to take the time to develop the capability for team self-management for very short-term projects. It may be better to have someone in a designated leadership role who will facilitate meetings, plan schedules, make sure the workload is appropriately divided, and act as the key interface with other teams. This is particularly true for short-term projects that are technically very challenging. Longevity of a team project is not a critical factor for self-management, however, if the members of the team already have self-management skills.

Management and Leadership Needs in the Alpha Program

In general, the greater the requirement for information processing, the more likely it is that adequate performance of management functions will not emerge informally within the team. Instead, designated team leadership and/or management roles will be required. What conclusion can be drawn about the need for team manager or designated team leader roles in the Alpha Program based on the contingencies that have been discussed? The information-processing complexity of the three component teams is relatively high, due to the number of members on each team (fifteen, thirteen, and seven, respectively), the number of disciplines represented (electrical engineering, mechanical engineering, systems engineering, and software engineering), and the relatively high amount of reciprocal interdependence among members of each team. In addition, the teams are not fully self-contained. The integration requirements among the component teams are primarily addressed by a software integrating team and a systems integration overlay team. The technical support work group is composed of three individual contributors who work across all three component teams. These individuals are self-managing for the most part, although they may need help in determining their priorities (given multiple requests). Although the competitive environment for the electronics firm is turbulent, this project is well under way and is being buffered from unnecessary changes. At this point, no one expects the kind of outside change that would lead to fundamental modification of the project's objectives and intended functionality, although change in customer requirements would not be surprising.

Technical excellence is perceived to be critical for Alpha's success, and engineering skill is valued and nurtured. There is a mixture of skills on each team, with some contributors needing help in getting up to speed. Although some technical mentoring can be done by more experienced members of each team, not all skill areas have a critical mass of experienced people. In particular, several recent-hire mechanical engineers are "green" and will need technical supervision, which will have to be provided from a mechanical engineering manager on the program management team.

The time-to-market objectives for this project assume a two-year development cycle. This is ambitious, given that similar projects in the past have taken three and a half years. In general, the complexity of the information-processing requirements within and among these teams suggests that team members will not be able to informally perform all management functions and that team manager or designated team leadership roles are therefore needed. Although much of the technical integration will be facilitated by the systems integration cross-team and the software cross-team, the complexity of the integration needed (both within and across teams) is extremely high. Each team already has one role with leadership responsibilities: the systems engineer. Alpha has decided to also designate a team leader to keep track of the specifications and the schedule, convene the team or subteams as needed, and deal with the customers. Functional managers on the management team will retain technical mentoring roles and monitor technical standards.

Team Leaders, Team Managers, Functional Managers, Cross-Functional Management Teams, and Alternative Management Structures

The previous section examined factors that call for formal leadership or management roles to support team functioning. In this section, we will differentiate team leaders from team managers. Then, we will discuss the role of the functional manager in the team-based organization. Finally, we will also discuss the role of management teams and the conditions under which it is desirable to have work teams report to management teams instead of to individual team managers.

Within the traditional organization, the debate about managing teams typically revolves around human resource control and whether the cross-functional team manager or the functional manager should have the "solid-line" reporting relationship of the team member. At stake is who has budget control, task assignment control, and review and pay authority for the individuals in the team. The notion is that if the functional manager has resource control, technical excellence and efficiency in the allocation of technical skills are preserved; and if the team manager (the program or project manager, for example) has resource control, team performance is optimized.

In a team-based organization, where teams are the core performing units, the design discussion must also address the reporting relationship of the team, weighing the related issues of who should have
responsibility for managing the team and how that determination
will affect the individuals within the team. That discussion is com-
plicated by the fact that, in a team-based organization, the concept
of the manager changes. Because many tasks previously performed
by a single manager are now spread among a number of locations,
including team members themselves, individuals can no longer think
of themselves as getting direction from their one boss. These tasks
are often performed by individual contributors and/or people in
quasi-managerial roles, such as facilitators, systems managers,
liaisons, and team leaders (Mohrman and Cohen, forthcoming).

The issue of team leadership roles and management roles is not
an either/or matter. Even when team leader roles exist within the
team, the team has to be in some manner embedded in the authority structure of the organization. The team has to have a manager
or managers who are responsible for linking it to the needs of the
larger organization and for ensuring that performance is adequate.

The discussion of team leadership, team manager roles, and
functional manager roles primarily revolves around by whom and
how the traditional supervisory tasks will be performed. A number
of different configurations are possible. Different leadership and
management roles will be discussed below.

Team Leaders

Team leaders are members of a team. They perform designated leadership functions that may include task management, boundary management, and technical leadership. Usually a team leader makes a
direct technical contribution as well, and he or she may be responsible for specific work tasks. Team leaders typically do not have hierarchical authority; that is, other team members do not report to them.
They do not have review and evaluation authority either, although
a team leader may be responsible for leading a participative review

process. Like other members of the team, leaders share responsibility for the performance management process (along with management). Because they do not have hierarchical authority, these leaders need to be able to be persuasive and to influence the other team members. Thus informal leadership skills are critical: the abilities to communicate clearly, resolve conflicts, build consensus, and recognize others are key skills.

Teams may have one or more members with designated leadership roles, and these roles may be temporary or permanent. The number and kinds of designated leadership roles depend on the factors discussed in the previous section—factors that determine the information-processing complexity of the team. At a minimum, designated leadership may be required to help the team have effective team processes, including holding meetings, making decisions, solving problems, and reviewing team performance. In addition, designated leadership may be required for achieving effective task integration and technical performance, integrating with other teams and units, and interfacing with management and with customers and suppliers. Although one team leader may play all these roles, there is some advantage to spreading the leadership responsibility out among different members. Shared leadership enhances the collective sense of responsibility and reduces the probability that a single team leader will simply be a supervisor called by a different name. In complex work settings, it may be difficult or impossible for one person to attend to all these roles, in part because many of them require different skill sets. Technical leadership, for example, requires deep technical knowledge; technical integration leadership requires interdisciplinary systems knowledge; team process leadership requires yet another set of skills.

The star model in Figure 5.2 depicts one possible configuration in which critical leadership functions are assigned to various team members. These roles may be permanent (for the life of the team), or they may rotate. This model makes sense only for teams with relatively long life spans, because it requires considerable investment

Figure 5.2. Team Leadership Roles in Star Configuration.

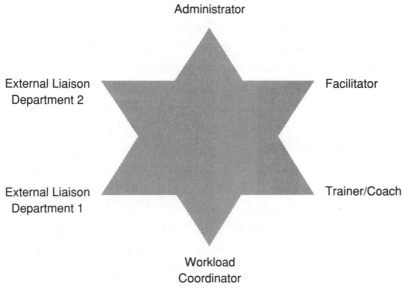

Administrator

External Liaison
Department 2

Facilitator

External Liaison
Department 1

Trainer/Coach

Workload
Coordinator

in developing the leadership capacity of various members of the work team. The team shown in Figure 5.2—a team we encountered in one of the organizations we studied—has several assigned leadership roles. The administrator is responsible for time sheets, vacation plans, meeting minutes, and other record keeping. The facilitator is responsible for leading all team meetings and consulting to team members when they have difficulty resolving an issue. The person in this role receives training in meeting facilitation and conflict resolution. The trainer/coach is responsible for working with team members on their technical skills and development plans and for obtaining external training resources for the team (or linking to the corporate training department) when appropriate. The workload coordinator tracks progress of the engineers and determines whether any changes in workload assignments need to be made. The external liaison for the first department is responsible for coordination with the marketing department. The external liaison for the second department is responsible for coordination with manufacturing. The individuals assuming both of these roles have had previous assignments in those departments and have informal networks there, expediting problem resolution. These liaisons do not make all the cross-department contacts, however. When team members need to work directly with others across departments, they do so, but they keep the liaisons informed. The critical linkages for this team happen to be with other departments. However, in other organizations they might be with other teams. In that case, boundary-spanning roles would have to be defined for the other teams.

Teams with a relatively long life span may have rotating team leadership roles. Rotation communicates a message of shared leadership and can be used to build self-management capacity in the team. The time that elapses between rotations needs to be sufficient for the new team leader to acquire expertise in the role. However, leadership roles for which the skills take a long time to develop may not fit a rotation model. This may be true, for example, of systems integration leadership roles. For new product development projects, rotation may be according to the project's life phase. During the design phase, the person assigned to the team leader role would be a design engineer; during manufacturing ramp-up, the team leader role would rotate to a manufacturing engineer; and during commercialization, the team leader role would rotate to a product marketer. This rotation of team leaders matches the change of primary tasks that occur during a new product's life cycle. Again, role clarity is important. It is imperative that the team, team leaders, and managers understand who will be performing necessary leadership functions.

The companies we studied handled leader selection in a variety of ways. Both management and the team have an interest in the selection of team leaders; both have a stake in ensuring that leaders have the requisite skills to perform the leadership task. In addition, management has an interest in making sure that organizational members have opportunities to develop skills that prepare them for new assignments. Selection of team leaders relates to career pathing, succession planning, and the development of management capabilities in the organization. The team has an additional stake in that leadership is a subset of the total tasks that the team is responsible for, and it affects the team's performance strategy and capabilities.

Both the team and management need to be part of developing the criteria for leaders. If the team selects the leaders, team members will feel ownership over their choice. Even if management selects the leaders, team members may still accept the people in their roles—if they feel the criteria are fair and the choices make sense. Ideally, though, the team has input into the decision. However leaders are chosen, role clarity is imperative. The team leaders, team members, and managers need to develop a shared understanding of the duties of the team leaders.

Team Managers

Teams are embedded in organizational hierarchies. Teams always report to a manager or a team of managers at a higher systemic level, even when layers of management are removed in the organization. Managers address issues from the perspective of the more inclusive business unit and link the team to the larger system. They do this through formulation and communication of strategies and priorities, allocation of resources, and development of organizational capabilities. They also play a major role in managing the performance of teams, making sure that the performance meets the needs of the organization.

Some team managers are highly involved in the day-to-day operations of the team; it is as if they were team leaders with position authority. Alternatively, team managers may manage a number of teams and be relatively uninvolved in the daily operations. In fact, they may manage teams but also be members of a larger business-unit or overlay team. At Analytico, for example, the functional team managers are also members of the product management team. At Netco, the industry business team manager is active in the coordination within the industry business team and also serves on the field office management team.

Team managers have position power. They are at a higher rank than team members, and the team (and possibly its members) may report to the team manager for operational direction. They have accountability for managing team performance and monitoring team effectiveness. Their influence is based on position and rank as well as on their ability to influence and persuade others. Their challenge is to be able to use their authority to help teams become as self-managing as feasible. Thus team managers need to skillfully balance performing certain task or boundary management functions to help the team effectively coordinate and encouraging the team to perform more of these functions over time.

Team manager positions often coexist with internal leadership roles. For example, both the design and process development teams at Analytico have an engineer serving as a systems integration leader to track technical integration issues and pull together team members to resolve them. A great deal of the interteam integration is led by those team members who have overlapping membership with other teams. In fact, the majority of the time of these members with overlapping membership is spent on cross-team integration issues. Although the team managers take responsibility for team meetings, agendas, and key issues, a great deal of the operational integration is done by the team members themselves, with different members playing leadership roles for different purposes.

The key question is how to divide responsibility between a team manager and his or her team members. There are certain responsibilities that managers cannot fully delegate to the team. These deal with linking the team to the broader organization and managing its performance toward that end. Even there, however, managers have to adopt a participative approach. Goal setting, budgeting, and certain performance management practices (such as reviewing performance and developing capabilities) have to be multidirectional, with considerable input from and influence exercised by the team itself. (These issues will be further discussed in the next two chapters of the book.)

Another function of team managers is to facilitate conflict resolution and mediate multiparty decisions when problems cannot be
resolved at a co-worker level. Peers can clearly integrate their activities with one another. They can be influential through persuasion
and may be able to resolve conflicts through negotiation and other
team processes. However, there are times when a team does not
have the bigger picture required to resolve differences of opinion,
when different functional priorities are mutually exclusive, or when
a decision involves trade-offs that have broader-scope implications.
Even a highly skilled team may reach impasse or need input from
managers at a higher systemic level.

The tasks mentioned above can all be handled by managers who
are largely external to the team. As we have noted, however, in
some situations it may be desirable to have a manager more active
in some of the traditional integrating functions—those that are
more tightly linked to the team's day-to-day operations. A manager
may even function as a team leader, with or without the other team
members reporting to him or her. Program and project managers
often have such team leadership roles.

As an example, consider the business leadership team for each
industry-specific team at Netco. This leadership team is composed
of a business manager and service, sales, and technical coordinators.
The coordinators are not at a higher organizational rank than the
members of the client teams. Each of the members of the business
leadership team is responsible for technical supervision and mentoring of the individuals in client teams from their functions. The
business manager is the leader of the industry team and has responsibility for integrating with the other industry managers and functional managers within the field office. The coordinators also have
clearly defined and differentiated leadership roles in the industry
team. Team members receive operational and technical leadership
from the leadership team, which is composed of individuals of different ranks.

The advantage of having a team leader who is a manager is that his or her credibility may be influenced by rank: this sort of manager may have an easier time getting things done than a team leader from the same organizational level as other team members. However, as we have noted, having two rankings within a team may cause the team to revert to the traditional, hierarchical way of doing things. Managers in team leader roles may have difficulty being participative; they may not have the skills to influence without being directive. They may not know how to develop the capacity of team members to do their own integrating. They may even be reluctant to do so, in those situations where their task is to work themselves out of a job as team members learn how to cover integration-related leadership functions themselves.

Hierarchical relationships within a team may be appropriate in complex team structures (such as those adopted at Netco) if there are subteams responsible for different components of a project or different clients receiving a service. These complex team structures may have a subteam that integrates the various components. Netco's leadership team is an example. In a sense, these complex teams contain more than one systemic level within their boundaries. For example, each industry-specific team at Netco has several client teams as well as a business leadership team. The business leadership team is responsible for the technical leadership of the client teams and deals with the allocation of resources and trade-offs across client teams. Because the business leadership team is responsible for a broader systemic level than each client team, having a higher-level manager exercising leadership in these integrating functions makes sense.

There are other sources of complexity that make it desirable for the team manager to play a more hands-on integrating role. Integrating with multiple internal and external technical partners, for example, may require hierarchical authority. Dealing with particular customers—those that work with many parts of the organization simultaneously, requiring an integrated interface, and those that demand a management interface—may also require a higher-level view.

A manager may have to adopt a more involved team leadership role if a particular team lacks the readiness or skills to perform the needed management functions and/or lacks members suited to serve in one or some of the required team leader roles. In this situation, one of the responsibilities of the manager is to help the team become more self-managing over time by developing members' capacity to manage their collective tasks, to integrate with customers and suppliers across team boundaries, to increase their technical skills, and to self-monitor their performance.

In general, a team-based organization should attempt to have as many of the traditional management functions as possible performed by team members or by lateral cross-team mechanisms (such as those described in Chapter Four) rather than by higher-ranked managers. Representative teams or other nonmanagement integrating teams can often be established to do this integration even at broader systemic levels than the teams they represent. (The systems integration team in the Alpha Program is an example.) This approach requires the team members to accept the authority of their peers in integrating roles. It also requires the integrators to have the necessary task management and boundary management skills. In those settings where complexity of information processing or a lack of team skills calls for a more active integrating role by managers, the managers need to develop a highly participative style in order to preserve the team members' sense of collective responsibility for team goals.

Functional Managers

Functional managers are in charge of organizational functional capabilities, such as software engineering, marketing, or manufacturing. Whether or not teams or team members report to the functional managers depends upon the logic of the team organization. When work teams are functionally based, they are likely to report to a functional manager who is also the team manager. At Analytico, the teams are cross-functionally composed, but they report to a manager in the function predominant at the stage of work performed by the work team. Work team members from different functions than their team manager also receive feedback from their own functional manager, who is a technical resource and provides technical review of work as an input to the team manager and the team.

When work teams are cross-functional and report to a project manager, functional managers do not have operational authority but are responsible for maintaining technical excellence by providing development opportunities, establishing technical mentoring, performing review roles where appropriate, and ensuring that technical processes are up-to-date.

The team-based organization requires that functional managers assume a new developmental role. In striving to provide teams with the technical expertise and support needed to function effectively, functional managers need to make sure that functional strategies are understood by people from their function whether or not those people report to them. They have responsibility for maintaining organizational technical expertise in a function, making sure that team members continue to acquire new functional knowledge and skills. This can be done in a variety of ways: making sure educational opportunities are available, establishing technical councils (like those that are present in Netco's field offices), providing direct coaching, providing performance review input, and influencing the staffing of projects to ensure that there are mentors and that people have adequate development activities. Through the organizational mechanisms functional managers set up, the opportunities for learning they create, the systems they develop, and their capacity to persuade and influence, functional managers carry out this developmental role. All this presupposes that the organization invests in its functional capabilities and provides the functional managers with resources to perform these tasks.

Functional managers also need to be able to effectively work with other managers in cross-functional management teams. In these forums, they help resolve trade-offs involving functional issues and exert influence to ensure adequate organizational investment in technical capabilities.

Cross-Functional Management Teams

Teams often receive direction and review from a management team. Cross-functional management teams are able to adjudicate the conflicts that arise across functions and make cross-functional trade-offs for products and services. The decision escalation process takes less time if cross-functional management teams rather than separate functional or disciplinary hierarchies are used. They can also be a far more efficient solution than dealing with cross-functional forums on an as-needed basis. Cross-functional management teams at the business-unit level can set business strategies and priorities that balance competing functional interests. Defining strategies and priorities establishes criteria that can be used by teams to determine appropriate trade-offs. Divergent interests can be evaluated and trade-offs determined based on the direction that has been set.

When the work teams are cross-functional, it is useful to have them report to management teams. This is true, for example, in the Alpha Program, where each component team reports to the program management team, which is composed of all the functional managers. It also may be useful when interdependence is high among functional or discipline-based work teams, requiring many issues to be escalated to a cross-functional forum. When work teams are predominantly functional or discipline-based, another possibility is to have teams report to a functional or discipline-based manager for day-to-day operational direction but to have an overlaid cross-functional management team to handle cross-functional trade-offs. The product management teams at Analytico are examples of this configuration. They make high-level trade-offs that cannot be made within the work teams even with guidance from the functional manager.

The decision to establish a cross-functional management team involves trade-offs. On the one hand, the deliberations of management teams involve several players and considerable transaction costs; these deliberations are expensive, given the costs of managerial time. In addition, if the work teams under the jurisdiction of a management team need close supervision, then the leadership provided by a management team may not be sufficient and a reporting relationship to a manager may be required. On the other hand, decision making in an organization without cross-functional management teams may be even more costly (and less efficient) due to the time spent using separate functional hierarchies, the waste of rework stemming from functional suboptimization, and the transaction costs when interdependence among functions is high. In addition, work teams that are relatively self-managing do not need day-to-day supervision. In most of the organizations we studied, the benefits of using management teams outweighed their costs.

A cross-functional management team can be a source of direction and review for the teams in the organization even if each team reports to one of its members or to a functional manager. The cross-functional work teams at Analytico are an example. Members report to a functional manager but get direction and review from a cross-functional product management team. In many organizations, one member of the cross-functional management team has primary responsibility for a team but operates within the overall direction of the management team. The management team is then on the escalation path for cross-functional issues that the team cannot resolve.

Because of their broad perspective, cross-functional management teams also serve as mini–general managers (Galbraith, 1994), as we have noted. Many issues that would traditionally have been escalated to a general manager can be resolved in this kind of team. However, a general manager role may still be needed. If functional leaders cannot laterally resolve difficult trade-offs, then a final escalation point is needed. The business-unit leader is often the leader of the management team—in other words, the general manager. That person helps with the integration issues within that team and between that team and the rest of the organization, plays a strategic leadership role, and is the final escalation point.

In the Alpha Program, the program manager is in the role of strategic leader. He acts as the leader of the management team and, when that team is unable to resolve conflicts, serves as a tiebreaker. The program manager, seeing his role as keeping the program on course, reminds the other members of the strategic direction for the unit and the objectives for the program. Fewer issues require his personal resolution now than prior to the reorganization, because most critical cross-functional issues that are escalated from the work teams are resolved by the management team.

Alternative Management Structures

How the organization distributes management functions between team managers and their teams determines how "flat" the organizational structure will be. Figure 5.3 depicts four possible management structures. These alternatives can be understood in either of two ways: as representing the management structures in different organizations or as reflecting one company's evolution over time to a flatter, more empowered organization.

In example A, each team reports to a manager. In this hypothetical case, the requirements for technical supervision, the number of issues that need to be escalated, and the amount of integration required within and between teams warrant a team manager. This is an organization that has not attempted to remove the first level of supervision, viewing the team management role as critical. The teams do not have a team leader, although there may be some members playing particular leadership roles.

In example B, the manager's span of control has increased: each team manager is responsible for two teams. In this case, the activities of the two teams are related, and the teams have considerable interdependence between them. They are also more self-managing,

Figure 5.3. Alternative Management Structures.

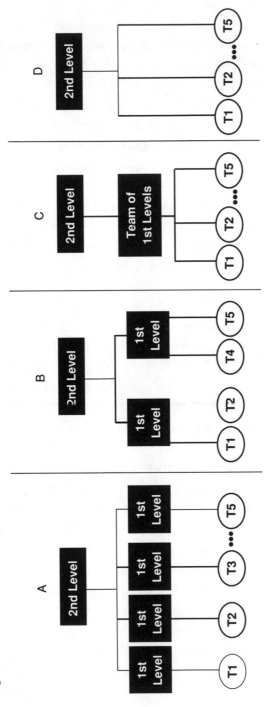

Key: T1 = team 1, T2 = team 2, and so on.

having picked up several leadership functions over time; they may have team leaders assigned to those functions. This is an organization in the process of reducing the numbers of managers and increasing employee involvement.

In example C, several teams report to a team of managers. In this case, each team may be cross-functional, with the team of managers representing those functions. Again, these teams are likely to be experienced and relatively self-managing, requiring less day-to-day involvement from their team of supervisors, and they have team leaders.

Finally, the structure depicted in example D has removed one level of management, and the teams have picked up several management functions. They have designated team leaders, but all the members perform certain leadership functions. The second-level manager (a role that may be filled by a management team) is more closely involved with the work teams than the other second-level managers depicted in the figure. These work teams are able to resolve many issues and other problems on their own, but they still rely on the second-level manager (or management team) to be a tiebreaker.

Role Clarity and the Charting of Responsibility

So far, we have identified various approaches to ensuring that all management and leadership tasks are carried out, and we have examined factors that should be considered in determining whether a team should have a designated team leader or a team manager who performs management tasks for the team. Our discussion does not assume an all-or-none state—that teams are either self-managing or not. On the contrary, self-management is incremental. Teams may pick up certain task management functions and not others. Managers may be responsible for boundary management functions with upper management, but team members may be responsible for linking directly with those from other teams with whom they are interdependent.

Similarly, more experienced team members may share responsibility for technical mentoring of those from their discipline with a discipline or functional manager. Teams may also share performance management responsibilities with their managers. Who has what assignments is no more important than clarity about that issue, however. Members of a team need to understand what management functions they are responsible for fulfilling and what they can expect from their managers.

When teams are first formed, they may not be ready to take on several management functions. After the members have worked together for a while and they have greater understanding of the technical tasks, they may be ready to expand their responsibilities. Thus the extent of self-management is dynamic. With time and experience, teams can take on more managerial functions, and managers should encourage them to do so. Managers play a key role in developing teams for self-management.

One tool that is quite helpful for determining and clarifying appropriate roles for the team and its manager(s) is responsibility charting (Melcher, 1967). Many self-managing teams, when first implemented, use this tool (Wellins, Byham, and Wilson, 1991). Exhibit 5.1 illustrates a responsibility chart that lists task management, boundary management, technical leadership, and performance management functions and identifies whether the team will be responsible for any listed function now, whether the team will be responsible for that function six months from now, or whether that function will be handled by a team manager or a team leader.

For teams that have both a designated team leader and a team manager, extra columns can be added that differentiate the team leader's from the team manager's role. Likewise, columns can be added to differentiate the roles of multiple team leaders. Team members and the appropriate managers need to discuss and clarify who is responsible for each activity. These negotiations may have to be done several times during the period when the team is learning how to handle greater leadership responsibility.

Exhibit 5.1. Sample Format for Responsibility Chart Dealing with Management Functions.

Task Management	Team Now	Team in Six Months	Team Manager or Team Leader
Assign work		X	
Balance workload		X	
Develop project objectives	X		X
Develop project work plan	X		X
Review & approve project objectives			X
Review & approve project work plan			X
Review & approve changes to objectives			X
Review & approve changes to work plan		X	
Solve problems	X		
Coordinate work with others on team	X		
Plan & lead team meetings		X	
Complete time sheets	X		
Schedule vacation	X		

Boundary Management	Team Now	Team in Six Months	Team Manager or Team Leader
Liaison with individual contributors outside the team	X		
Liaison with other teams		X	
Liaison with suppliers		X	
Liaison with customer		X	X
Liaison with upper management			X
Liaison with professional organizations	X		

Exhibit 5.1. (cont.) Sample Format for Responsibility Chart Dealing with Management Functions.

Team Leadership	Team Now	Team in Six Months	Team Manager or Team Leader
Train employees new to discipline	X		
Mentor employees from same discipline	X		
Consult on technical difficulties	X		
Enforce technical standards			X
Assign people to future projects			X
Provide career counseling			X

Performance Management	Team Now	Team in Six Months	Team Manager or Team Leader
Develop team goals	X		X
Determine individual goals		X	X
Review team performance		X	X
Survey customers about team performance		X	
Provide input for performance appraisals	X		
Conduct performance appraisals		X	X
Handle disciplinary problems		X	X
Recommend improvements	X		
Develop and monitor budget			X

Reporting Relationships

The concept of reporting relationships takes on a different meaning in team-based organizations. Individuals are part of teams as performing units. The effective teams in our study had managers or management teams that took responsibility for making sure the team had clear direction, reviewing team performance, and creating a context in which the teams could be effective. In the new sense, these teams "reported" to those managers or that management team.

The concept of individual reporting relationships unfolds differently in each setting; individuals in teams receive different kinds of direction and feedback from a variety of sources, depending on the organizational structure. In Chapter Seven, on performance management, we will see that individuals negotiate their task responsibilities with the team, not with a manager, in the team-based organization. They get feedback from team members about how they are meeting their team commitments. They may get technical feedback from a team mentor or from a functional expert who is a manager. They may get help integrating their work from a liaison or a systems integrator. So whom do they report to?

For both the team and the individual, as we will see in Chapter Seven, direction setting and performance management are multi-directional processes, which makes it difficult to think in conventional terms about reporting relationships. Direction and feedback come from many sources, including managers, co-workers, other teams, and customers. Performance reviews reflect input from multiple sources, and decisions about consequences reflect that myriad of perspectives. Ultimately, consequences depend on whether the team is accomplishing its organizational mission of producing products or services that deliver value to the customer and to the organization and whether the individual is able to execute his or her responsibilities to the team.

In the Alpha Program, team members maintain their reporting relationship to the functional manager, despite the fact that they receive operational direction from their team and their team leader. The functional manager, who reviews technical performance and provides development and career advice, is ultimately responsible for making sure that the teams are populated by individuals who can perform the needed technical functions.

At Analytico, the team manager provides operational direction to the team, whose members then together work out plans and provide each other with on-line operational direction. Everyone in the team reports, in the operational sense, to the team manager. Members of the team from different functions than the team manager, however, receive technical feedback and review, as well as development and career assistance, from a manager in their own discipline. Ultimately, decisions about moving a person off a team are jointly made by the team manager and the functional manager, but the team is as likely to initiate such action as anyone else.

At Netco, individual reporting has been left intentionally vague. The teams receive some operational direction from the leadership team, and individuals get technical input from their coordinators, who are their peers. Reviews are pulled together by the coordinators with a great deal of input from customers, team co-members, and the coordinators themselves. Although it has not been made formal (and had never happened when we studied Netco), the head of the field offices felt that if it were necessary to fire a team member, the coordinators, industry business heads, and functional managers would be jointly involved in making the decision. Again, though, such action is likely to be *initiated* by the team itself.

Mature work teams in routine settings often have responsibility for their own personnel functions, including reviewing, rewarding, and taking job action. In knowledge-work settings where teams are dynamic and individuals have multiple memberships, the processes of dealing with performance problems, moving people in and out of teams, and determining career development are likely to be more fluid and multidirectional. They are likely to entail team input and initiative, although management would be involved in the ultimate disposition of any performance issue. This is because any one team may see only a portion of a person's performance over time (or even at any one time), since people move between team assignments and often serve on multiple teams.

The key in a team-based organization is to have processes, with input from multiple sources, that arrive at a good picture not only of the technical tasks the person can do but also of how and how much the person is contributing to the success of the performing units: the teams. This theme will be echoed in a number of the remaining chapters of the book.

Key Issues

The most important concerns related to management structures and roles are these:

1. Determining the extent to which teams should assume management responsibilities is a design choice and depends upon task complexity and the corresponding information-processing requirements. Some guidelines:

   Put as many self-management roles as possible into the teams.

   Involve the teams in determining how various leadership tasks will be performed.

   When possible, use lateral rather than hierarchical cross-team integration.

   Create management roles (managers or management teams) to link work teams to the larger organization and make large-scope decisions.

2. A management team or a member of a team designated as a team leader or a team manager can perform integrating roles.

3. Functional managers have a special responsibility for developing people from their discipline, irrespective of reporting relationships.

4. There are three reasons for considering having more than one hierarchical level in a team:

   The team is responsible for performance at multiple systemic levels.

   The team is dealing with a complex array of partners and/or customers that are best dealt with by a manager.

   The team lacks the readiness or skills to perform the needed management functions or lacks a member who can serve as a team leader.

5. Responsibility charting is a helpful tool for clarifying responsibilities of team members, leaders, and managers.

6. Team leader alternatives include permanent roles, rotating roles, and the sharing of designated leadership functions.

7. The amount of team self-management should increase over time as teams develop the capability to perform additional management functions.

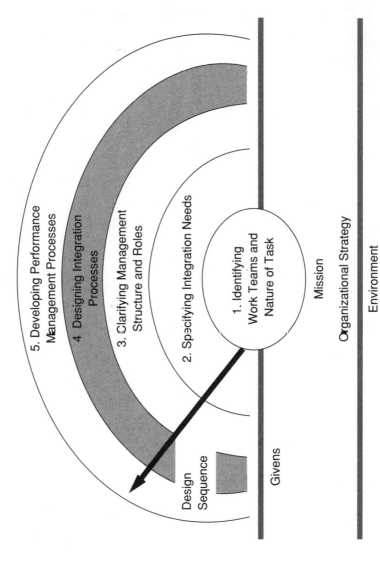

Figure 6.1. Step Four of the Design Sequence: Designing Integration Processes.

6

· ·

Step Four

Designing Integration Processes

Many organizations have made the mistake of establishing teams but failing to implement or redesign the processes required for teams to be successful. Organizational processes create a context in which lateral integration can occur within and across teams and across the levels of the organizational system. This chapter deals with three integration processes that our research found to be particularly important for shaping the context for effective team functioning: the processes of direction setting, information distribution and communication, and decision making. The chapter then provides a framework to underpin the development of systematic approaches to these processes.

These three processes are important in all organizations, not solely in team-based organizations. However, team-based organizations face particular challenges in these areas. We will not try to be exhaustive in our description of these processes; rather, we will emphasize the aspects that are particularly important in team organizations.

These processes are central to the ability of the organization to create teams that are able to make a difference in the attainment of goals through the interaction of team members with one another and with other teams. They are the essence of empowerment, which was defined earlier as entailing both direction and capability. They provide the context in which people with different specialties and roles in the organization go through the divergence/convergence cycle of interdependent work and develop shared understandings of what they are trying to accomplish. These shared understandings of the organization's direction then serve as the foundation for integrated task performance, allowing participants to align their efforts.

Direction Setting

The traditional hierarchy relied on direction setting that cascaded through the various chains of command of the organization. Each chain translated corporate direction into direction for that part of the organization, its specificity increasing as the direction was passed down. Thus the direction received by the technical core of the organization was both narrow and specific. Indeed, in our research, it was not uncommon to talk to highly skilled and experienced individuals who were uninformed about organizational direction beyond their immediate job assignment. In several organizations in the early stages of the transition to teams, we saw "team" members who were unaware of even each other's goals and assignments. Little wonder that lateral integration in these traditional organizations was the purview of managers, often those relatively high in the organizational hierarchy. Little wonder, too, that direction was often fuzzy: managers could get away without giving clear direction because they could count on being able to resolve ambiguous issues themselves.

Team-based organizations rely on clear direction and broadly held knowledge of that direction. If issues are to be resolved laterally—that is, within and between teams—and if cross-functional teams are to be able to make complex trade-offs on issues that cannot be easily handled from the perspective of a single discipline or function, people must work with a similar and rich understanding of the direction of the organization.

What can an organization do to establish and communicate clear direction? Let us turn now to that question.

- *Define a strategy, communicate it, and operationalize it at all systemic levels.* Strategy includes the mission of the organization and its plans for applying its resources to ensure that it can accomplish that mission in its environment. Ideally, strategy informs the trade-offs that are made throughout the organization: business units translate the corporate strategy into a business-unit strategy, teams of all kinds translate it into a team strategy, and so on. At Analytico, for instance, the corporate strategy calls for leveraging technology and process development across multiple products and product lines and for creating families of related products that address different segments of the market. Members of particular design or development teams need to know both the general business strategy and the strategy for their team's product, in order to be able to resolve difficult trade-offs. One of the explicit responsibilities of each product-line coordinating team in that organization is to articulate the micro-strategy for the product line and for each of the products within it. This is not done unilaterally; rather, members of the product teams are given an opportunity to give input. In a team environment, it is management's responsibility to ensure that both the macro- and microstrategies are articulated, broadly shared, and understood and that those strategies reflect information from organizational performers as well as information from the environment.
- *Align goals vertically and laterally.* Strategy gets translated into goals. In an organization that is a system of teams, the goals are for performing units (for example, individuals, teams, or product lines) nested within each other as well as for the organization as a whole. These unit goals, in combination, must add up to the business goals. This raises issues of fit in two areas: between systemic levels (the goals of a lower-level unit, such as an individual or a team, must fit with the goals of the higher-level business unit in which that individual or team is

embedded) and between units at the same level within a larger unit (the goals of all the teams in a business unit must fit with each other, and the goals of all the individuals within a team must fit with each other). This means that the goal-setting process must be both vertically and laterally conducted (see Figure 6.2).

We will again use Analytico to illustrate this issue of fit. The members of the design and development teams operate within two logics: the logic of their product, which drives to optimize the success of the product, and the logic of their discipline, which pushes for optimized processes and the reuse of design elements. To achieve a vertical and lateral fit, Analytico must achieve a workable compatibility between the functional goals and the product goals. This may mean, for example, that the teams share the goal of leveraging technology and process development across multiple products. In other words, leveraging technology would be not simply a func-

Figure 6.2. Goal Setting as a Vertical and Lateral Process.

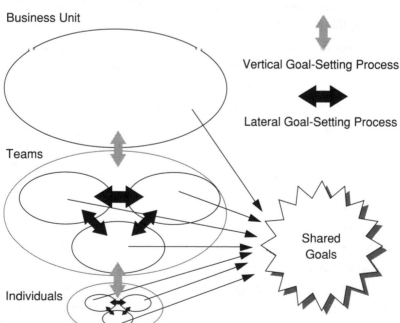

tional goal but a team goal as well. Likewise, reuse of design elements might become a team metric.

Compatibility must also be achieved across units to make sure that units are not working at cross-purposes, that their goals aggregate to the larger-unit goals, and that interdependent units have consistent goals. Where a unit needs support from another unit, this support must be included in that other unit's goals. This requires that the individuals in teams collaborate in the setting of goals for their team and for each other and that interdependent teams have both a process check to make sure that their goals are compatible with one another and a way of negotiating between competing focuses in order to accomplish compatibility.

The fit of organizational goals and the way in which they are established are particularly important factors in team members' confidence in their ability to accomplish the goals. In our study, this confidence was in turn strongly related to team effectiveness. Team participation in setting team goals was also related to team effectiveness. The goal-alignment process must therefore be two-way: it must involve a negotiation between parties regarding what is possible, given the resources that can be committed. The effective teams we saw often had "stretch" goals—goals that everyone agreed would require unusually high levels of performance. But those goals were set through a process that involved the team; the team understood the organizational strategy or customer requirements that called for high levels of performance and participated in deciding how to accomplish them.

In the team-based organization, the goals of the larger organizational unit are shared by all members of performing units within it. This concept is fundamental to the creation of the capacity to optimally integrate across individuals and teams because it underpins the motivation for the individuals and teams to integrate their work rather than optimize their subpiece. Operationalizing this concept requires a system of feedback and consequences for goal attainment at all levels. The component of this system involving rewards will be described in Chapter Seven (and is discussed briefly below). Here it is important to note only that managers must treat all members of the unit as owners of the unit's goals—a departure from the traditional viewpoint, in which unit managers own unit goals and members are responsible for only their microgoals.

- *Align support service goals.* A special case of goal fit is the alignment of the goals of shared support services with the goals of the teams and other performing units that they serve. Teams cannot be held fully accountable for their performance if they depend on support services that cannot or will not deliver service in a way that facilitates the ability of the team to accomplish its goals. Shared services are suppliers to teams; consequently, their goals should be aligned with the needs of the teams. Team-based organizations handle this alignment in two ways. First, they create service "contracts" (explicit statements of the services to be delivered and the standards for delivery) so that the goals of the shared service incorporate the needs of the teams. Second, they establish conditions that help ensure that the goals of the operating units are goals of the support services as well; for example, they may base part or all of the rewards for support services on the performance of the operating units those services support. Technical support group members might each negotiate a service contract specifying the parameters of the service they are committed to deliver to each team so that their own goals take into account the goals and plans of the teams. In addition, a bonus or merit pool might be based on the performance of the operating teams and the whole business unit against its targets.

- *Choose goals that are measurable.* The data from our study indicate very clearly that having measurable team goals is related to team and business-unit effectiveness. These goals include performance targets, such as cost, quality, schedule, revenue, and profit; they also include such goals as reusing a certain amount of software code, earning a particular percentage of revenue from new products or new customers, and achieving an order of a certain magnitude from a particular new customer. These latter goals have a qualitative aspect to them, but they are stated in such a way that team members and managers will know without ambiguity how they are doing with respect to their goals.

• *Assign rewards in accordance with organizational goals.* The reward system is a direction-setting element of the organization because it influences the course of organizational effort. We are using the term *rewards* very broadly here to refer to desired outcomes such as increased compensation, acknowledgment and recognition, and career advancement and growth opportunities that accrue to organizational members as a result of certain behaviors or performances. What gets rewarded sends a message to organizational members about what is valued in the organization—that is, the behaviors that management *really* wants and that move one ahead. Someone who continues to be rewarded for individual performance irrespective of that person's team performance will continue to direct his or her efforts to individual accomplishments and may not attend to the integration requirements of the team.

• *Do not assume that direction precludes empowerment.* The issue of direction has been particularly troublesome in organizations that see themselves as moving toward self-managed or empowered teams. Managers are often reluctant to provide much direction, for fear of violating the spirit of empowerment. Our research suggests, however, that providing direction is critical to the empowerment process. In fact, not providing direction is disempowering (Hackman, 1990). However, the sort of direction required is different from the traditional notion captured in the phrase "directive management"—a practice in which managers tell subordinates what to do and how to do it and monitor very closely the daily work activities. The direction that is key in team-based organizations is based on broad knowledge of where the organization is headed, its strategy for getting there, and the criteria and priorities that result; and it is the translation of that broad direction into local goals that aligns the various performing units of the organization and the individuals within teams.

Supporting this view is the fact that team members in our study indicated that they were much more likely to receive information relevant to the way they performed their day-to-day work from their co-workers than from their managers. Thus managers' influence is largely exercised by the goal context they set, not by daily direction.

- *Plan collectively.* Team member involvement in the planning process is related to team effectiveness. Ineffective teams in the companies we studied tended to have managers who developed and "kept" the plans, allowing little team input or influence. The plans often were accomplished through individual interaction between the manager and each team member, with the manager serving as the integrating mechanism (in a role much like the traditional one described in Chapter Five). These were the situations in which team members, feeling no sense of commitment to the official plan, were most likely to develop a "shadow" plan—one that they believed was more realistic. This mode of operation fails to take advantage of one of the most important sources of performance leverage that is afforded by establishing a team: the ability of the members to develop performance strategies that are flexible, that they can control, and that they believe will work. A common observation from team members was, "I can understand why we need to have stretch goals, but management needs to give us some leeway in how to accomplish them."

This does not mean that organizational planning tools are irrelevant in a team environment. Nor does it mean that management disappears. In fact, the most effective teams we saw used systematic planning processes for determining responsibilities and for scheduling and integrating their work. PERT-charting (or some other form of scheduling) and other project management tools are important to team success. For example, task responsibility charting, mentioned in a management context in Chapter Five, can be used to create a systematic display of the expected contributions from each participant, while quality functional deployment (QFD) can be used to specify the responsibilities of each function within the team for meeting the requirements of the customer (Hauser and Clausing, 1988). Such tools are formal processes for specifying responsibility. Frequently, they are computer-based, electronically connecting project participants together and fostering shared agreement regarding a planning and decision-making process. Exhibit 6.1 illustrates a generic form of task responsibility charting (in a partial example taken from Netco's field offices).

Plans, regular updates and reviews of progress against plans, and determination of steps needed to address discrepancies are part of the process of effective teams and underlie their ability to become more effective over time. This planning and review cycle is a team responsibility and a core team process. The role of management in the planning process is to ensure that it is happening in a systematic manner, to ensure that the plans fit with the organization's needs for team performance (which may require an approval process), to periodically review with the team its progress against plans, and to be available to help the team problem-solve when obstacles to plan attainment arise.

• *Facilitate flexibility and responsiveness*. In knowledge-work settings, goals, plans, and even strategy may change frequently, requiring goal-setting and planning processes that provide for periodic revisiting of goals and plans and include mechanisms for renegotiating and updating them. As one of Netco's client teams works with the client in the initial stages of system implementation, for example, the client may develop a better understanding of its needs and initiate changes in the contract, requiring a revisiting of business team plans.

Information Distribution and Communication

The design model described in this book is based on the information-processing needs of the organization. It has as its fundamental premise that organizational structures and linking mechanisms should connect performers who need to collectively process information and

Exhibit 6.1. Sample Format for Responsibility Chart Dealing with Cross-Functional Planning.

	Customer/Task Requirements			
	Requirement 1: Gain Familiarity with Client Needs	Requirement 2: Develop Proposal	Requirement 3: Deliver Proposal, Make Sale	Requirement 4: Prepare Final Contract
Contributor (or Function) 1: Industry Consultant	Participate in client meetings. Provide industry expertise to help resolve system design requirements.	Provide information to service and technical contributors for developing specifications of proposed system. Draft system overview.	Support sales agent in final meeting with client or in proposal revision.	No role.
Contributor (or Function) 2: Sales Agent	Convene and lead client meetings. Provide cost information.	Lead internal process of gathering information for proposal generation. Provide costing information. Finalize proposal.	Deliver proposal and make sale (or manage proposal revision process).	Draw up and present final contract.

| Contributor (or Function) 3: Engineer | Participate in client meetings. Provide technical information about system capabilities. | Generate technical information describing proposed system. Draft technical overview. | Support sales agent in final meeting with client if needed or in proposal revision. | No role. |
| Contributor (or Function) 4: Service Technician | Participate in client meetings. Provide technical information about service requirements for different configurations. | Generate service information for proposed system. Draft service requirements section. | Support sales agent in final meeting with client if needed or in proposal revision. | No role. |

make decisions because they have task interdependencies, deal with complex trade-offs or deliberations on issues where multiple points of view are relevant, and integrate the work constituting a process that delivers value to the customer.

The fundamental difference between a team-based organization and the traditional organization in this regard is that, in the former, an increasing amount of the information processing required to integrate the work in the organization is performed laterally rather than hierarchically. This means that information regarding the bigger picture—information relevant to how the various parts fit together—must be widely held throughout the organization. Again, merely establishing teams will not accomplish this. A properly designed team organization will enable greater ease of on-line and informal communication between people who have to work together to get the job done, but the structures alone will not ensure that people are working with needed information. The communication processes must be designed to make relevant information available to all performing units without completely overloading the system with irrelevant information.

Information needed for interdependent individuals and units to resolve trade-offs and arrive at a shared course of action is especially important. The goals and priorities of the organization and its parts, plans for accomplishing them, feedback regarding performance, and changes in any of these are central pieces of the communication system. An especially vital aspect of the information system is feedback from internal and external customers, since customer information is useful in resolving differences. The customer viewpoint, which exists independent of the views of any of the diverse organizational contributors to a decision, is generally considered critical to organizational success and can therefore be seen as a neutral and mutually valued perspective upon which to base decisions. Many successful teams told us that their ability to get past critical junctures marked by internal disagreement was the result of maintaining a focus on the customer and having good data regarding customer preferences.

The sharing of relevant information must be multidirectional. Big-picture information needs to be shared hierarchically (from higher systems to lower systems) but also laterally (from one performing unit to another). For example, Netco's client teams need information regarding the industry strategy so that they can determine whether it makes sense to sell service at a lower profit margin in order to secure a foothold with a very large customer. The trade-off is not independent of how the other client teams in the industry business team are doing, since the business team has profit and revenue targets as a whole that can be accomplished by allowing one client team to concentrate on revenue and another on profit margin. The leadership team relies on receiving information from each client team concerning its workload and staffing needs so that it can sensibly distribute contributors across teams. The technology development team depends on receiving information from each client team regarding technical development needs to better service clients in that particular industry. In turn, the technical council for the field offices depends on receiving such information from all the business teams.

Figure 6.3 illustrates this multidirectional communication dynamic in an information flowchart. A chart of this nature can be used to depict the communication flows that need to be formalized. Creating a high-level flowchart during the design of a team organization permits communication responsibilities to be written into the charter of every team.

Management's responsibility is to ensure that the proper communication flows are formalized and that they are functioning as intended. In some cases (such as the sharing of strategy and performance feedback), management does the communicating. In other cases (such as the exchange of task-relevant information between teams), management creates conducive conditions and ensures that communication happens but does not necessarily participate in it.

Information technology has enabled the emergence of more laterally oriented organizational forms and team-based organizations (Morton, 1991; Galbraith, 1994). Our research found that the

Figure 6.3. Partial Communication Flow: Netco Field Offices.

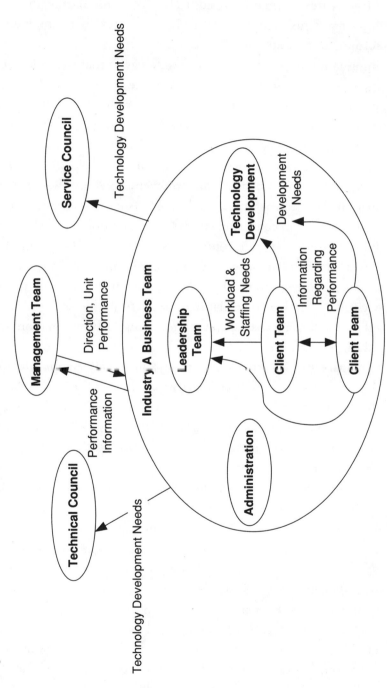

effectiveness of these organizations is related to how well they employ the new technology. The most effective business units were those in which members felt they had adequate computer tools, were connected electronically to the people with whom they were interdependent, shared common computer languages, and had access to shared data sets.

One tool for the coordination and integration of work within the traditional organization is the vertical information system, which enables managers to receive aggregated data from below them in the organization upon which to make decisions and take action. The higher in the organization the manager, the broader the information that is accessible. That tool needs to be retained in the team-based organization. In the laterally integrated organization, teams and individuals at higher systemic levels still need access to broad and aggregated data, for they are making decisions that have a broad scope. Furthermore, the hierarchical control in a team-based organization is exercised in large part by monitoring results and process indicators rather than by becoming involved in the details of operation. For this purpose, vertical information systems are even more important than ever. However, the team-based organization calls for equally robust lateral information systems.

Distributed information systems are the enablers of team decision making. The team-based organization relies on people to make operational decisions laterally, which requires that information be broadly diffused and data sets broadly accessible. Teams and team members who are making decisions that used to be made hierarchically in the organization need access to much of the information that was previously shared only at management levels. Furthermore, the information systems that are used within and across teams need to be compatible with one another. Managing integrated processes optimally requires that the information systems of the various parts of the process be integrated. The effective management of concurrent cross-functional processes requires that the data bases of various functions be accessible to one another and that they be manipulable to address cross-functional issues.

The importance of electronic connectivity is magnified when electronic communication is the major mode of operation, as in team-based organizations in which the interdependent parties are not co-located. As organizations establish business units that have responsibility for processes that cut across the organization, this is increasingly the situation. Another issue becomes particularly salient in these situations: the norms for communication and for task accomplishment when electronic communication and shared data bases are utilized. These norms include response expectations, guidelines for not overloading the system with irrelevant information, documentation standards, and confidentiality rules, to name a few. Other studies have found that, particularly in physically and organizationally distributed organizations, effectiveness is enhanced when these norms and guidelines are formally established and agreed to by all parts of the organization.

Decision Making

The transition to teams is often motivated by the desire to improve the decision-making capabilities of the organization. One desired outcome is more timely decision making, which enables better cycle time. Teams can facilitate this outcome by reducing the amount of process time or transaction time entailed in moving decisions through the hierarchy to a level that has authority over all involved participants and the amount of time lost as the operating level awaits such decisions. Moving decision making into the teams that include the interdependent participants facilitates ease of access for decisions involved in the integration of work. In addition, creating teams that represent various perspectives close to where the work is done and close to the customer improves the quality of decision making, since competing perspectives are represented in decision-making forums and participants in these forums are knowledgeable about operational issues and customer requirements.

In our study, timely decision making was indeed found to be

strongly related to the effectiveness of both teams and the larger business units in which they are embedded. However, a number of organizations told us that they were perplexed by the fact that their teams,
far from facilitating faster decision making, appeared to be slowing
things down. In response to that concern, one of the questions we
investigated was this: What can the team-based organization do to
contribute to timely decision making? We discovered that several
aspects of the way an organization goes about decision making are
related to the ability of the organization to make timely decisions: the
clarity of decision-making authority, the involvement of appropriate
parties in decision making, and systematic decision-making processes.
Each is discussed below.

• *Clarity of decision-making authority.* Three factors in a team-
based organization can cause ambiguity in the locus of authority for
particular decisions. The first is the coexistence of a team-based
design and a functional organization, with the hierarchy of both the
function and the team systems representing a different potential
locus of authority and escalation path for particular decisions.
Within the team hierarchy, on the one hand, an operating team may
be mandated to make operational decisions about how team members go about their work. On the other hand, a manager in the functional hierarchy may be given organizational authority over work
processes and may make decisions that constrain the integration of
work in cross-functional settings by stipulating certain decision
processes or work plans (or even overriding technical decisions made
by teams).

The second source of ambiguity of authority lies in the conflict
between the intent of team-based organizations to empower teams
(and move decision making as close as possible to where the service
and products are produced) and the fact that all decisions cannot get
resolved at the team level. As discussed above, issues of broader scope
need to get resolved through mechanisms of broader scope, such as
integrating teams. In addition, some team-based organizations exist

in very dynamic environments, where changing competitive requirements and/or changing customer expectations may result in changes in micro- or macrostrategy that reverse team decisions and result in rework. For example, a product design team at Analytico may have to modify the design of a component because of the introduction of a new process in the factory that results in a significant decrease in the cost of manufacturing the products of the division.

Finally, ambiguity surrounding decision-making authority may be a symptom of a poorly designed team structure—one in which the domains of multiple teams are so intricately intertwined that the decisions of one team are by definition decisions about how the other teams will go about doing their business. This intertwining happens when an organization artificially segments consideration of different aspects of the same issue—an electronics program that houses customer responsiveness in one team and technical development in another, for example. The team attending to customer responsiveness during the product development process will find itself unable to make an agreement with the customer that requires a change in technical performance without members of the technical development teams that have to deliver on the promise.

Organizations that take the time to specify decision-making authority for the different teams and roles in the team-based organization are better able to make timely decisions. This authority is best clarified through responsibility charting for decisions and through the specification of escalation paths (and the decision situations that trigger them).

Exhibit 6.2 illustrates a partial decision-making responsibility chart, using the Alpha Program as an example. This chart lists the various parties potentially involved in a decision and their role in the decision, ranging from having authority to make the decisions (D), to having authority to make recommendations (R), to having authority to give input (I), to needing to be informed (N), to remaining uninvolved (U).

Exhibit 6.2. Sample Format for Responsibility Chart Dealing
with Decision-Making Authority.

	Changes to Specifications	Software/Hardware Trade-offs	Technical Design	Individual Design Task Assignments
Management Team	D	I	N, I	N
Functional Bosses (as Individuals)	I	U	N, I	N
Design Team	I, R	D	D (within box)	D
Software Integrating Team	N	I	D (interface decisions)	U
Systems Integrating Team	I, R	I, R	D (systemwide fit issues)	U
Escalation Path		Design team to management team	Design team to integrating teams	To functional bosses

Key: D = the authority to decide, R = the authority to recommend, I = the
authority to provide input, N = the need to know, and U = uninvolvement.

The final line on the decision-making responsibility chart indicates the escalation path for the decision. An escalation path—the path to be followed if the first group with authority is unable to come to agreement—raises the trade-off in question to a systemic level with a broader scope of responsibility. For example, if the design team at Alpha fails to make a decision about the software and hardware trade-offs of its box, the decision can be escalated to the management team. Following an escalation path does not necessarily mean giving up authority over the decision. The management team may work with the design team to resolve the issue, providing a fresh perspective and perhaps a broader context for the decision.

For the escalation path to work effectively, there have to be clear norms for its application. Teams cannot be made to feel that they have failed if they escalate a decision, nor should they be required to give up their ownership of the issue. The most effective escalation of decisions leads to collaborative decision making across levels rather than to a hierarchical decree.

Another norm that is critical is response time. The slogan of one company we studied was "No decision should remain unresolved through the weekend," signaling the intention of the management team to be available every Friday morning if any of the operating teams needed management's viewpoint in resolving an issue or its help in removing a barrier to performance.

• *Appropriate decision involvement.* The decision-making responsibility chart illustrated in Exhibit 6.2 gets at another facet of decision making that relates to timeliness: decision involvement. Failure to involve the appropriate perspectives in a decision may well result in a poor decision and a lack of commitment by organizational contributors. However, it may also result in delayed decision making—despite the fact that a subset of relevant parties often goes ahead and makes a decision precisely because the participants want to "get on with it." Frequently, a decision made with inadequate involvement will keep being "unmade" until the relevant parties have had input. At Alpha, for example, if a hardware/software design team decides to alter the design to put functionality in the software rather than the hardware and does not consider input from the system integration team regarding the impact of that decision on the integration of the three boxes, the design team should know that the decision may have to be reversed later. Both the integration of the three boxes and the integration of the software may be affected in ways that the design team fails to anticipate.

In the teams we studied, the phenomenon of the "unmade" decision was most likely to crop up when teams had mixtures of fully dedicated and partially dedicated members and when organizations were unable to fully staff a team at the outset. Fully dedicated team members were likely to discount the commitment of the absent or partially dedicated members, making decisions without waiting for their input and perspective. We especially saw this with respect to the marketing perspective in new product development projects undertaken by technology-driven firms. Marketers, who were busy handling the logistics of product release on another project, would arrive on the team relatively late in the concept development phase. Frequently, the R&D contributors had progressed quite far, making decisions that assumed market understanding. Rework (and hard feelings) often resulted when the marketing perspective was added to the equation. The systematic specification of decision-making responsibility can help an organization avoid the delays and the rework that result when decisions are unmade, as well as the considerable hard feelings that ensue when the viewpoints of relevant parties are ignored.

Hard feelings also result when a team mistakenly feels that it has complete authority over certain decisions, when in fact it is required to get input from beyond its members or has only recommending authority. Especially in the early stages of transitioning to a team-based organization, unrealistic expectations of autonomy may cloud the decision-making processes in an organization. To minimize that danger, decision authority should be clearly specified in each team's charter.

• *Systematic decision-making processes*. In our study, we found that the use of systematic decision-making processes was the aspect of decision making that related most strongly to the timeliness of organizational decision making and related most directly and strongly to team and business-unit effectiveness. Systematic decision-making processes specify the way in which an organization will make certain decisions, including the steps to be followed, the data to be considered, and possibly the parties to be included. They represent a shared understanding of how the organization makes decisions. An example of systematic decision-making processes are the various multistep processes for solving organizational quality problems that are specified in total quality management approaches. Other systematic processes might include costing mechanisms in the field offices, trade-off analyses in the electronics program, and quality functional deployment in the consumer electronics division.

Organizations derive at least two benefits from the use of systematic processes, in addition to the quality of the decisions that result if the processes are optimal for the task. One additional benefit is that there is shared understanding of how decisions are made, which facilitates the process of diverse participants working together. The second benefit is that, to the extent that participants agree about *how* to make the decision, they are more likely to agree to the decision itself (if the process is followed). Both of these benefits relate to the ability of diverse participants, each of whom may carry different discipline thought-worlds and decision algorithms in their heads, to agree across their disciplines in a relatively efficient manner.

The Importance of Integration Processes

This chapter has discussed integration processes: direction setting, communicating, and decision making. These are important in all organizations, not just in team-based organizations. The tendency may be to dismiss this discussion as "fundamentals of management" and to say, "Of course, but we've always done that well." Although this may be true, it is probably best not to assume that the practices that served managers well in the traditional, hierarchical organization will meet the needs of the team-based organization.

In the hierarchical organization, management could get away with somewhat sloppy processes, precisely because managers existed as a very active court of last (and sometimes even first) resort in the information-processing and decision-making arena. This resulted in a vicious cycle. Managers did not need to provide operating contributors with sufficient direction, information, and clarity of decision-making authority to be able to resolve decisions at the lower levels precisely because the major way in which managers controlled the organization was to make many decisions themselves, even about the details of task performance. They personally integrated the organization, so subordinates did not have to have the big picture. As a consequence, the operating contributors were unable to make decisions that took the big picture into account and were thus not viewed as trustworthy to make many decisions. Sloppiness of organizational processes in the hierarchically oriented organization was relatively invisible, except to the subordinates in the organization, who felt disempowered by unclear direction, loose planning, partial communication, and unclear decision-making authority.

Our study results make it clear that the transition to a laterally oriented, team-based organization taxes the processes of the traditional hierarchy. In almost all of the nonroutine work settings we examined, team members reported that their work involved large amounts of interaction with diverse contributors beyond their team. They had to cross many organizational boundaries in order to do their jobs. In addition, much of the work involved the collaboration of people representing different functions and multiple disciplines. The formal organizational processes are more highly related to organizational effectiveness when these conditions are true than when work involves less complex interdependencies.

The paradox is that, in complex knowledge-work settings, *the organization must structure itself to make easier and more likely the informal processes that are required for multiple contributors to integrate; at the same time, the organization must, as much as possible, formalize the processes required to create a context where integration is possible.* These processes, as we have noted, relate to direction setting, communication and information sharing, and decision making—processes by which all participants share an understanding of where the organization is headed and gain a common picture of the means to be employed in getting there.

Other processes that are at the core of the ability of the organization to create a common understanding and get people "pointed in the same direction" are the processes by which performance is managed in the organization. These processes will be the focus of the next chapter.

Key Issues

Key issues in the design of integration processes for a team-based organization include the following:

1. Teams cannot operate effectively if they do not have direction. The direction context must make clear the priorities and criteria that enable a team to make trade-offs. The direction context is a management responsibility that includes

   Clear systemwide strategy

   Goals that are vertically and laterally aligned

   Goals that are measurable

   Rewards that motivate the behavior/performances needed for team and business effectiveness

   Planning and review processes that assess progress against direction

2. Effective teams have access to the task-related information required to do their jobs. In a lateral organization, the information streams required to support teams go in all directions.

Communication responsibilities should be part of a team's charter.

3. Information technology is the enabler of the processes of the team-based organization. Computer connectivity, common languages, and shared data bases provide the technological foundation for collaboration. Appropriately distributed information enables teams to make decisions once reserved for management.

4. Effective teams achieve timely decision making. This outcome depends on the appropriateness of the team design and of the decision-making processes in the organization. Important aspects include

   Clarifying the locus of decision-making responsibility

   Ensuring appropriate involvement in decision making

   Having common, systematic decision-making processes that provide a foundation for collaboration

5. Organizational processes are more important in team organizations because managers have less active involvement in day-to-day operations than their counterparts in traditional organizations.

Figure 7.1. Step Five of the Design Process: Developing Performance Management Processes.

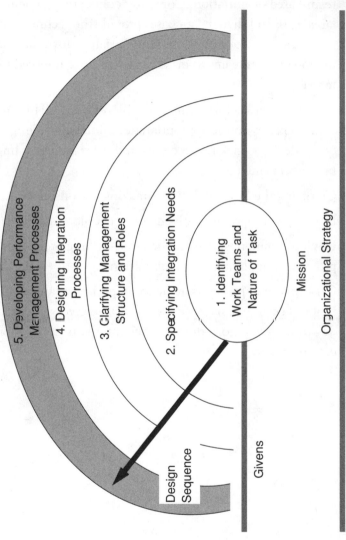

Design Sequence

5. Developing Performance Management Processes

4. Designing Integration Processes

3. Clarifying Management Structure and Roles

2. Specifying Integration Needs

1. Identifying Work Teams and Nature of Task

Mission

Organizational Strategy

Environment

Givens

. . . .

7

Step Five

Managing Performance

This chapter is meant to help organizations that are using teams or that are changing to a team-based environment to establish performance management practices that are appropriate. The emphasis is on the elements that must be considered in designing such practices, not on the process of design itself. As seen in Figure 7.1, devising performance management practices is the fifth and final step in the team design sequence. This chapter describes what those performance management practices should look like. It begins with a definition of what performance management is and a discussion of who should do performance management in team-based settings. It then presents a detailed description of each of the four major performance management processes: defining performance, developing for performance, reviewing performance, and rewarding performance. Each process description is accompanied by principles that should be followed and general practices that might be established to carry out that process in team-based organizations. Performance management practices are described for both team and individual performance.

What Is Performance Management?

In this section, we give a brief overview of performance management. Subsequent sections go into more detail about how performance management can be applied to teams.

There are many models of performance management in the literature. The one used here has been developed and tested in organizations in a number of studies, including our study of teams in nonroutine settings. This model is best thought of as a way to conceptually keep track of all the issues and practices that fall under the domain of performance management.

Performance management is the set of processes that have to be done in order to make sure that what people do and work at in the organization will obtain the results that the organization needs. These processes can be put into four categories: defining, developing, reviewing, and rewarding. Figure 7.2 illustrates these four processes as a cycle of activities surrounding and having an effect on performance. The organization creates formal systems and practices to foster these processes, which themselves are often a combination of formal and informal practices. Our research found that how these processes are done relates to performance.

Performance management processes take place at all levels in the organization and are applied to all levels of performer. In team organizations, the performance of at least three levels of performer (or performing unit) must be managed: the individual employees, teams of employees, and entire business units. For example, in the Alpha Program, the individuals, the teams, and the program are all performers, as are the company as a whole and its large business units (such as divisions). In the consumer electronics division, individuals, teams, product lines, and the division itself are performing units within a larger company. In this chapter, we will consider only three levels, in order to keep the discussion as simple as possible.

The process of defining performance establishes what performance is supposed to be—what performers are supposed to do. Traditionally, organizations have relied on such things as job descriptions, goals, and standards to define the performances that need to be achieved. Business-unit strategies, business plans, team goals, and team missions are also examples of performance definitions. Aspects

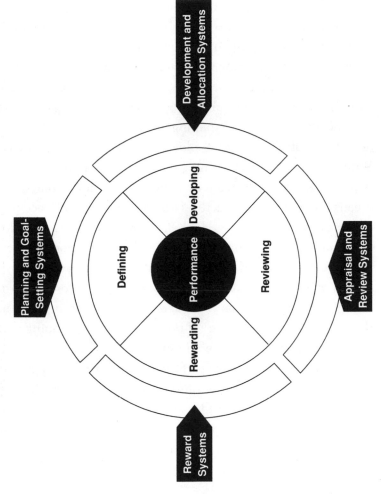

Figure 7.2. Performance Management Model.

of the defining process that are used with all levels of performer include planning and goal setting.

The process of developing performance includes mechanisms used to develop the capability of the performer and the situation so that the defined performance can be achieved. At the individual level, this process can include such formal practices as classroom training and such informal practices as on-the-job coaching. Developing can also mean providing the individual performer with the tools and resources needed to do the work, such as technologies, systems, and time. Teams, too, can be developed as performers: the organization can enhance their technical skills by providing training or by adding new members, by offering training needed for good team processes, and by allocating useful technologies, budgets, and other resources. Similarly, business units can be developed to help achieve their defined performance. Team or business-unit development often means the redesign of structures and processes to enhance performance capabilities. In the Alpha Program, for example, the design of a team-based organization was intended to develop new performance capabilities in the business unit. This development was viewed as necessary to attain the goals that were set for the program. Many of the practices that come under the rubric of "organizational development" are examples of the process of developing performance as applied to teams and business units.

The process of reviewing performance describes and evaluates actual performances against criteria that were set down during performance definition. The traditional performance appraisal is a prototypical example of the practices often employed in the formal reviewing process with individual performers. Likewise, project teams often undergo project reviews, and business units sometimes receive corporate "report cards." These formal review practices are heavily supplemented by informal practices that happen every day. Performers may see directly the results of their own performance, and they may receive data (such as weekly budget reports or daily sales figures) that provide ongoing feedback. Customers, clients, managers, and fellow performers often note how well a particular team or individual is doing and sometimes give feedback. Done well, the formal review process is merely a periodic, systematic look at performance in an environment that has rich performance information available all the time.

The process of rewarding performance entails mechanisms by which performers have their needs more or less satisfied as a result of their performance. Some rewards are intrinsic in nature: people can, for example, get a good feeling simply by performing well, either as individuals or as members of effective teams and business units. Other rewards are extrinsic: formal reward and compensation practices can be designed so that performers get something of economic value, for example, as a result of their performance. Teams and business units can get rewards just as individuals can—for example, in the form of team recognition, incentives, profit sharing, or gainsharing.

Designing performance management practices for teams and in team settings means designing practices that achieve alignment among the levels of performers as well as among the performers at any one level. Figure 7.3, with a bull's eye indicating performance, illustrates the fact that overall performance is a composite of performances at multiple levels of the organizational system; overall performance is optimized to the extent that the various performances are aligned. There are two aspects of this alignment: first, all the performers at each level must be going in the same direction; second, performers at each level must be aligned within the context of the next level up.

Individual-level formal performance management systems are prevalent and firmly embedded in modern organizations. They embody philosophies about what is and is not equitable and are central to the self-esteem of employees. These individual-level practices of reviewing and rewarding can work at cross-purposes with the concepts and philosophies needed for successful team performance management to the extent that they perpetuate the custom of managing

Figure 7.3. Alignment of Performance Management Processes.

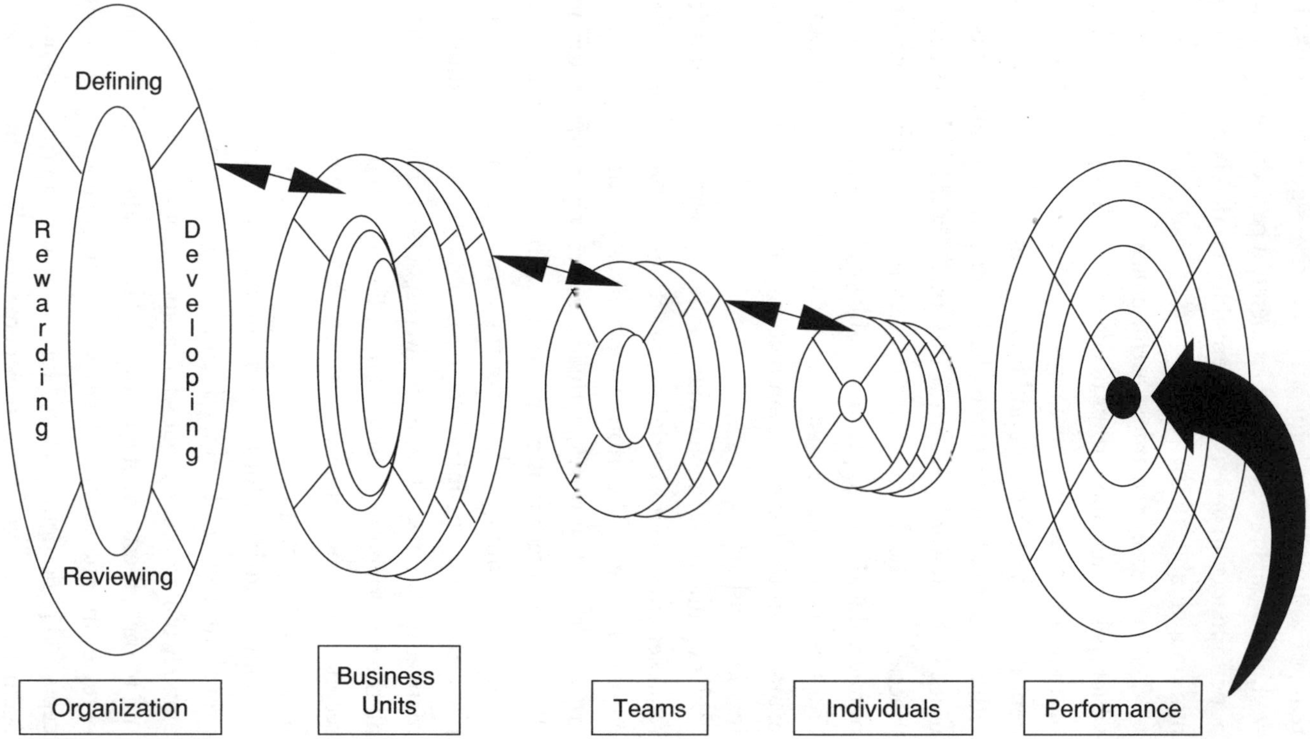

an individual's performance as if it could be considered in isolation from the performance of the team that the individual is part of.

Ultimately, the prevalent incompatible, individual-level systems will have to become more team-oriented. But this transition is a tall order in most corporate settings. Because of this, team-level performance management practices are not often as well developed or as formally adopted as corporate practices. Most team performance management is done in informal ways or in pockets of the organization that have been allowed to experiment with new practices. As teams become more established in organizations, they will engender a reevaluation of traditional practices. Until then, ways must be found to supplement, tailor, and/or patch traditional practices so that they are more compatible with the new team practices. By these adaptive means, managers of team-based organizations can ensure that team performance management processes are occurring even before the individually oriented corporate system is overhauled.

Who Should Do Performance Management?

Performance should be managed by those who have a stake in the performance. In a team-based organization, the same types of stakeholders are potentially present whether the performer in question is an individual, a team, or a business unit: the team itself and its members, the team's customers, co-performing teams (other teams that the team is interdependent with), and the managers that are responsible for the team and the performance of the business unit as a whole.

Managers traditionally manage the performance of their subordinates. Managers represent the larger system and have a stake in how well performance contributes to it. For business units, managers represent the larger corporation and may be at the executive level. For teams, managers represent the business unit that the team is part of. For individuals, managers represent the team(s) and/or business unit(s) that they belong to.

Internal and external customers have a direct stake in performance, since they are the recipients of it. Individuals, teams, and business units all have customers—individuals or groups that receive products or services from them. In general, the performer/customer relationship is sequential in nature: the performer performs and the customer receives the results of that performance.

A team's customers might be part of the business unit or reside outside it. In the case of a team producing a component for use by another team in the creation of a multicomponent system or the case of a team producing a software tool or methodology for use by other groups in the business unit, the product of the team is delivered to other teams so that they can do their work. The relationship is essentially that of supplier-customer, even though both parties are within the same business unit. On the other hand, the client teams in each Netco field office deliver services and products directly to external customers.

Co-performers have a different kind of stake in the performance. They work with the performers to achieve performance of the larger system. Team members, for example, are co-performers with one another in the accomplishment of the team's performance. Teams themselves often must work with other teams in order to accomplish the performance of the larger business unit. Information and work pass back and forth between co-performers and sometimes are produced jointly. Co-performers depend on each other's performances to get their own work and the work of the larger unit done.

In the Alpha Program, the three teams that are interdependent in the creation of the three boxes are co-performers. They must learn to work together to get their tasks accomplished. Teams can have co-performers that are outside the boundaries of the business unit and the company. An electronics team might have to co-perform with a vendor or partner team to develop its component, if the business unit does not have the resources internally to accomplish what the vendor can and the nature of the component requires ongoing reciprocal interaction between vendor and team for both of them to do their work.

Performers themselves have an obvious stake in their own performance. They have a direct responsibility for it and are quite liable to reap the consequences of it. They have a unique insight into how the performance was created and how it might be improved.

Every organization is an intricate network of these interrelated performers and stakeholders. Figure 7.4 depicts how performers are embedded within larger performing groups and suggests the complex interrelatedness of performers and stakeholders. Different stakeholders bring different perspectives to the management of performance.

The distinction between co-performer and customer is important. These two stakeholders have different stakes in the performance of the team and get involved with performance management for different reasons and with different outcomes. In our study, we found that co-performers' involvement in each other's performance management led to improvements in the processes and procedures used to co-perform. Customers, on the other hand, are usually less interested in the processes used to deliver and more interested in the results. Our data show that customer involvement in performance management is related to performance but not to improvement of performance capability. In fact, too much customer involvement can get in the way of process improvements and development of the team.

Performance management of individuals by peers is an example of co-performer performance management. Team settings that use peer evaluation often find that peers are initially resistant to evaluating each other. They worry about creating conflicts among themselves that will be counterproductive. On the other hand, our research shows that when peer evaluation and feedback are used well, they result in process improvements.

Performance management by managers tends to be done from the perspective of the larger performing units. Thus it provides alignment among the levels of performers. Performance management by the other sources may result in misalignment unless there is management perspective that reflects the viewpoint of the larger system. For instance, self and co-performer performance management tends

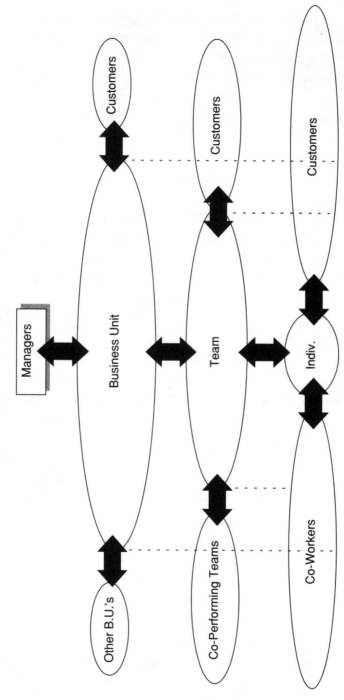

Figure 7.4. Levels of Performers and Sources of Performance Management.

to focus performers on the ways they perform rather than on what they produce. Thus their results tend to drift from the needs of the outside entities that have a stake in them. Customer performance management tends to pull results in the direction of the customers' needs, and this may guide performance in directions that are not in the best interests of the larger organization. A team, for instance, might be strongly oriented to servicing a particular customer or set of customers. If that customer group is not an important part of the larger organization's market strategy, the team's activities may actually be detrimental to business-unit performance (though highly effective with the customer group).

Another example requiring a balance of the organization and team perspectives is where a team contains individuals with skills needed elsewhere in the organization for something of higher priority than the team's immediate task. In this case, it might make organizational sense to sacrifice the performance of the affected team. Because staffing decisions at the business-unit level often work contrary to staffing desires at the team level, it is important that reliable performance management processes are in place to ensure that such decisions are made correctly. Is the movement of human resources really resulting in better business-unit performance, or is it simply a matter of raiding one team for the sake of another one no more or less organizationally important? This issue is especially crucial given our finding that a common source of team failure is loss of resources required along the critical path of the work. If managers are to play this resource allocation role effectively, they must engage in a two-way dialogue with the team.

Performance management by managers only is neither adequate nor generally viable. In many team settings, managers are so distant from the day-to-day performances of individuals and teams that they cannot know enough to properly define, develop, review, or reward performance. They are often reduced to relying on information supplied by the performer to make performance management judgments. Even when managers are close enough to the situation to make sound judgments from their perspective, this is not enough in team settings, because managers do not always adequately understand the lateral needs of co-performers and customers. In team settings, manager-conducted performance management must be coupled with performance management by the lateral stakeholders.

In summary, performance management in team-based settings is considerably more complex than that in more traditional, hierarchical settings. Performance must be consciously managed at at least three levels of performer: individual, team, and business unit. In addition, there are four stakeholders in performance at each level: the performers themselves, their co-performers, their customers, and their managers. The performance management practices at each level of performer by each stakeholder must be orchestrated in order to achieve alignment.

In the following sections, we suggest what team-based performance management should look like. Addressing each of the four performance management processes (defining, developing, reviewing, and rewarding) in turn, we develop a general outline of practices. The most important thing is that each of these processes *happens*, not that the processes are formalized into an organization wide performance management system. Depending on the setting, the new team-based practices for each process may or may not be formalized. In an organization that is transitioning to teams, different units will be at different stages. Even units that are not ready for formal team performance management practices, however, will experience a performance boost to the extent that the practices tied to the four processes are informally happening.

Defining Performance in Team Settings

Our research continually confirms that, among the four processes of performance management, it is defining performance that has the greatest impact on subsequent performance. But this is not the case when definition is done only at the individual level in team-based knowledge-work settings. When individual performance is defined in isolation from that of the other individuals with whom the performer must work and without an understanding of the performance required of the larger group and the business unit, it is often quickly made irrelevant by the realities of the context in which the individual works. Defining team performance in the context of the business unit and then defining individual performance in the context of required team performance is the most effective approach.

The following list summarizes what should be included in the process of defining performance in team settings. (Remember, performers can be individuals, teams, or larger units.) Many of these process elements were described from a different perspective in Chapter Six.

- Establishing the general direction and role for the performer

- Identifying the needs of stakeholders

- Clarifying the deliverables and services that are to result and the tasks that are to be accomplished

- Establishing goals and objectives

- Establishing metrics that can be applied

- Planning how the work will be carried out and organized by the performer

- Identifying the skills, tools, and resources needed by the performer

Let us now consider each of these elements in turn. Although each applies to any performing unit, whether business unit, team, or individual, our emphasis in this discussion is on the team.

- *Establishing direction and role.* Performers at all levels must start with the general direction performance is to take and the role that the performer is to play. When the performer is the business unit, this general direction might be expressed in its mission and strategy. The mission and strategy of the Alpha Program, for example, is to supply high avionics components to an external customer using cross-functional teams to achieve greater speed to market. Within the program (which is a business unit within a larger organization), a team might have a general mission that translates into a task that requires it to play a role within a larger set of teams. For instance, the team might have the task of developing an electronic box with a certain functionality that is to be integrated with two other boxes designed by two other teams to form a larger-system component that is to be delivered to a customer. A software engineer in that team might be expected to design and program a particular kind of application needed in one of the boxes—a role that makes her highly interdependent with other members of her team as well as some members of other teams.

• *Identifying needs.* The direction setting and planning done at a higher systemic level provides the framework within which the next level's performance is defined; in turn, its planning process leads to definitions at the subsequent level. Building on the foundation laid by direction setting, each performing unit must identify the performance needs of its stakeholders: business managers, customers, and co-performers. The team, for example, articulates how its performance has to contribute to business-unit strategy, what is important from its customers' viewpoints, and what will be required to coordinate effectively with co-performers. In short, the team's planning must have an outward as well as an inward focus.

• *Clarifying deliverables, services, and tasks.* Once performance needs are established, the business unit, team, or individual should clarify the deliverables and services that can meet these needs and/or the tasks that need to be done. The needs of stakeholders serve as a reference point for the definition of services and deliverables, requiring performers to look beyond their personal and discipline-based assumptions and preferences and providing an impetus for diverse participants to come to agreement.

- *Establishing goals and objectives.* Goals and objectives for meeting needs should be set at each level, reflecting the performance definition done thus far. These goals should reflect not only the task requirements for delivering products or services but also stakeholder needs. The dual inward and outward focuses should pervade the defining process.

- *Establishing metrics.* Once this level of specificity is reached in defining performance, metrics and various measurement approaches can be defined to determine the extent to which performance occurs as designated. The dual inward and outward focuses can be continued by including metrics such as customer satisfaction that reflect stakeholder perspectives and perceptions.

- *Planning and organizing work.* Once performance results are defined, the definitional process at each level must turn to planning how the performance is to be carried out and how the teams involved should organize, both within and among themselves, for its achievement. Performance definition also involves clarifying the roles individuals and teams need to perform. Thus the process of defining team performance leads to the process of defining the performance of its individual members.

- *Identifying necessary skills, tools, and resources.* As the performing units become more concrete in their defining and planning processes, they can make a realistic assessment of whether they have the resources, including skills, tools, and personpower, to carry out their plans and achieve their performance goals. The defining process includes planning for use of and acquisition of these resources.

Our research has repeatedly shown that the degree of specificity with which performance is defined up front and the degree to which performance measures are put into place are strongly related to subsequent performance. But this finding involves a caveat: the definitional process must use both vertical and lateral mechanisms that result in shared definitions, and the appropriate stakeholders must be involved in any planning that leads to the definition of team performance. This is the essence of defining performance in a team setting.

Several principles should be kept in mind by those establishing the various components of performance definition listed above. First, performance definition should be done in a vertically integrating manner; that is, each performing unit (whether an individual or a group) should define performance within the context of the larger organizational system. For instance, a software engineer's performance might be defined as creating an application with a certain functionality that is to integrate with other hardware and software applications into a system designed to perform in a certain way for the customer. This approach is different from giving that software engineer a set of design parameters specific to his or her application and disconnected from the role the application is to play. In the latter case, it is entirely possible for the engineer to do his or her task without knowing how it fits with the larger system.

Second, in order to achieve lateral fit, performers should define their performance in collaboration with co-performers. Teams must collaboratively define performance with other interdependent teams; individuals must collaboratively define their performance with co-workers. And lateral fit cannot be achieved independent of vertical fit. At Alpha, for instance, the teams that are to produce the avionics component might first work out their interteam responsibilities and any interteam processes required to deliver the needed component and achieve the goals of the business. This interteam planning—the lateral process of collaboration—defines the goals and roles of the teams relative to one another. Each team can then work out its intrateam designs and make plans to achieve team goals. In the process, members must also collaboratively work out their individual goals and roles.

Third, the definition of performance for any single performing unit must protect against overextension that will work against overall organizational performance. One of the realities of team-based settings is that individuals often belong to many teams at the same time. In our study across eleven organizations, the average was over six teams for each individual! While we do not recommend that individuals belong to so many teams, multiple-team membership is a fact of life. One of the major problems with this reality is that it tends to stretch individuals way beyond their capabilities; each team demands more of the individual than is available. This may occur because performance definition fails to explicitly define the individual's various roles in the context of the performance needs of each team. The individual's direct manager may take only business-unit needs into account in defining the performance of the subordinate, not the needs of each team. To combat the tendency toward overextension, when individuals belong to multiple teams, they must reach explicit agreement with each team about their total performance commitment in all teams.

Fourth, customers—whether internal or external, direct or indirect—are ultimate stakeholders in the performance at issue and should therefore have a prominent role in its definition. There are many ways that customers can have input, ranging from interviews by team members, perhaps as focus groups, to written statements of needs by customers, to joint definition between customers and performers of what performance needs to be.

Fifth, in an organization striving for employee empowerment, teams and individuals should be active participants in the defining of their performance. They should be active stakeholders in the goal-setting process, working with managers and other teams. For maximum effectiveness, internal team planning and the setting of individual goals and roles should be largely team-defined. Our research results reveal that it is when teams self-define their performance that performance is enhanced, not when managers define performance for them.

Sixth, the definition of performance must be treated as a dynamic process. A common situation in team-based settings is constant change. Teams are often constituted and reconstituted for various purposes. Even when teams are relatively intact and permanent, goals and tasks can change—as customer needs change, for instance. The important thing is that there be mechanisms, as performance needs change, to ensure that teams and individuals are in concert with these changed needs and can redefine performance accordingly.

Figure 7.5 presents a general model that can be used in designing a team-level defining process. The team must perform its own internal defining process; but, equally important, it must also engage in a defining process with its stakeholders, the most important of which is the business unit. Figure 7.5 shows putting the team in the context of the overall business direction as a key role for business-unit management and shows working out how the team will go about accomplishing its performance requirements as a key role for the team. The definition of goals and metrics is a mutual process.

Figure 7.6 presents a general model for the individual-level defining process. The individual participates in the planning process of the team(s) of which she is a member and, with each team, mutually defines her contribution. She then integrates these roles into an overall performance definition, making each team aware of her overall performance commitments.

Parts of the individual- and team-level defining process may already exist in an organization transitioning to teams, in the form of business planning practices, for instance, or project start-up procedures. They may or may not be formalized. Almost certainly, however, existing practices will not completely cover all the aspects that appear in Figures 7.5 and 7.6. To do a complete job of defining performance, organizations will have to develop additional practices as needed. This does not mean that the defining process must be extensive and laborious. It should be in scale with the performance being defined: large, complex projects require comparable up-front investments in defining what performance is to be; small, short-duration projects should not invest inordinate amounts of effort and time in defining performance. Nevertheless, as we have noted, the defining process has a great impact on subsequent performance. Although practically no one spends enough time on it,

Figure 7.5. Team-Level Defining Process.

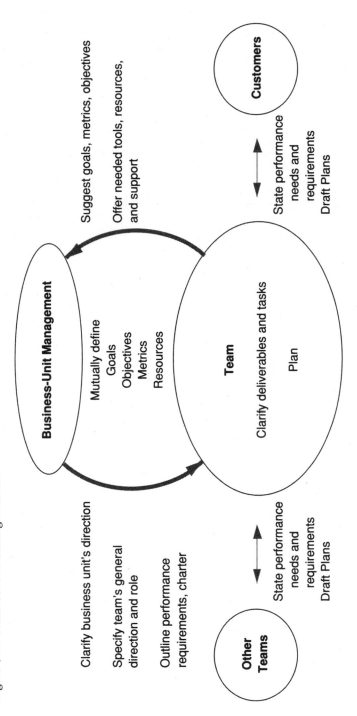

Figure 7.6. Individual-Level Defining Process.

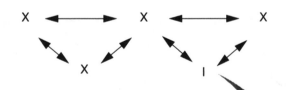

Team

Mutually defines with business-unit
management: goals, objectives, metrics

Assesses resource availability

Plans application of resources to tasks

Members

X ⟷ X ⟷ X

X   I

Mutually define each member's
role and contribution

Member I

Combines roles and
expected contributions
to team or teams into
overall definition of
own performance

because of a desire to "get on with it," complete definition pays off in the long run.

Care must be taken to avoid the tendency to think of defining as an administrative burden that impedes performance. It is just the opposite, if done well. Overdocumentation is wasteful, but insufficient documentation of what performance is to be leads to incompatible understandings and expectations and contributes to project delay. There is a need to define performance multiple times for an individual on multiple teams. However, the results of the individual's total defined contribution to all his or her teams (shown at the bottom of Figure 7.6) can simply be attached to any required performance management form. The defining process is done to plan performance, not to create an administrative hoop of performance management paperwork.

Developing for Performance in Team Settings

In traditional performance management systems aimed at the individual, there is often a section of the form (and perhaps a subprocess) referred to as "development." For the most part, a subordinate and/or manager identifies the subordinate's developmental needs and prescribes training classes or other learning experiences. In most cases, this is an underutilized and cursorily done section of the form. The developmental "fix" is almost always seen in terms of new skills to be acquired by the individual performer.

In team-based settings, the developmental process needs to take on a much more important and broader role in performance management. When the team is considered a performer, the meaning of *development* changes. What does it mean to develop a team? It can mean that each of the members develops additional skills, including social, team-oriented skills, in order to perform better. But team development can also mean adding new team members with the appropriate skills or replacing members to get a better skill mix. Thus team development becomes a human resource allocation process.

Development of a team does not occur just through skill acquisition in any of the above forms. Teams can also develop in many organizational ways: teams can perform better by changing the way they go about their work, the way they internally organize, and the way they relate to their stakeholders. Thus development is also an organizational development—or OD—process.

Finally, in this day of total quality management and the process-based organization, we are coming to accept that, even for individuals, a major part of performance is a function not of the performer but of the tools, systems, and resources the performer has (Deming, 1986). This fact is even more apparent in team settings than in the traditional organization. Thus development has come to also refer to the acquisition and allocation of necessary tools and other resources for the teams and their members.

The following list summarizes the practices that should be included in the development process:

- Organizing work and roles according to plans

- Acquiring and allocating the necessary skills, tools, and resources for the performers

- Establishing necessary relationships among performers and stakeholders

- Changing the situation and context to facilitate performance (for example, the processes and systems used)

The starting point for development should be the organizing plans made and the skills, tools, and resources identified during the defining process. Development is the actual organizing, not the drafting of organizational plans; it is the acquiring of skills and resources, not the identification of skills and resources needed.

Organizing and acquiring resources are internally focused aspects of development. Other development endeavors need to be more externally focused, however. Our research findings consistently remind us that the context in which the team finds itself has as great an impact on its ability to perform as internal competencies do, and probably greater. Thus the team must work to develop its context. In particular, the team and its members must establish the appropriate relationships with co-performers, customers, and managers and work to establish organizational systems and processes that are supportive.

There must be a balance between internal and external development. Too often teams focus internally in their development efforts in the mistaken belief that team capabilities are the primary determinant of performance. Most of the stakeholders in the team's performance labor under the same belief. Therefore, teams must take the initiative in developing relationships with their external stakeholders.

If resources are needed, teams should work with management to achieve them. Management is ultimately responsible for allocating resources and must do so from a businesswide perspective, but team needs must be voiced, not left to chance in the belief that they will be perceived by some sort of management omniscience.

If there are important interdependencies with other teams, the team should proactively work to establish the right kind of relationships with those teams to manage the interdependencies. (These are the kind of relationships that were discussed in detail in Chapter Four.) Such relationship development with co-performing teams is the source of business-unit development as a whole.

Many products and services are not capable of being delivered to the customer in a simple fashion. In order for delivery to be successful, a complex technology transfer process may need to take place, the customer may need to be trained and reorganized, or the customer may need to get interactively involved with the development of the deliverable. Each of these situations demands that a relationship be established with the customer to ensure successful delivery. Customers are often blind to this need even though it can decisively determine performance success.

New systems and processes may be needed to enable goal attainment. For example, one technical support team that we studied worked with its internal customers to develop a work request and prioritization process to enable the team to channel its activities to the highest-priority tasks. This system replaced the old manager-centered system where the team responded to customers yelling the loudest at its manager rather than negotiating work directly with the customer based on an evaluation of organization-wide priorities. The new system was required to support the team's customer satisfaction objectives because in the previous system the team had little input into how work was prioritized and could not manage its responsiveness to customers.

Figures 7.7 and 7.8 illustrate general models of the developing process (team and individual, respectively). As with the defining process, there may be existing organizational systems for doing the various things enumerated in this section, but they are unlikely to cover all the necessary aspects of developing in a team-based environment, and they may be inappropriately structured and/or fail to address stakeholder relationships. Development may or may not be time-consuming, depending on the adequacy of existing skills, resources, relationships, and integration processes, but it should not be overlooked as a performance management process. It is a prime source of performance improvement. Failure to spend time on resource allocation needs, for instance, is a central cause of performance failure in team settings.

We have from time to time mentioned the concept of empowerment, which we defined in Chapter Two as "the capability to make a difference in the attainment of individual, team, and organizational goals." This definition has two major components: capability and direction. Thus empowerment is primarily a function of the defining and developing processes of performance management. Defining provides direction, and developing provides capability. Because empowerment is essential in team-based environments, considerable time must be spent (especially in the transition period)

Figure 7.7. Team-Level Developing Process.

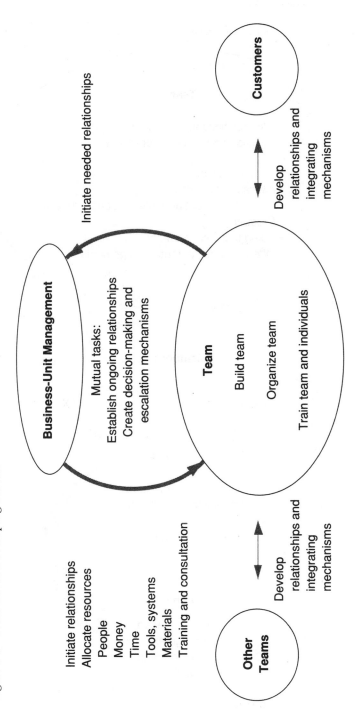

Figure 7.8. Individual-Level Developing Process.

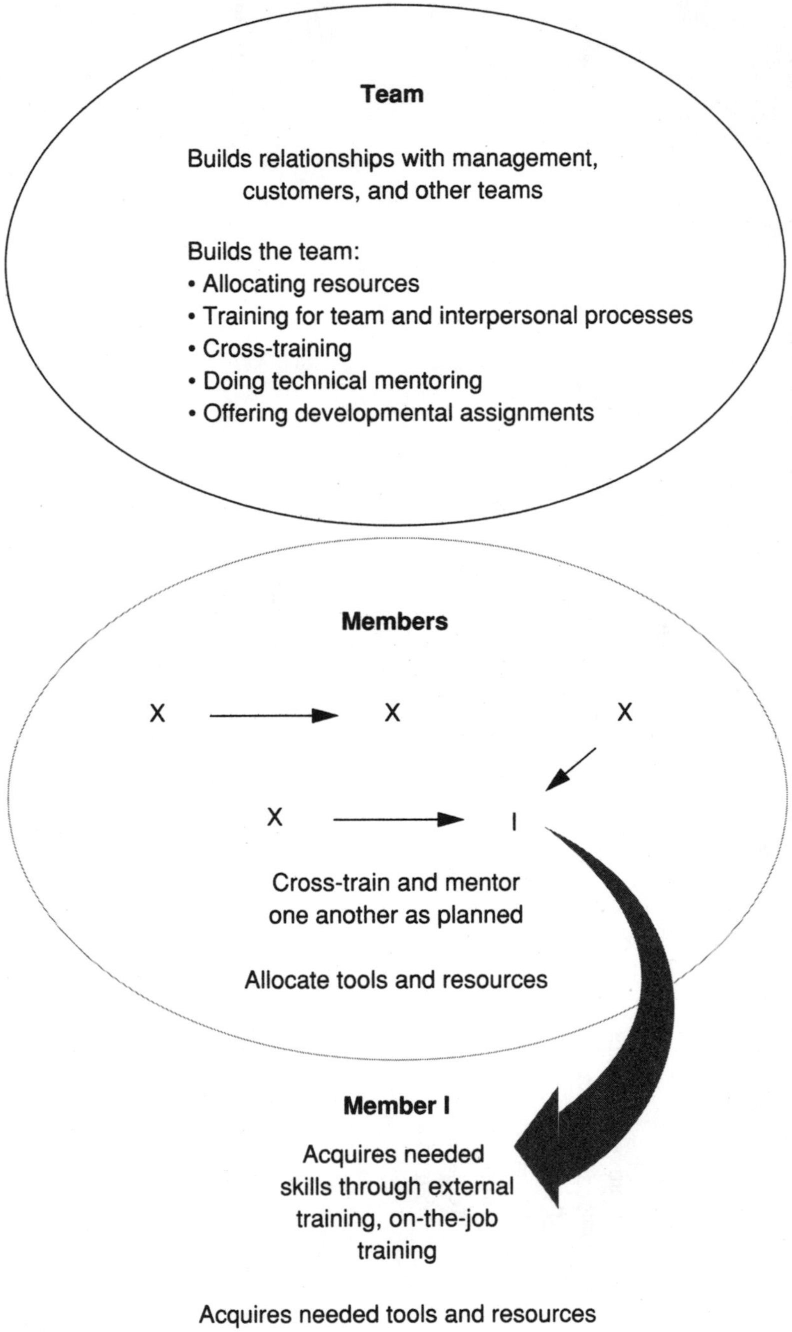

Team

Builds relationships with management, customers, and other teams

Builds the team:
• Allocating resources
• Training for team and interpersonal processes
• Cross-training
• Doing technical mentoring
• Offering developmental assignments

Members

X ⟶ X   X

X ⟶ I

Cross-train and mentor one another as planned

Allocate tools and resources

Member I

Acquires needed skills through external training, on-the-job training

Acquires needed tools and resources

on team development—that is, on helping teams acquire the empowering capabilities they need.

Reviewing Performance in Team Settings

Performance review feeds into all other aspects of performance management:

- It can be used directly to affect performance by feeding back information to the performer to clarify what adjustments in performance are necessary, assuming the original performance definitions are still intact.

- It can be used to identify where performance definitions are no longer valid and to suggest new ones.

- It can reveal that performance is falling short because of deficiencies in the performer or the situation that need to be corrected through some type of developmental process.

- It can be used to determine a fair reward for the performer so that desired performance will continue.

Each of the various performance management uses to which review can be put requires a different lens through which to review performance. In large part, these perspectives match the ways performance should have been defined. The following list enumerates the different aspects of performance that should be reviewed.

- Assessing the skills and resource adequacy of the performer (business unit, team, or individual)

- Evaluating how the work is organized and carried out by the performer

- Judging how much the performance contributes to the performance of the larger system

- Appraising how well the performance meets the needs of its stakeholders

- Determining progress from base-line measures of performance, as well as goal attainment

All these elements are relevant for feedback purposes, since all provide information that can be used by the performer to adjust performance. For developmental purposes, we are interested mainly in the skills and resource adequacy of the performer and how the performer goes about organizing and carrying out the work. For defining purposes, it is important to know whether the performance is contributing to the performance of the larger system and how much the performance is meeting the needs of its stakeholders. For reward purposes, we might consider reviewing all the above; but we must do so using metrics in a fair and just way, taking into account changes in the business requirements and situation that result in alteration of what is possible or desirable.

The aim of performance review is to discern, as much as possible, the organizational value of a performance. In view of this goal, review must entail evaluating the direction performance has been going as well as its magnitude. As formally practiced in organizations, performance review too often slavishly evaluates performance in terms of original definitions instead of in terms of emerging definitions that more closely reflect the direction performance needs to take. Consequently, performers may spend time on activities that are no longer a high priority.

On the other hand, performers sometimes pursue emergent goals without properly evaluating the degree to which those goals represent value to the organization. For instance, a design team may begin to pursue design options for technical reasons without ascertaining whether the new technical functionality meets customer needs. In such cases, review must evaluate the performance's direction and perhaps redirect performance back to the originally defined goal. There should be flexible opportunities to review performance definitions (goals) during the performance cycle to prevent this misfit between needs and activities.

Because each of the stakeholders of performance tends to review performance from a unique perspective, the information gleaned through their various reviews tends to be more useful for certain purposes and less useful for others. Thus a complete review needs to strike a balance among the various stakeholders.

Self-review by teams, including peer review conducted by co-performing team members for one another, is useful for team development. Using peer review for reward evaluations is a more difficult issue. Some organizations we studied reported that team members were not willing to carry out review tasks of this sort, while others reported having successfully established peer review systems. There are two different reasons we have seen that team members may refuse to review teammates for reward purposes. First, co-workers can see evaluations of one another as divisive. They fear that negative evaluations of co-workers will create conflicts among each other that will negatively affect the ability of the team to perform. Second, team members come to view the team's performance as truly a team phenomenon to which all members contribute. They see themselves as so interdependent with their fellow team members that it is impossible to judge the contributions of individuals; consequently, they do not believe that it is possible to separate team from individual performance for purposes of rewards. However, these same teams can comfortably review one another's performances for purposes of improving the team's overall performance.

Just as reviews of and by co-performing individuals are associated with team development, reviews of co-performing teams tend to support business-unit development. That is, teams tend to focus on how they need to relate differently in order to more effectively integrate their work.

Even in team-based organizations, managers are generally involved in team and individual reviews. When managers review team performance, they tend to focus on the team's contribution to the business unit and make comparisons among teams. They do the same things when reviewing individual performance. This focus on contribution to business is useful for maintaining alignment among the levels of performers. The tendency to compare among performers has two sources in our experience. First, because managers are responsible for resource allocation across business units and teams, they must be aware of the relative competencies of various performers. Second, the allocation of scarce resources to individuals and teams creates "fixed pie" decision situations: not all people and teams can get all the resources they would like. Sometimes resources need to be allocated to the performers who are having performance problems, as part of a remedy. Other times, as in the case of rewards, resources go to the better performers.

However, comparative reviews among different performers who have to work together can be divisive, especially if there is a requirement that a summary review differentiate among them. Studies of some organizations that have used rankings of individuals to determine pay have shown that such ranking processes get in the way of teamwork (Mohrman, Mohrman, and Worley, 1990). Similarly, if co-performing teams are ranked against each other, we should expect this ranking to create competition rather than cooperation. For this reason, it is recommended that managers rate competencies and keep inventories of skills but keep this process separate from the performance rating, maintaining the latter as a judgment of actual performance in comparison to defined performance.

Customers judge performance in terms of whether the product or service is delivered and how well their needs are being met. Even in a customer-oriented organization, customers' judgments may be at odds with those of other stakeholders (such as managers or the team itself). Thus individuals, teams, and managers must constantly balance these different stakeholder reviews.

Finally, performers should be held accountable only for performance over which they have control. This is a staple of individual performance management and applies equally well to teams. Team members will balk at being held accountable (either as individuals or as a team) for team performance unless they feel that they have control over the mechanisms for achieving performance. This control includes being able to organize themselves and being able to have some influence over who their teammates are and over other team resources.

Figures 7.9 and 7.10 offer models of the team-level and individual-level reviewing processes. They portray the team as involved in a two-way review with co-performing teams and with business-unit management. The team's ultimate review comes from business-unit management, who must orchestrate a process by which the multiple perspectives are considered. The team is also engaged in a process by which team members' performances are reviewed in the context of their contributions to the team. This team review should be an integral, formal part of an ultimate individual appraisal, if such an appraisal is done.

Reviews should be done periodically (and relatively frequently) to make sure performance is on track, to make sure performance definitions are still appropriate, and to look for further development that might be needed. Yearly, formal performance appraisals should be thought of as summaries of reviews done more frequently. As with the other processes, reviewing should not be out of proportion to the work itself. Nevertheless, it is necessary for effective performance. Reviewers should use any existing procedures that are available, adapting them as needed, make sure all stakeholders and issues are covered, and remember that time spent on defining performance well minimizes the time spent in reviewing.

Rewarding Performance in Team Settings

Reward systems present special problems in team-based settings. Reward systems are most often corporate-wide, but team settings often constitute only a portion of the organization. Evolving team settings

Figure 7.9. Team-Level Reviewing Process.

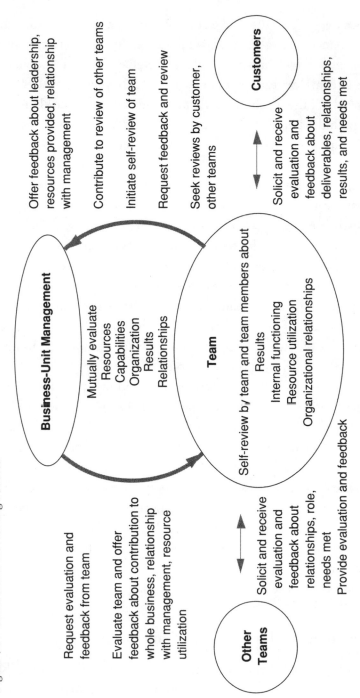

Business-Unit Management

Mutually evaluate
Resources
Capabilities
Organization
Results
Relationships

Offer feedback about leadership, resources provided, relationship with management

Contribute to review of other teams

Initiate self-review of team

Request feedback and review

Seek reviews by customer, other teams

Customers

Solicit and receive evaluation and feedback about deliverables, relationships, results, and needs met

Request evaluation and feedback from team

Evaluate team and offer feedback about contribution to whole business, relationship with management, resource utilization

Team

Self-review by team and team members about
Results
Internal functioning
Resource utilization
Organizational relationships

Other Teams

Solicit and receive evaluation and feedback about relationships, role, needs met

Provide evaluation and feedback

Figure 7.10. Individual-Level Reviewing Process.

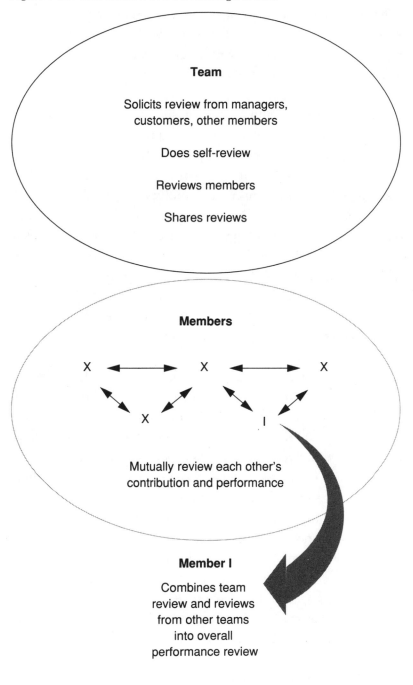

are therefore trapped within a reward system that was designed for a different kind of organizational logic. This section is concerned with what can be done within this type of context in the short term and with the design of longer-term goals for team-based reward systems. We begin with a review of what we learned from our study in team-based settings.

Despite their commitment to teams, most of the companies we studied had not moved completely toward reward systems that were compatible with the new team approach. They continued, by and large, to use the traditional merit-pay system aimed at individual employees as the core compensation and reward practice. This is in part because it is hard to change corporate-level practices for any reason and in part because organizations still lack complete understanding about what kind of compensation and reward practices make sense in team-based settings. Although traditional merit pay was still widespread, some of the organizations we studied had developed additional sources of rewards—primarily special awards programs—and they had made some alterations to merit-pay practices to better suit their needs.

In the organizations we studied, we measured the degree to which employees were rewarded for their individual performance, for their team's performance, and for their organization's performance. There was wide variation in practices across organizations, business units, and teams; employees experienced very different patterns in how and how much they were rewarded for individual, team, and organizational performance.

We found that the more people were rewarded for their individual performance, the worse team performance was. On the other hand, the more people were rewarded for team performance, the better their team's performance was, the better their business unit's performance was, and the more process improvements the teams and their business unit had made. Apparently, rewards for individual performance are detrimental to team performance, while rewards for team performance lead not only to better team performance but also to better unit performance.

When we took a closer and more complete look at the role that rewards play in team settings, we got a fuller perspective. In particular, we found that much of the impact of team reward practices was due not to the rewards themselves but rather to the processes by which team performance was defined and reviewed. Good practices for rewarding team performance require good practices for defining what the performance should be and for measuring, reviewing, and evaluating the performance. The positive impact of team reward practices on performance is due largely to the fact that team reward practices are built on practices by which team performance is well defined and reviewed. Rewarding for good performance in and of itself achieves only a small improvement in performance. The main impact comes from defining and reviewing. On the other hand, basing rewards on team performance helps greatly to achieve alignment in the performance management of teams, because it gives people a strong signal about what is valued in the organization.

The significance of the above finding is that, even in the absence of team rewards, managers have access to two key influences on performance: the processes of defining and reviewing performance. Both of these processes also lead to development of improved capability in the team and in the business unit.

But this finding does not mean that rewards are irrelevant. On the contrary, rewards for individual performance have a disruptive effect on team performance. To further complicate matters, rewards have a great impact on employees' sense of pay equity and their satisfaction with work in general. In the organizations we studied, the more people were paid for individual performance, the more they felt fairly paid and satisfied with work, even though the performance of their teams was adversely affected! This poses a dilemma for team performance management. If individually based reward practices, while not conducive to team performance, are important for employee satisfaction, employees' sense of fairness must be related to the logic of the traditional merit-pay system. This logic, based on individual contributors as performers who are managed as individuals by hierarchical superiors, is contrary to the logic of team organizations.

However, our findings show that team rewards also are related to employees' sense of being fairly paid and lead to general satisfaction. As people work in team-based settings, they begin to adopt the logic of the new organization and perceive reward practices that are consistent with that new logic as fair. This change in viewpoint takes time; it comes only after people live within the new system. Consider one team we studied: a high-performing team of chemists. They had become so aware of their interdependencies with one another that they were unable to separate out their individual contributions to the team's performance. When management initiated the annual exercise of ranking individuals for pay purposes, the members of this team refused to allow themselves to be ranked differently. They demanded that management rank them all at the same level within the larger group of employees being ranked. In essence, they demanded that, even within the individual merit-pay system, they be rewarded as a team. This is what seemed fair to them.

Another example of this logic shift has occurred with quality circles in many organizations. As circles solve organizational problems and thereby contribute substantial savings to their organization, many go the next logical step and wonder aloud why they are not being rewarded as a group for the savings they generate as a group (Lawler and Mohrman, 1985).

The challenge for organizations that are transitioning to teams is to merge the traditional notions of what constitutes fair rewards with the emerging notions of fairness. In the beginning, employees are reluctant to give up their traditional sources of self-esteem and feelings of individual contribution and sense of fair treatment. It feels wrong that they should be rewarded for what the group accomplishes, especially if the team is held back because of weak individual performances from others or if the team succeeds because of their own extraordinary performance. At the same time, many team members will identify the individually oriented reward systems as a barrier to team effectiveness. As the transition to teams progresses, people will gradually come to see traditional individual merit-pay systems, especially those that rely on ranking, as divisive. There will be increasing demand for pay systems that acknowledge the contribution of the individual without pitting teammates against one another; and there will be increasing demand that teams should be rewarded for what they have achieved as teams. Managers need to help this shift in logic to take place.

There are two fronts on which new reward practices can be brought about. First, companies can work to change the organizational (often corporate) compensation and reward practices. A number of these formal practices, including skill-based pay plans, team bonus systems, profit sharing, and gainsharing, are highly compatible with team settings. Many organizations are working toward establishing various combinations of these compatible practices. Even in organizations that have significant team-based efforts, however, these practices are slow in coming.

The second front is pragmatic and immediate. It involves supplementing and amending existing practices so that they minimally disrupt the functioning of teams and thereby contribute to the transition from individual logic to team logic.

The list below offers various approaches to rewarding performance that foster effective teamwork. The list moves from those practices that can be rather easily implemented within existing pay practices to those that require major changes in or additions to normal compensation practices. One could take the order to be roughly chronological also, in that the top items could be done first and the bottom items could come later. The chronology does not have to be adhered to, however. (Profit sharing and gainsharing, for example, can be implemented regardless of where an organization is in the transition to teams.)

Practices That Adapt Existing Merit-Pay Procedures

- Make teamwork and contribution to the team more important.

- Minimize the competitive focus on individual performance.

- Tie together the fates of people who must work together.

Practices That Focus on Team Performance

- Offer special team awards.

- Initiate a bonus pool based on team performance.

Practices That Focus on Unitwide Performance

- Initiate gainsharing.

- Initiate profit sharing.

Before changing reward systems, managers should establish team performance management practices for defining, developing, and reviewing. These account for the lion's share of influence over performance. If effective, they are empowerment practices that can be rewarding in and of themselves.

There are a number of adaptations to traditional merit-pay systems that can positively support performance in team settings. The first set of adaptations often used are aimed at acknowledging teamwork as an important aspect of performance. Managers who are officially responsible for appraisals can take the individual's teamwork behavior into account by adding the appropriate dimensions to the standard form. These dimensions can even be weighted to ensure that they are given enough priority. Managers who do not have first-hand information about the person's team-oriented performance can use input from co-workers, peers, and customers.

The next set of adaptations are often implemented in order to minimize the negative impact that focusing on individual performance can have on team performance. As we have noted, the practice of ranking team members against each other in determining the distribution of salary budgets tends to put team members in competition with one another. If it is politically impossible to abolish comparisons among individuals, organizations sometimes resort to

minimizing comparisons by putting people in one of three categories
for pay purposes: a small group that is clearly unable to perform at
the level needed, a large group that meets standards, and another
small group that is clearly performing at an exceptionally high level.

Focusing on individual performance can detract from team performance in another way: it can orient people too much to their
own set of performance goals and responsibilities without considering how they might be contributing to or interfering with the team's
performance. On the other hand, people want to be recognized for
what they bring to the organization as individuals. Therefore, organizations are increasingly changing the basis for merit ratings from
recent past performance to the level of skills, knowledge, and competencies that the individual has achieved. This has the effect of
transforming pay-for-performance merit-pay systems into pay-for-
skills merit-pay systems. In such systems, pay increases are given for
development of skills and may be based on whether and to what
degree developmental goals have been reached.

A third set of adaptations to merit-pay systems is designed to tie
the various fates of team members together so that their orientation is
away from themselves as individual performers and toward their joint
performance with others. The easiest way to do this is to use joint performance measures as one indicator of the performance of individuals. For instance, all individuals involved in a project could be partly
rated by the level of the project's performance. A variation on this
approach is to give each person an individual performance rating and
then weight it by the performance of the team or teams to which he
or she belongs.

Organizations can move even further to a team logic by distrib-
uting pay for performance at the team or larger unit. Many organizations make their first forays into team-based bonuses by adapting
existing special awards programs. Usually, team rewards do not
remain the team's as a whole. They are distributed to the members.
Sometimes this distribution is automatic; perhaps everyone gets a
bonus that is an equal percentage of their base pay or an equal cut of

the bonus pool. Sometimes the team might determine the distribution; perhaps the team jointly identifies members that are especially deserving of a larger or smaller cut. Team input and agreement are important in determining whatever distribution practice is used. Often team-based bonuses are available in addition to, rather than instead of, individual rewards.

Finally, organizations can implement reward practices at the business-unit level that are very conducive to performance management in team-based settings: gainsharing and profit sharing. These orient employees to the larger performing unit by making it in everyone's interest to improve the performance of the enterprise as a whole. They are reward systems that thoroughly embed the logic of sharing in the group's performance by allowing everyone to share in the economic value of that performance. Our research, as well as that of others, shows that well-designed practices of this type lead to a high degree of perceived fairness. These types of bonuses can be given along with team bonuses and individual rewards.

Special Issues in Team-Based Performance Management

Team-based organizations often represent a departure from a functional logic, but performance still rests on the maintenance of discipline expertise. In some cases, such as Alpha's technical support group, functional specialists may be individual contributors supporting teams. In others, they may be housed in shared services teams. In most knowledge organizations, the management of the technical performance and of the technical capabilities of the organization are key challenges. These issues are addressed in this section.

Performance Management of Individual Contributors Who Are Not Team Members

Even in team-based organizations, there will be employees who are not members of teams. These may be scientists exploring the outer limits of a technology or one-of-a-kind support specialists (such as a process consultants). In general, these individuals will either be placed within an organizational unit and be working in the service of that unit or be servicing various teams in a supplier capacity (or both). In any case, the performer is an individual with a set of people and groups who have a stake in his or her performance. These stakeholders should be identified and incorporated into the performance management process. Essentially, the practices of performance management for such an individual are abbreviated versions of those suggested in our discussions of defining, developing, reviewing, and rewarding performance, with the individual contributor taking the role of the team. These individuals participate in defining, developing, and reviewing practices with their customers, other teams, and their unit's management. They should be eligible for individual and business-unit rewards; and if the teams they service are eligible for team-based performance rewards, they may be given a bonus based on the average of the bonuses awarded the teams serviced.

The Role of the Functional Manager

In traditional organizations, the functional manager is the supervising manager responsible for performance management of individuals. As individuals become team-based, and as these teams are managed more and more as business units and/or as teams oriented toward products, programs, or customers, the role of the functional manager as a direct manager of performance will disappear. Business-unit management, program management, and customer-service-unit management will take on the responsibility of orchestrating performance management processes. What, then, will become the performance management role of functional managers? Essentially, the new role will be one of managing technical/functional development of the employees. This will involve assigning employees to an area and giving input about an individual's skills, capabilities, and needs in this area. It will also involve assuming responsibility for orchestrating the processes by which individuals further develop their skills. This new role will be played out in conjunction with and in support of performance management by business-unit management.

Performance Management of Functional Teams

Often in team-based organizations, people belong both to project teams and to functionally based teams (also known as "home teams" or "centers of excellence"). Individual work assignments may be to projects in the center of excellence. On the surface, these functional teams appear to be simply continuations of traditional functional departments. In reality, however, there are important differences. The most fundamental is the fact that they are managed as teams. Their sources of interdependence are different as well, since their work—having to do with development of technology for the company or providing teams and projects with advanced technical services, for example—is often done on a consulting basis. Although these teams are interdependent with those they consult to, they also have their own functional team goals to achieve.

The performance management of functional teams, like their overall management, parallels that of any other team. The major difference lies in their multiple customers. One "customer" is the organization's management, since these groups nurture technologies that are key corporate resources. In fact, functional team performance should be judged mainly in terms of organizational value. The other teams that house the various functional specialists on a business-unit and project basis are also "customers"; as such, they can judge the functional team in terms of the extent to which the technology it develops and the services it provides meet the needs of the teams. Both corporate management and business teams should have input into the goals and reviews of the performance of these functional teams.

Performance Management of Shared Service Teams

Shared service teams are groups that provide services to a variety of teams in the organization. Good examples are human resource

(HR) management teams (offering HR systems and system support as well as expertise and consulting in HR management issues), information system teams (maintaining, developing, implementing, and providing consultation about information technologies used by other teams), and support service teams (supplying graphic and printing services). These services are not always organized in teams; when they are, however, they are legitimate teams as long as there are strong interdependencies among their members. Within a shared service, members may be constituted in teams to meet the needs of particular internal customers. The major consideration here is the fact that the customers of these teams are the other teams of the business unit. Otherwise, the performance of these teams can be managed like that of any other team.

Key Issues

Key issues faced by team-based organizations as they attempt to manage performance effectively include the following:

1. Performance management consists of a cycle of activities that encompasses defining the work, developing the performers, reviewing performance, and rewarding performance.

2. The major immediate impact on performance comes from the way work is defined and reviewed. The reward component of performance management depends on having performance definition and review in place.

3. Rewards direct behavior and impact members' sense of being equitably treated.

4. In team organizations, performance management is no longer a dyadic boss-subordinate matter. (In fact, dyadic performance management can work against team performance.) Active roles in performance management are played by peers, customers, and other stakeholders.

5. In team organizations, performance management must be

conducted for performing units at multiple levels: the team, the business unit, and the corporation. Teams have shared goals, and collective performance must be managed.

Part III

. . . .

Implementation Concerns

The organizational design framework for team-based organizations that was presented in Part Two raises a number of issues that surround both the design and the processes required to make it work. These issues relate to the significant cultural change necessitated by the transition to a team-based design, the extent of the new understandings and skills required to make this design work, the changes in organizational systems that are called for to provide a foundation for new integration and performance management processes, and the magnitude of the change, implementation, and learning processes required.

Part Three addresses a number of these general issues. Chapter Eight provides a conceptual framework for the responsibilities of the different systemic levels of the team-based organization. In the traditional role breakdown in the hierarchical organization, the technical core has conducted the transformation processes of the organization, middle management has controlled those processes, translated direction into operational meaning, and buffered the technical core from uncertainty, and executive management has worried about institutional issues and strategy (Thompson, 1967). Some of these roles continue in the team-based organization, and others change. Control, strategy, planning, and dealing with uncertainty all become shared responsibility throughout the organization. Likewise, people at all levels worry about how to organize, and learning goes on at all levels. This chapter deals not only with responsibilities at different systemic levels but with the skill-building requirements underlying those responsibilities.

Chapter Nine revisits the notion of *empowerment*, which has been mentioned repeatedly in earlier chapters. This term is used with great frequency in most team-based organizations, and its interpretation has (ironically) caused such paralysis in some settings that we felt it deserved special attention. The chapter debunks some of the myths of empowerment, provides a definition that relates to the team-based organization, and talks about what managers and teams can do to make it a reality.

Chapter Ten addresses the systems that have to be developed to support a team-based organization. Information technology has enabled the lateral organization to become more than a normative fiction; the absence of adequate information technology can seriously impede organizational efforts to function more laterally. Team-based organizations depend on new distributed information systems, common languages and data bases, and new financial and performance management systems that fit with the team-based structure. The development and maintenance of these systems are key sources of organizational learning, with joint line/staff development teams serving as key learning forums. The development of these systems points out in bold relief the tensions, the trade-offs, and the need for balance between global and local planning and systems development and between commonalty and the local optimization of systems and processes. These issues are key to the capability of the team-based organization to achieve responsiveness, flexibility, and lateral integration.

Chapter Eleven provides a view of implementation as a learning process. It discusses some of the major implementation challenges faced by organizations that are becoming team-based. Implementation is depicted as an iterative process that no organization gets completely right the first time. The challenge is to have in place the learning processes that reveal where the organization gets it wrong or incomplete and that then continue to bring all aspects of the system into alignment with the new model. A team-based organization is in its essence a learning organization, and top management is charged with leading the learning process.

The final chapter draws some summary observations about where this is all leading. It hits head-on some of the tensions that make the transition to teams difficult and offers suggestions for the kinds of research and development required to make more wide-spread application of team-based models feasible.

. . . .

8

Identifying New Responsibilities and Skills

The team-based organization has been depicted as a system of teams, in which teams with a narrower scope are nested in business units with a broader scope (such as programs, field offices, or product lines), which in turn are nested in a larger organization. This chapter draws on the design model presented in the preceding five chapters, as well as our study findings, to present an overall view of the responsibilities of work teams and management teams at these different systemic levels in a team-based organization. It presents a brief overview of responsibilities at three levels: the team, the business-unit management team, and the organization's executive team. It also presents some findings regarding successful management teams and discusses the implications of the team-based organizational structure for the role of managers in general. Finally, it gives an overview of the skill requirements for team members and for managers in a team-based organization.

Team Responsibilities

Effective teams perform several functions related to managing themselves and integrating their work. These functions apply whether the teams are work teams, integrating teams, or improvement teams. They also apply to management teams. These functions are illustrated in Figure 8.1.

Figure 8.1. Self-Managing and Integrating Functions of All Teams.

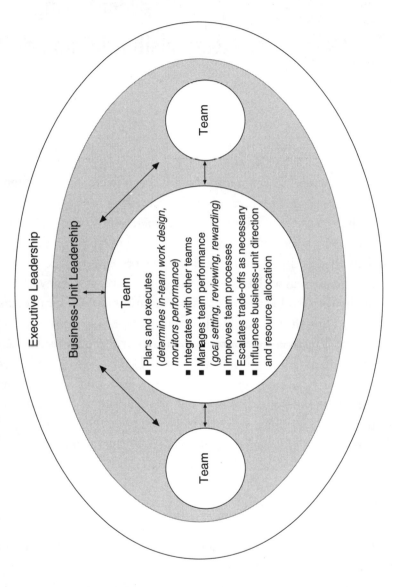

Executive Leadership

Business-Unit Leadership

Team

Team

Team

- Plans and executes
  (*determines in-team work design, monitors performance*)
- Integrates with other teams
- Manages team performance
  (*goal setting, reviewing, rewarding*)
- Improves team processes
- Escalates trade-offs as necessary
- Influences business-unit direction
  and resource allocation

- *Planning and executing their work.* Teams determine how they go about their work, including who does what, using both formal and informal processes to integrate their work and monitor their progress and to deal with issues that arise.

- *Integrating with other teams.* Teams work with other interdependent teams and/or individuals to make sure that their work fits together.

- *Participating in their own performance management.* Teams work with their manager and/or the management team to set goals, review performance, develop their capabilities as a team, and determine rewards. The previous chapter described a number of ways in which these performance management tasks may happen, but the cardinal point is that performance management is a shared responsibility of the team, its managers, and key stakeholders (such as internal or external customers).

- *Improving team performance.* When teams participate in their own performance management, they tend to become more skilled at working together and at finding ways to do their work more effectively. This increased skill may involve cross-training or changes in the work processes that are used (including the way team members relate to external stakeholders).

- *Escalating issues as necessary.* When teams encounter issues that are beyond their scope and/or that cannot be resolved internally without the help of a broader perspective, they raise these issues to the management team or another broad forum for help.

- *Influencing business-unit decisions.* Each team learns as it goes along. It offers technical and customer knowledge and a perspective that should be taken into account in business-unit-wide decision making, particularly regarding direction and resource allocation. Creating conditions that enable teams to be empowered involves both giving them authority over issues within their scope and providing opportunities for them to influence decisions that are made at a broader scope.

These team responsibilities may be carried out by a team with or without designated leadership roles or manager roles, as we noted in Chapter Five. Even when a manager performs some of these responsibilities with or for the team, the important issue is that these tasks have to be performed at the team level of the organizational system. The focus of these activities is the team and its relationship to other parts of the system.

Now we turn to the skills required by teams as they carry out these responsibilities.

Team Skills

In order to adequately perform their responsibilities, teams need members with the appropriate mix of skills. These skills go beyond what is required in a traditional organization. They fall into six categories.

- *Technical or functional competence.* People in all organizations need to be technically competent. They need to have the body of knowledge that defines competence in their field and be able to apply this knowledge to the project or task at hand. In other words, they need both a conceptual and a practical understanding of their field. Conceptual knowledge is usually acquired through formal education; practical knowledge about how to do tasks is acquired through experience. Neither conceptual nor practical knowledge is static.

Technical competence includes some additional nuances in a team setting (Mohrman and Cohen, forthcoming). In order to have credibility in a team setting, team members need to be willing and able to keep up with the technical changes in their field. This may take more individual initiative in a team setting than in the traditional organization, because team members are not tightly linked to a functional manager. In addition, since team members broaden and deepen their technical knowledge through lateral interactions, they need to be able to learn from their experiences and the feedback of others.

When members are selected for a team, chances are that not everyone will have the full complement of technical skills required for the collective task. This does not have to be a major obstacle if team members are committed to development and if resources are available for needed learning. If some of the team members are experienced technical contributors, mentoring relationships can be established (although this responsibility needs to be factored in to the total workload of the mentor). If internal technical mentoring is not possible, relationships with external functional resources will have to be established.

A team's skill mix is as crucial as its skill level: team members must have the collective knowledge required to produce the team's product or service. Although internal development can supplement existing skills, it cannot compensate for the absence of key disciplines. A pharmaceutical team charged with the commercialization of a new drug, for example, should consist of physicians, marketers, and clinical researchers. It would be a mistake to have only physicians on this team. At Analytico, the product-line marketing team would not be able to compensate for the lack of a technical writer to prepare product marketing documents.

• *Cross-training.* In teams composed of members from different specialties, should there be any cross-training? The prototypical work team from a manufacturing setting often has people cross-trained on a full set of team skills. Full cross-training is inappropriate for most knowledge-work teams, however, because the in-depth, specialized knowledge required is expensive to obtain. Certainly, the pharmaceutical company should not cross-train its marketers as physicians (and vice versa). On the other hand, it is not unusual to have R&D engineers cross-trained in manufacturing process engineering, generally through a rotational sequence of roles in the organization. Physicians can get some exposure to the marketing worldview by going on customer visits. Teams require members to have, at a minimum, enough understanding of the skills of their teammates to be able to discuss issues and trade-offs as the team goes through the cycle of considering divergent views and arriving at convergence on a direction. Familiarity across disciplines provides a basis for communicating across the thought-worlds of the different disciplines.

How much cross-training to do depends on the need for specialization, the comparability of skills, and the need for flexibility. It is easier for two programmers to be cross-trained on each other's applications than it is for a technical writer to be cross-trained as a programmer. The greater the cross-training, the more team members can substitute for one another. This creates flexibility and the capacity to adjust to differences in workload across members. Figure 8.2 illustrates the contingencies involved in determining the degree to which cross-training should be done.

• *Interpersonal and conflict resolution skills*. Working effectively with others requires the ability to communicate clearly, to listen, to feel free in expressing ideas and feelings, and to be willing to disagree. Over thirty years ago, Rensis Likert and Douglas McGregor described these skills as critical for effective teams (Likert, 1961;

Figure 8.2. Cross-Training Contingencies.

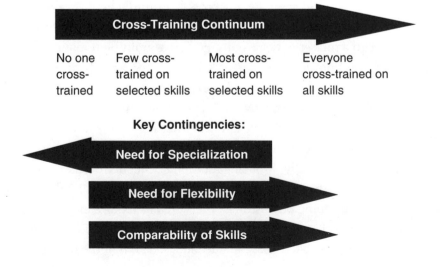

McGregor, 1960). Most approaches to team building emphasize the development of interpersonal skills, and many companies offer training in them (for example, Dyer, 1987).

Conflict resolution skills may be at the center of what is required to work collaboratively in the lateral organization. People in teams from different disciplines view their worlds in dissimilar ways. They have distinct bodies of knowledge, attend to different aspects of information, and have different preferences. These differences are frequently the source of conflict. What is required to successfully resolve conflict is the ability to transcend differences, to develop a shared understanding, and to work for mutual solutions. Conflict resolution requires team members to be open about their feelings and frustrations and to listen to others' feelings and concerns (Van Berkholm and Tsovold, 1981). It can be facilitated by decision-making tools that systematically guide the surfacing of information and foster analysis that leads to solution. Conflict will be resolved productively only if a team has shared goals. Conflict resolution skills are not a substitute for either an appropriate team design or shared, clearly understood goals.

• *Decision-making skills.* In order to make decisions about how to do work, deal with the issues that arise, and determine solutions to problems, teams need decision-making skills. In our research into knowledge-work teams, we discovered that teams that use systematic decision-making processes are much more likely to be effective than teams that do not. Systematic decision-making processes are disciplined ways of collecting data, evaluating alternatives, and determining outcomes. Team members need to learn and become proficient at the decision-making processes they use. Decision-making skills can be learned on the job, but only if the team and its members receive good on-the-job training and facilitation and if team members take the time to orient new members.

Using systematic decision-making processes requires team discipline and commitment. Many teams abandon their use of these processes when confronted with a tight deadline or other extreme performance pressures. This is usually a mistake, because decisions made on the fly often get undone, resulting in rework and added time. Although the use of systematic decision-making processes is strongly related to timeliness of decision making, it is important that these processes not be cumbersome and that they fit the work to be done. Teams that experience the benefits of good decision-making processes are likely to be committed to their use.

• *Learning skills*. Team members need to be open to learning. Scientific and technological advances mean that team members need to be willing to acquire new knowledge to stay current in their fields. In addition, working with people from other disciplines requires a capacity to develop an understanding of different ways of viewing the world. This entails learning some basics about the frameworks and language of the other disciplines. A team adds value through a synthesis of disparate perspectives. Whether or not cross-training formally takes place, some cross-discipline learning must occur in multidiscipline teams.

Developing interpersonal and conflict resolution skills also entails learning. Even team members who have effective interpersonal skills in the traditional organization may feel the need to further refine them when placed in team settings. Personal development is enhanced in teams that are reflective about how well members are working together and in which team members get feedback from multiple sources. Individuals who learned well in a classroom may not be as effective at learning from co-workers and from feedback. Deriving action plans from such feedback, for example, is a skill that may need to be taught. Teams may not know the behaviors required to examine their own functioning and make team-level development plans. An expert facilitator may help a team establish these learning skills and coach individuals.

• *Leadership skills*. Team members will be put into various leadership roles, including that of team leader, technical mentor, systems integrator, and liaison. These leadership roles require skills of informal influence, meeting management, and communication that are similar to (but more sharply honed than) those required by a member who is not in a leadership role. Leadership in the technical integration process, for example, might require a broad technical knowledge to allow the leader to "translate" across the worldviews of various contributors. Leaders also need to be skilled at the kinds of processes that enable a team to move through the processing of divergent information and the building of convergence around a shared direction. Some leaders may need to learn models and tools for this.

These are the skills that all teams need to effectively carry out their responsibilities. Management teams have additional responsibilities and need added skills. In the remainder of the chapter, we will consider the responsibilities of management teams that are accountable for tasks at the two higher systemic levels: the business unit and the organization.

Management teams offer a collective service: they provide management and leadership for the organizational unit for which they are responsible. That service includes clarifying direction and building capability (see Figure 8.3).

The shared goal of management teams is business performance.

Figure 8.3. Business Management Team: Creating the Context for Effective Teams.

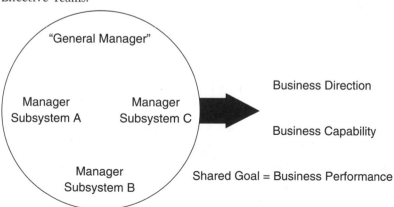

The business-unit management team builds the context in which the work of all the different contributors in the business unit is optimally integrated. The executive team for the larger organization has a similar set of responsibilities, but for the organization as a whole. After discussing management team responsibilities in more detail, we will discuss the skills that managers must develop in a team-based organization.

Business-Unit Management Responsibilities

Business-unit management teams are responsible for creating the conditions within which teams can operate effectively. This means providing the direction and developing the capabilities that allow teams and team members to effectively integrate their work laterally. It entails creating the context in the work unit for effective team performance. Figure 8.4 illustrates four major categories of responsibilities that are particularly important in a team-based organization: designing the work unit, aligning business-unit goals and activities with the corporate strategy, modeling the norms required for a successful team-based organization, and orchestrating performance management processes.

Designing the Work Unit

The management team is responsible for the design of the work unit's structures, including the work teams, integrating teams, improvement teams, and customer interfaces. Team organizations tend to have structures that are more dynamic than traditional organizations, because the appropriate configuration of teams may change with changes in market, phase of project, product mix, and so forth. Temporary teams are established for special purposes and with a limited life. Managers have to find the proper balance between time spent on various improvement-oriented activities and time spent in work teams.

Figure 8.4. Business-Unit Leadership Team Responsibilities.

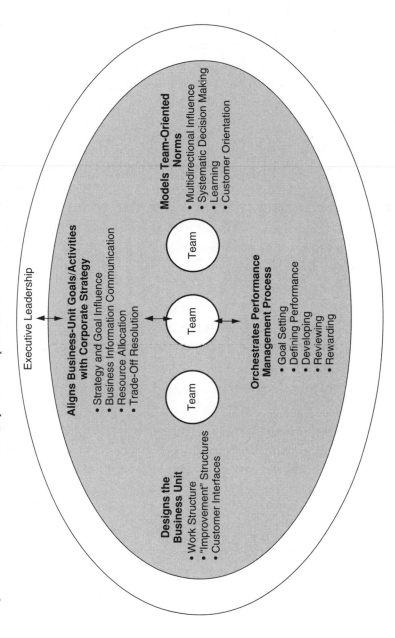

Team organizations have a tendency to establish more and more teams. In our study, individuals were in an average of 6.7 teams—a stretch that often caused conflicting priorities and worked against the effectiveness of all teams. Management must carefully monitor the resource adequacy of the teams, establish teams to address the highest-priority activities, and make sure that teams are properly designed and chartered to minimize interteam interdependence. Improperly designed or chartered teams and an excess of teams can result in paralysis rather than effective lateral coordination.

As noted above, it is the responsibility of the management team to make sure that all teams are properly chartered. Each team should work collaboratively with the management team in determining its charter, but management must ensure that the charter addresses the needs of the business. The charter should specify outcome and process requirements, the resources available to the team, team authority, and team constraints. Exhibit 8.1 offers a generic format that can be used in drafting a team charter.

Another structural feature that must be carefully designed is the various customer interfaces. It is not unusual for managers in traditional organizations to personally manage the customer interfaces. Customers come to the managers with requests and complaints; managers then carry this information to the appropriate parties. Team organizations, on the other hand, often build in direct contact between customers and teams—contact that is not filtered through levels of management.

It is important that management foster upward communication about how the design is working and initiate redesign when there are problems. Although we argue that the design of the unit is the responsibility of the management team, design should be done with input from the business-unit members. In the companies we studied, management-determined designs often had to be redesigned after the operating teams discovered that they did not fit certain aspects of the work.

Exhibit 8.1. Sample Team Charter Format.

Organizational Goals:

Business-Unit Goals:

Team Mission (products or services, including support
  to other teams):

Team Goals (parameters of products or services):

Stakeholders

    Customers:

    Managers:

    Co-Performers:

Resources:

Authority:

Requirements for Integration with Other Groups:

Escalation Path:

Review Processes:

Aligning Business-Unit Goals and Activities with the Corporate Strategy

The management team must work to create shared understanding of
what the organization is trying to accomplish and agreement about
how it will go about it, including how people with different knowledge bases will work together to integrate their perspectives. There
must be a shared understanding that enables all business units to be
aligned in carrying out the organization's strategy: each business-unit
management team must then make sure that the goals and activities
of the business unit and its teams are aligned with the organization's
strategy. One of the findings of our study has particular relevance to
the issue of alignment: the effectiveness of management teams is particularly sensitive to their ability to achieve shared understanding
internally. In other words, management teams cannot effectively
align the business unit they manage if they do not themselves have
a shared understanding of the unit's goals and priorities and agree
about the way the unit will go about accomplishing them. Many

struggling teams we spoke with reported that they were getting conflicting messages from different members of their management team. Teams cannot offset such disagreement from their managers.

Achieving shared understanding and alignment entails a number of activities:

- *Influencing organizational strategy and goals.* Executive management must be made aware of the business unit's technical and market situation through an upward influence process so that it can plan for the company. For example, the councils in the Netco field offices keep upper-level management informed of their technology needs, which become part of the company's planning for technology development.

- *Communicating business information.* The management team makes sure that business-unit members have information required for making trade-offs, including knowledge of the business strategy and goals and of organizational progress against goals. At Analytico, for example, the management team needs to keep all teams aware of the strategy for development of and reuse of technology and notify them of progress in that arena.

- *Allocating resources.* In the traditional organization, resources are allocated largely by a budgeting process through which managers make determinations about what resources will be required in their areas and argue their case (based on their internal needs). In a team-based organization, on the other hand, resources are allocated to teams responsible for a service or product as the result of a resource allocation process that is in part a determination of organizational priorities (and is therefore part of the alignment process). Together, the members of the business-unit management team determine resource allocations based on strategy, with input from the various teams. For example, at Netco the allocation of resources across industry teams should reflect the corporate strategy for expansion into key industries as well as the internal needs of each industry team. In this way, the corporate technical development activities and each field office's market development will fit with one another.

• *Helping resolve trade-offs*. By helping to resolve trade-offs when teams in the business unit are unable to resolve issues (within or across teams), the business-unit management team helps keep the organization aligned. Team impasse may occur when individuals working within different frameworks are unable to find common ground. Such an impasse may reflect lack of information, lack of clarity about criteria, lack of ease with decisions that optimize one criterion while minimizing another, or inability to get beyond conflicting self-interests. The management team, because it is specifically charged with optimizing the business unit, can provide a perspective that helps resolve the issue. If, for example, a design team at Analytico is unable to resolve a trade-off between reusing code (knowing that reuse will result in patchworking and some functional inefficiency but will save design hours and costs) and building the code from scratch (so that it can be optimized to a particular application), the business team may be called upon to help break the impasse. Organizations in our study reported that teams, as they matured, tended to use this kind of escalation path less frequently, because they developed the internal skills and the necessary perspective for resolving increasingly complex issues. This development is most likely to occur when the management team resolves *with* the team rather than *for* the team.

Modeling the Norms Required for a Successful Team-Based Organization

The transition to a team-based structure requires a change in culture for most organizations. The behavior that the management team models is the strongest determinant of whether the behavioral norms of the organization will change. We will mention only a few of the most important norms below.

• *Openness to multidirectional influence*. Given the premise that one advantage of teams is that interdependencies can be worked out laterally, the lifeblood of team organizations is openness to multidirectional influence. Management teams must model such openness and encourage their subordinates to do the same.

- *Systematic decision making.* Because systematic decision-making processes provide a foundation of shared understanding about how issues are decided in the organization, it is crucial that management teams model their use. In our research, however, we found that management teams are often rated lower than other teams in the application of these processes.

- *Learning.* Given the dynamic nature of team organizations and most organizations' relative lack of experience with them, learning is another key norm. Management teams must spearhead the learning process by soliciting feedback about how the organization is working and being open to change.

- *Customer orientation.* Management's attitudes toward customers will be reflected throughout the organization. Since many organizations are moving to teams in order to increase customer responsiveness and since team performance is a function of multi-stakeholder feedback (including feedback from the customer), the norm of customer orientation is paramount.

In short, the business-unit management team must model the kinds of processes and attitudes that are required for teams to be successful.

Orchestrating Performance Management Processes

The management of performance in a team-based organization is executed by multiple sources and at multiple levels. Performance management includes two aspects: a directional aspect (in the goals that are set, the ways in which the work is defined, the review of performance, and the rewards that are given) and a capability-building aspect. We made the case in Chapter Seven that performance management is a responsibility shared between team members, their managers, their customers, and their co-workers.

The business-unit management team's responsibility is orchestration of the various performance management practices. The management team needs to ensure that appropriate practices are in place for individual, team, and business-unit performance management. In the area of team performance management, the management team may be a major player, since the assessment of team performance against goals is sometimes best made by this group collectively, particularly if the management team is cross-functional.

Through the cycles of performance management, the management team becomes aware of the development needs of various teams and of the business unit itself. It works with teams to determine needed development approaches and determines the same for the business unit as a whole. The management team also makes sure that teams, which are generally at various developmental stages, get the support they need and get developmental help to become more self-sufficient.

The importance of both formal and informal performance management practices cannot be overemphasized. Management in organizations that are introducing teams often takes a hands-off stance; the management team watches helplessly in frustration as teams flounder. Although it is true that teams will not develop if managers continually jump in to prevent errors, it is also true that the performance of the business unit as a whole will suffer to the extent that a team is allowed to flounder unnecessarily. This is particularly true if other teams rely on the performance of a floundering team.

The management team has responsibility for ensuring that there is an effective performance management system in place, including a review and feedback component. When the management team becomes aware that a team has performance problems, it needs to provide timely feedback and offer any necessary support in resolving problems. It is not the responsibility of management to stand by and watch a team crash. On the other hand, managers dealing with a struggling team should collectively problem-solve with the team rather than making decisions for the team. The management team manages by results, and the discussion with the team has to be around what is necessary to achieve results.

This also means that managers must determine whether their uneasiness about the performance of a team stems from a true performance problem or from their own preference for how something should be done. If a team finds a different technical solution to a problem than managers anticipated, but one that meets the performance requirements of the system, for example, management intervention would be inappropriate. Hierarchical intervention in this situation, especially if couched as a command, would damage a team's confidence that it can (and will be allowed to) perform effectively; it would reestablish traditional, hierarchical norms.

Executive Management Responsibilities

In a team-based organization, the executives are members of the executive management team, with responsibility for managing the overall performance of the organization, including the various business units, the shared services of the organization, and other structures that integrate business units. At Analytico, for instance, the executive management team manages the two product lines (each of which has a network of teams) and the two integrating councils that cut across product lines (the R&D council and the manufacturing council).

Executive management teams operate significantly differently from the traditional general manager's staff. In the traditional structure, each individual had responsibility for a piece of the organization, represented that piece in discussions and decision making, and individually managed that piece. The executive management team, on the other hand, has collective accountability for managing the whole organization. That is its charter.

The executive management team is responsible for creating the context within which team-based business units can operate effectively. This means providing overall business direction and leadership in developing organizational capabilities for team effectiveness and fostering lateral integration across teams and business units. The importance of leadership from this team cannot be overestimated. Unless the macrocontext is brought into alignment with the team approach, organizational members will be caught in the tension between the new and old ways of operating.

Figure 8.5 illustrates the executive responsibilities in a team-based organization. These responsibilities parallel those of the business-unit management team (Figure 8.4), but they are carried out on a broader scope—that is, for the organization as a whole. The performances of all the business units combine, often in an interactive way, to constitute total organizational performance. The executive team must create a context in which this is likely to happen effectively.

The executive team in a team-based organization has the following four major clusters of responsibilities: setting and communicating corporate strategy and goals, designing the organization's structure and systems, orchestrating performance management of the business units, and modeling team-focused norms. These functions characterize executive groups in traditional organizations as well, but their importance is magnified in a team-based organization; in fact, our research found them to be critical for creating the context for an effective team-based organization. Furthermore, it is important that the executive team be aligned in performing these functions.

• *Setting and communicating corporate strategy and goals.* The executive management team sets and communicates the organizational strategy and goals and orchestrates a process designed to achieve a shared understanding of the strategy and alignment of the goals of the various units of the organization. Strategy is the umbrella under which all business units operate. Executive team tasks that stem from this responsibility for strategic direction include allocating resources between business units and shared services to

Figure 8.5. Executive Leadership Team Responsibilities.

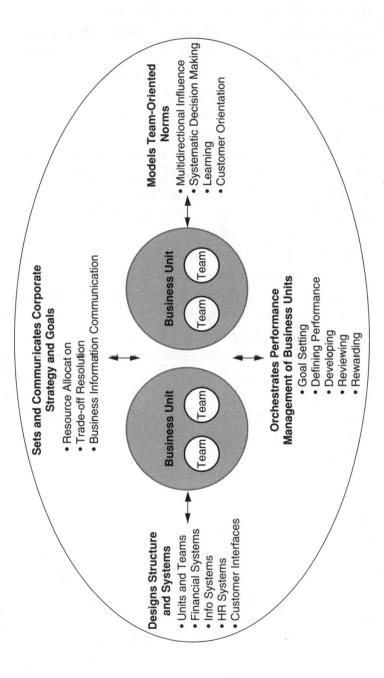

Sets and Communicates Corporate Strategy and Goals
- Resource Allocation
- Trade-off Resolution
- Business Information Communication

Models Team-Oriented Norms
- Multidirectional Influence
- Systematic Decision Making
- Learning
- Customer Orientation

Designs Structure and Systems
- Units and Teams
- Financial Systems
- Info Systems
- HR Systems
- Customer Interfaces

Orchestrates Performance Management of Business Units
- Goal Setting
- Defining Performance
- Developing
- Reviewing
- Rewarding

Business Unit

Team

Team

Business Unit

Team

Team

enable business units to attain their mission, communicating and ensuring understanding of the strategy and priorities, and making high-level trade-offs among various competing preferences that cannot get resolved laterally at a lower level.

• *Designing the organization's structure and systems.* The executive team also has responsibility for designing the macrostructure of the business and determining the nature of its key systems, including financial, information, and human resources. (These systems will be described in more detail in Chapter Ten.) This responsibility requires executive understanding of the logic of a team-based organization, for the structural arrangements and systems that serve a hierarchical, segmented organization well do not meet the needs of a team-based organization. For example, staff services must be designed to be maximally attuned to business-unit operational needs. Human resource systems must foster the capability and motivation of people to work collaboratively. Information and financial systems must distribute information broadly in order to enable lateral decision making at lower levels and to provide performance feedback to teams. The logic behind these structural arrangements and systems is a departure from the past, requiring redesign. Leadership for the direction of these new systems and priority for their redesign must emanate from the executive group.

• *Orchestrating performance management of business units.* The executive team is also responsible for orchestrating the performance management of the business units and business-unit management teams. At this highest level of the business, they provide the cross-functional management of cross-functional business-unit teams. This role is critical if functional members of cross-functional business-unit teams are to be required to optimize the business-unit performance rather than the functional performance.

• *Modeling team-oriented norms.* Finally, the norms established by and modeled by the executive team will become the norms of the organization as a whole. What executive team members expect from one another will be the expectation they communicate to the organization. The ways in which they address cross-functionality internally will set the context for how cross-functional issues will be resolved organization-wide. Their norms concerning multidirectional influence, learning, decision making, and customer orientation will be reflected down to the lowest levels of the system.

Management Team Effectiveness Issues

Although management teams are responsible for managing the overall performance of the business unit or organization, business performance itself is clearly a result of the performance of the entire network of performing units. The outputs of the management team itself—the "products" and "services" that it provides to the members of the business unit or organization that it manages—are described above and illustrated in Figure 8.6. Also shown in Figure 8.6 are the internal dynamics of management teams that we found to be particularly important in enabling management teams to perform effectively.

In general, management teams in our study were perceived to be (and perceived themselves to be) less effective on almost all team process dimensions than the work teams, improvement teams, and other integrating teams we studied. It appears that many management teams advocate teams for the performers they manage but fail to attend to their own team effectiveness. In some cases, they do not even acknowledge the need to perform as a team. As a consequence, they do not invest in creating the internal management dynamics required to effectively provide the context needed by the teams in the organization.

The internal dynamics that we found to be especially likely to differentiate between effective and ineffective management teams all relate to management's ability to provide common direction in the organization. They fall into three categories: the ability of the management team to develop a shared understanding of where and how they are leading the organization, the extent to which the team plans and sets goals collaboratively, and the extent to which the

Figure 8.6. Management Team Outputs and Dynamics.

KEY INTERNAL PROCESSES:	KEY "SERVICES" & "PRODUCTS":

KEY INTERNAL PROCESSES:

Developing Shared Understanding
   Clarifying Values
   Concretizing Issues
   Ensuring Decision Involvement
   Clarifying Decision Responsibility
   Resolving Conflict

Planning and Goal Setting

Managing Own Team's Performance
   Team Goals, Reviews, and Rewards
   Team Feedback to Members
      and Input to Goal Setting

KEY "SERVICES" & "PRODUCTS":

Direction
   Strategy
   Goals
   Priorities
Design
Information
Resource Allocation
Performance Management of
   Teams and Units
Norms
   Learning
   Influence and Participation
   Systematic Decision Making
   Customer Orientation

team is managed (and manages itself) as a team. These dynamics will be described briefly below.

• *Developing a shared understanding.* A number of the management teams we studied failed to provide common direction. Different managers communicated different priorities and even goals to their units. Work team members reported receiving conflicting information concerning something as basic as how much importance to attribute to the teams that they were in. One executive team had some members who saw the team structures as existing for "communication, not execution," and others who saw the teams as mini-businesses, accountable for the operations and results of whole pieces of the organization. Teams lower in the organization cannot resolve conflicting understanding within the management team, and the resulting context of conflicting messages works against their own ability to resolve issues laterally.

• *Collaboratively planning and goal setting.* Effective management teams spend time as a team developing integrated plans and goals. Although these might be developed for each piece of the business, they are not finalized until they have been integrated. Members have input into each other's plans and goals and make sure their plans are supportive of one another.

• *Managing team performance.* Management teams, like all teams, have to assess the extent to which they are accomplishing their shared goals, and they are more effective if they are held collectively accountable. They have to develop ways to give feedback to one another, since their behavior both in the team and outside of it influences the team's performance and the performance of the various pieces of the organization. Team-level goals and rewards reinforce collaboration in the team.

These key internal processes are not unique to management teams. In fact, we have made the case throughout this book that all effective teams have them. However, they are especially important for management teams for two reasons: first, because management teams tend not to operate in accordance with these processes; second, because these processes are critical to the capability of the management team to provide a common direction, thereby allowing teams throughout the organization to be effective. In other words, ineffectiveness and lack of agreement at the management team level reverberate throughout the organization.

The New Manager

By now it is evident that the role of the manager in a team-based organization is significantly different than the managerial role in a segmented, hierarchical organization. And this difference goes beyond the variations in management style that have been emphasized in many earlier treatises on managing teams. Managers, individually and collectively, need to operate in a different mode in the team-based organization, and the content of the management role includes new facets and demands new capabilities.

Figure 8.7 illustrates the facets of the "new manager"—that is, the manager who can effectively manage in a team-based organization. The new manager will have to be able to both manage teams and be an effective team member; that is at the heart of the job. We have made the case that managers are likely to be members of teams that manage and of other integrating and improvement teams in the organization.

In order to effectively manage team-based organizations, managers will have to learn the skills required to design team structures and to make sure that teams are developed as effective performing units. Business-unit and executive team managers will have to design entire team-based organizations and create an organizational context that allows teams to be effective. This will require knowledge and skills that go beyond the structural aspects of teams and team dynamics to include the other components of organizational design.

At this point in the evolution of team-based organizations, the design of the organizational system as described in this book is still a new frontier. The logic of the team organization is still a foreign one, and a threatening one at that. The knowledge and experience underpinning the organizational transformation is patchy. For these reasons, managers of team-based organizations are also in the business of managing large-scale change: fundamental change in the character of the organization. Crafting such a change process and stimulating the organizational learning required for functioning in this new manner is integral to the management of team-based organizations as long as they are a departure from the status quo.

Management Team Skills

In addition to the knowledge and skills required by all teams, management teams at the organizational or business-unit level need some particular skills in order to carry out their responsibilities.

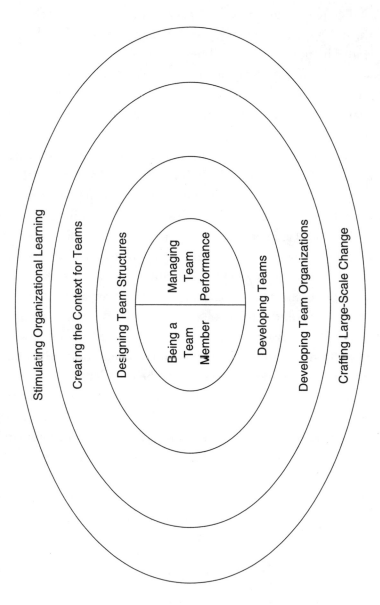

Figure 8.7. The New Manager.

Stimulating Organizational Learning

Creating the Context for Teams

Designing Team Structures

Being a Team Member

Managing Team Performance

Developing Teams

Developing Team Organizations

Crafting Large-Scale Change

These skills can be broken down into three categories: leadership skills, coaching skills, and skills in the area of organizational design and change.

- *Leadership skills*. Almost all the treatises on leadership emphasize creating a vision for the organization (for example, Bennis and Nanus, 1985). Management teams have the responsibility for creating and implementing processes by which that vision becomes a shared organizational vision—for example, a vision-building process that involves other parts of the organization (Block, 1993). This approach to create an organizational vision implies a commitment to communication, participation, and working through differences.
- *Coaching skills*. It has become fashionable to describe managers of teams as coaches and facilitators. Often missing, however, is a delineation of what it means to coach or facilitate in a team environment. The primary goal of team coaching is enabling teams to learn how to manage themselves. Managers can work toward this goal in the many ways discussed below.

Management teams can encourage work teams to develop goals, objectives, and work plans consistent with broader business strategies (although they charter teams by defining parameters for performance). They can also encourage teams to take their share of the responsibility for performance management processes.

If teams are to become self-managing, they need to be able to regulate their behavior; this regulation in turn requires team members to be aware of how well they are performing and what they can do to improve performance (Manz and Sims, 1989). Managers can help teams become more self-aware by asking the right questions and making sure feedback mechanisms are in place (Fisher, 1993); they can teach teams how to use systematic decision-making processes and encourage an attitude of continuous improvement. Managers can also ask teams to do their own tracking of performance and to analyze the reasons for any shortfalls. If managers are able to work in a participative fashion with teams to determine reasons for performance problems and to develop corrective action, the teams can take responsibility for improving performance.

Finally, managers can often provide technical mentoring. This requires an ability to provide information, teach skills, make resources available for technical development, and encourage teams to seek out those resources.

• *Skills in the area of organizational design and change.* Management teams cannot adequately perform their role as designers of the work unit without knowledge of organizational design. Management teams should understand basic principles of organizational and work design, including team design, team effectiveness, and the performance management processes. They also need to understand the processes involved in organizational change. Their knowledge needs to be both conceptual and practical. (The latter implies an in-depth understanding of their own organization and an openness to learning from their experiences in redesign.) This knowledge about organizations is in addition to their functional or technical knowledge. Management teams need to view such knowledge as important and legitimate for them, rather than solely the province of human resource or organizational consultants. Managers need this knowledge about organizational design and change in order to create the conditions for effective work teams and to help in the ongoing process of making sure the structural configuration meets current business needs.

Key Issues

Key issues concerning the distribution of roles in a team-based organization include the following:

1. Teams plan and execute their work, participate in their own performance management, and manage their interfaces with the rest of the organization.

2. Management teams create the context for effective team performance, establishing the direction, the design, and the norms. They also charter and orchestrate the performance management of teams and other units under their jurisdiction.

3. Effective management teams have internal dynamics that enable them to provide shared leadership in the organization.

4. Team-based organizations place new demands on team members and managers, often requiring extensive skill development.

Defining Empowerment
for the Team Environment

This chapter revisits the concept of empowerment, which has been discussed throughout the book. We first summarize key myths or partial truths about empowerment believed by many managers and employees in the team-based organizations that we studied. Then we contrast these partial truths with our own definition of empowerment and discuss its essential elements. Finally, we discuss how the organization can provide these essential elements and offer some examples.

Myths About Empowerment

Empowerment has become a fashionable concept, written about in the popular business literature and talked about in many corporate halls. It has become a catchword in the 1990s for many organizations needing to dramatically improve their performance and hoping that empowering their employees will give them that performance edge. This need to do something different and the desire for a quick fix have generated several myths about empowerment. We will discuss seven.

• *Empowerment is a business strategy.* Some organizations that have increased the use of teams and teaming mechanisms describe empowerment as a key business strategy. Companies following an empowerment strategy expect all teams—simply by virtue of their existence—to be empowered, and they believe that the result will be high performance. Rarely do these organizations define what they mean by *empowerment* or explain how it relates to strategy.

A business strategy is an organization's plan for applying its resources to ensure that it accomplishes its mission; that strategy defines how the organization will deliver value to its customers and maintain an advantage over its competitors. For teams to be empowered, they must understand the business strategy and the relationship of their goals to that strategy. In other words, empowerment includes both an understanding of organizational and team direction and an alignment between them. It is not possible to be empowered without knowing what one is being empowered to do. Empowerment is not the same as the business direction, but it does require knowing the business direction.

- *Empowerment is an individual characteristic.* One notion of empowerment is that it is an individual characteristic: empowered people take initiative, encourage self-expression, demand commitments, and take responsibility for their actions (Block, 1987), and empowered teams are composed of empowered individuals. This notion leads managers either to declare that they cannot do anything to empower others (because people must empower themselves) or to exhort people to behave differently and take risks. In both cases, the organization is taken off the hook; the organization does not need to change in order for people to be empowered. Yet behavior in organizations is a function of organizational policies, practices, structures, and systems—in short, organizational design—and the interaction of that design with individual skills, motivations, and behaviors (Mohrman, 1993). Of course, individuals do vary in their tendencies toward being proactive and taking risks, but the way that organizations are designed and managed can have a strong impact on individual behaviors.

- *Empowerment is a substitute for organizational design.* Like the previous myth, this one also involves wishful thinking and the belief that it is possible to empower teams and achieve performance results without changing the organization. In reality, however, empowerment is a function of organizational design; without conditions that foster it, it cannot exist. Access to relevant performance information, for example, is critical for empowerment: people cannot responsibly be given the authority to make decisions if they lack requisite information. This issue of information access is a function of organizational design; corporate information systems determine who has access to information. In similar fashion, all other organizational policies, structures, systems, and practices strongly influence the way that people and teams behave in organizations. Empowerment is not a substitute for organizational design; instead, organizational design is vital for empowerment.

• *Empowerment means complete autonomy.* One of the most serious misconceptions about empowerment is that it means complete autonomy. From this perspective, people, teams, and business units are empowered when *they* determine what to do and how to do it. Yet, as we have discussed throughout the book, teams are embedded in larger business units. Their goals and objectives are a function of the business unit in which they are embedded. Thus no team can have complete autonomy over the determination of its goals. Goal setting is a two-way process in which the larger business unit sets constraints and defines opportunities and then negotiates at multiple levels. In addition, work teams in knowledge-work settings often are interdependent with other teams and with people outside the teams; they typically are not self-contained. Thus goal setting and decision making frequently involve lateral processes as well. No work team can have the authority to make decisions that go beyond its scope. Integrating teams can be set up to make decisions of a broader scope, but their authority depends on their mandate. No team is an island; consequently, no team can have complete decision-making autonomy. Empowerment does imply, however, having the authority to make decisions within the team's scope and to influence decisions made elsewhere that impact the team's work.

The scope of decision-making authority needs to be clearly defined before a team can be empowered.

• *Empowerment requires that management stand aside.* We have seen many managers abdicate their role and responsibilities in their confusion about what it means to empower teams. Management becomes so fearful of limiting autonomy or constraining initiative that it defines its role as getting out of the way. With this belief, managers are less likely to provide direction, coaching, or feedback. If teams fail, managers frequently conclude that empowerment does not work. They then revert to a directive style of management, telling teams not only what to do but how and when to do it. This negative performance cycle and self-fulfilling prophecy can be avoided if managers define their role as providing direction and helping to build capability so that teams can be empowered.

• *Empowerment is self-management.* Self-management is the extent to which the members of a team perform their own management functions, including task integration, boundary integration, technical management, and performance management. Many managers believe that self-management is equivalent to empowerment; consequently, they transfer tasks inappropriately. In our view, a team can be empowered whether management is conducted by outside managers or by team members. The question is whether the leadership formula and the management structure fit with the work demands of the team. If management is performing tasks a team could perform for itself with equal effectiveness, the team is not empowered. On the other hand, the fact that a team is self-managing does not guarantee empowerment.

• *Empowered teams are the same as effective teams.* Empowered teams have the capability to make a difference in the attainment of their goals. Effective teams accomplish their goals efficiently, contribute to the effectiveness of larger business units in which they are embedded, continually improve their capabilities, and achieve high commitment from their members. Effectiveness refers to *outcomes*, including business, learning, and human outcomes. Empowerment, on the other hand, describes a set of directed capabilities. If designed appropriately, empowered teams are likely to be effective teams. Not all empowered teams, however, are effective teams. Teams with good capability and direction can fail to jell, and they can get off track. Management should not lose sight of the need to continue to monitor the effectiveness of all performing units, whether empowered or not.

These misconceptions about empowerment may create problems for those implementing a team-based organization. They may result in a lack of understanding of management's critical role in empowering teams: to provide direction within which teams and individuals operate, to develop team capabilities, and to design an empowering organizational context. They may distort the relationship between teams and managers, producing teams that view any management intervention as interference with their rightful autonomy. Anarchy and poor performance may be the consequence. In the remainder of this chapter, we will review a definition of team empowerment that addresses the embeddedness of the team in a larger organizational system and describe what managers and teams can do to enhance empowerment.

Empowerment Defined

The definition of empowerment that we have used throughout this book is *"the capability to make a difference in the attainment of individual, team, and organizational goals."* Thus empowerment has two major aspects: direction and capability. These are the two essentials of power; if we lack either one, power disappears (Burns, 1978). If we know what we are trying to accomplish (that is, we have direction) but lack capability, we will not accomplish our goal. For example, if a software design team has the goal of completing a fully compatible systems architecture in three months but does not have the necessary programming skills, it will not be able to accomplish its goal. Similarly, if a software team has state-of-the art programming skills but no clearly agreed upon product definition, it will not be able to successfully execute its design task. We will discuss both direction and capability in the pages that follow.

Direction

Having a clear organizational direction is empowering for two major reasons. First, it focuses attention and energy. People know where they are supposed to be going, and they can work with others to get there. If there is no direction, or if the direction is unclear, collective energy gets so dissipated that coordinated action cannot occur (Hackman, 1986). This issue is embodied in a story frequently told about a white rock. In one version, a manager and his group of direct reports went on a hike and agreed to meet at the white rock in three hours if they got separated. In three hours, the group had not coalesced at the white rock; several individuals were lost. The problem was that there was no white rock. There were several different rocks of various shades of off-white, beige, and gray, but none stood out as the meeting place. Since this experience, this manager and his subordinates often spend time clarifying the "white rock" for any change effort they are undertaking. They have a better understanding than most of why a clearly defined and understood direction is critical for empowerment.

Second, having a clear organizational direction provides an opportunity for individuals to relate their personal objectives to organizational objectives. Individuals derive meaning from being able to make a difference in activities, including work, that matter to them; that meaning connects people to their work and is motivating (Kahn, 1990). Organizations are in business to make a profit by delivering value-added products and services to customers. The tasks that individuals and teams do are determined by business objectives that are aligned with that goal. However, individuals can derive personal meaning from their interpretation of organizational objectives; they can fulfill their own aspirations in the process of working to meet business objectives. Personal goals vary, but they may involve having opportunities for learning, growth, accomplishment, affiliation with others, recognition, rewards, and career development. To the extent that organizations define a clear direction, individuals can relate their personal aspirations and their own developmental direction to organizational goals (Waterman, Waterman, and Collard, 1994).

Vertical and horizontal alignment among individual, team, and business-unit objectives is critical for empowerment, because alignment creates shared direction. Alignment cannot occur without understanding, and understanding requires two-way communication. In order for members of a team to effectively set team goals, they need to understand business-unit goals and priorities. Likewise, individuals cannot develop their goals without an understanding of team goals.

This mutual understanding occurs in the context of a multidirectional dialogue in which managers share their higher-level goals (providing opportunities for questions, input, and possible revisions), customers and other key stakeholders offer their viewpoint, and team members have the opportunity to influence higher-level goals. Team participation in higher-level goal setting is crucial; it helps team members understand goals across systemic levels and helps to ensure that team objectives can be compatible with unit objectives. Teams might, for example, help management see that modifications in the business-unit goals are needed. Team members also need to have influence over the determination of their own team goals. Shared direction is developed by team members participating in team and business-unit goal setting.

Our study found that a clear, well-aligned organizational direction contributes to employee beliefs about empowerment. A few of our survey questions addressed the issue of team efficacy, the belief of team members that their team could make a difference in the attainment of goals—a belief reflective of our definition of empowerment. We found that a clearly defined, well-understood business strategy, goal alignment at multiple systemic levels, and measurable goals were positively related to efficacy. In addition, co-workers' planning and goal setting also were positively related to efficacy. This sense of efficacy is strongly related to multiple performance outcomes. Teams whose members were confident that they could accomplish their goals were more likely to perform well, to be part of business units that performed well, to have satisfied members, and to demonstrate continuous improvement.

Capability

The second key aspect of our definition of empowerment is the capability to make a difference in the attainment of goals. Teams are empowered when they have the following:

• *The knowledge and skills (technical, business, interpersonal, and organizational) required to contribute to team and business-unit performance* (Lawler, 1986). Members of teams need to have the technical competence to do their part of the collective task and the willingness to continually learn so that they do not become obsolete. A basic understanding of business and the economics of the firm is important for grasping strategic direction. In a team-based environment, problem-solving, conflict resolution, decision-making, and organizational development knowledge and skills are as important as technical knowledge and skills. A human resource allocation system that provides access to people with the right skills should be in place so that teams are composed of members with the appropriate skills.

• *Information about goals and performance results at multiple levels: organization, business unit, and team* (Lawler, 1986). In addition, information about competitors, customer requirements, resource availability, and upcoming technology and organizational changes supports empowerment. (This kind of information is in addition to information about ongoing work processes required to do one's job.)

• *The material resources, including space, time, and equipment, required to perform work well.* Without access to the appropriate tools and resources, people cannot perform well. In our study, we found adequate resources to be an important component of capability.

- *The authority to make decisions about how the team does its work and to impact decisions made elsewhere that affect the team's work.* Decision making should take place where the expertise resides. This is generally as close as possible to where services and products are produced and often involves multiple interdependencies.

Our study found that these capability factors contribute to team members' belief that their team can accomplish what it sets out to do. Specifically, teams with access to the right mix of people and skills, information about team goals and performance results, decision-making authority, and reliable resource commitments have a strong sense of efficacy.

Empowering Teams

Since empowerment consists of having both direction and capability, anything that can be done organizationally to set direction and to build capability is empowering. Among these means are performance management systems, various integration processes and structures, strong support systems, management structures and roles, and thoughtful team design. In addition, managers and teams themselves can do things that foster empowerment. In this concluding section of the chapter, we offer some examples of how empowerment can be fostered and some of the issues that arise as organizations strive for empowerment. We start with suggestions and issues for direction setting and then move on to capability building.

Suggestions for Direction Setting

In any organization, senior management has the responsibility for setting direction, for defining the business it is in, and for formulating high-level plans for successfully operating that business. In a team-based organization, business direction has to be broadly and deeply shared, owned, and understood, and teams and team members need to understand how their activities relate to the broader business strategy. By involving teams and employees in the strategy formulation process, organizations help employees develop a shared understanding of the strategic direction and their relationship to it.

There are different methods by which to involve employees in the strategy formulation process. The executive management team can invite input or reactions from study groups or task forces with representatives that cut across organizational functions and disciplines or from existing teams and contributors at multiple levels in the company. (Other stakeholders, such as customers, may also be involved.)

Once strategy is formulated in the team-based organization, it should be communicated clearly and widely to all relevant stakeholders. Again, this can be done using a variety of communication mechanisms, including question-and-answer sessions, electronic mail, newsletters, memos, and white papers. Media advertising can be used to communicate the organization's strategic intent to a wider constituency. Education sessions can be used to help employees understand the strategy. The form of communication matters less than the fact that regular communication occurs.

The performance management of teams provides opportunities to communicate and review the business direction at multiple systemic levels. Each time a new team is established, the team's charter should include a description of the company's goals, the business unit's goals, and the team's preliminary mission and goals. As part of defining performance, teams should participate in determining their mission and goals, but participation needs to occur within the context of well-understood business goals. The training used to develop teams can provide information that increases understanding of strategic and business-unit objectives. The review process is critical, because it offers the opportunity to provide teams with feedback about how they are performing on their objectives (and how the business unit and company are performing). Finally, rewards can be designed that recognize achievement of team and business-unit objectives. Thus the organization can intentionally manage team performance in a way that focuses attention on the business direction.

Issues in Direction Setting

In knowledge-based organizations, business direction frequently changes. Team goals and objectives also change frequently, in response to changing customer or competitive requirements. When direction changes, there must be mechanisms in place to communicate the change to all stakeholders. Teams must receive enough information and feedback from customers, managers, and others so that they understand the reasons for change. Then they must adapt and modify their objectives and plans in accordance with the changed requirements. If it is difficult for a team that has been operating for a while (and therefore has established routines) to make necessary changes, managers or others may have to help team members adapt to the changed circumstances. This may include working with the team on establishing new objectives, asking for revised work plans and ideas for improvement, and making sure feedback mechanisms are in place to let the team know where it stands on addressing the changed requirements. It also may include changing the composition and skill mix of the team.

In a team-based organization, a common problem is a lack of alignment between what a team actually does and what it should be doing. In other words, the team goes off and does its own thing. This problem has two primary causes. First, the up-front definition of performance may have been inadequate; in other words, the team may not fully understand what it is supposed to do. Rather than spending the time to clarify direction with management and others, the team may take action based upon its limited understanding of business direction. In this case, managers need to work closely with the team on clarifying business direction and specific team objectives. In a discussion of specifics, differences in understanding emerge and can be reconciled. Second, the team may understand what it is supposed to do and have clear agreement on paper but disagree with the defined direction (and therefore fail to act in accordance with it). When the performance direction differs from the alleged direction, considerable dialogue between managers and the team is again required. Managers need to question the team's activities and its reluctance to hike to the appropriate white rock, but they must also be open to input from the team that indicates its destination should be the glacial lake. Managers and teams should never ignore questions of direction, because the cost in time, resources, and rework can be considerable. Slippage in alignment is inevitable during the course of work performance. Therefore, creating shared agreement about direction is an *ongoing* process, not an event that happens just at the beginning of a project.

A similar problem occurs when individual activities are not aligned with the work of the team. In other words, individuals go off and do their own thing. In the ideal situation, a team is aware of this problem and can work with straying team members so that their contributions help the team reach its mutual objectives. Peer feedback can be very effective and powerful. However, if a team does not directly address this issue (or is unsuccessful in its attempt), it may be up to managers to make sure that individual alignment occurs. Again, managers need to work together with team members so that they openly address this issue. Managers should not sidestep the team, simply telling the wayward team member what to do. Consensus about direction is built from open discussion of specific alignment problems. Sometimes the lack of alignment within a team is due not to internal team issues but to a lack of alignment among managerial objectives. This is particularly likely for overlay teams—those representing different disciplines or functional areas. These teams have the responsibility for surfacing the problem, and managers have the responsibility for working with one another on defining shared business objectives. It will not help to work on the problem only within the team if the members are responding to different directives from their managers. Managers must work laterally with their peers on creating a shared business direction, in order to create the infrastructure for team alignment.

Another direction-setting issue concerns the unwillingness of teams to accept stretch goals—those requiring unusually high levels of performance. If team members believe that goals are not achievable (particularly if they have had no involvement in setting them), they will neither accept the goals nor work toward them. For example, several new product development teams that we studied said that the schedules that they agreed to with their managers were unachievable and that they were using their own private "shadow schedule." On the other hand, teams we studied that had participated in setting their own stretch goals, in response to strategic, competitive, or customer requirements, were more likely to have unusually high levels of performance. This argues for managers' working closely with teams so that they understand the competitive realities that call for stretch goals and making sure that team members are involved in the goal-setting process.

The final issue concerning direction setting that we address here is a consequence of believing in mistaken notions about empowerment. If empowerment is viewed as complete autonomy, teams reject the right of management and others to set direction that constrains them. If management views its role as standing aside (in an effort to fully empower teams), it will abdicate its responsibility to set direction. Empowerment demands that managers lead the effort to define and communicate a clear business direction and make sure that team goals and objectives are set and aligned with business imperatives. This view of empowerment needs to be communicated and understood throughout the team-based organization.

Suggestions for Capability Building

Teams develop capability by having the knowledge and skills, information, resources, and authority needed to accomplish performance objectives. What organizations can do to move these conditions downward to all employees has been discussed extensively by Lawler (1986, 1992) and Lawler and Mohrman (1989). Rather than repeat that discussion here, we will simply provide examples particularly relevant to the team-based organization.

- *Knowledge and skills.* Managers are responsible for making sure that an effective human resource allocation system is in place so that members can be assigned to the appropriate team. In a team-based organization, team members need to have some understanding of the knowledge bases of their teammates, and they may need to be cross-trained in more than one specialty. Thus they need opportunities for learning across disciplines, including rotational assignments (when they make sense). The organization can adopt reward systems, such as skill-based pay, that encourage cross-training or the learning of new skills. The organization can make sure that "just-in-time" training is available so that teams can receive help in problem-solving, conflict resolution, and decision-making processes when needed. It can also ensure that development opportunities exist for team leaders and managers who are learning new roles.

- *Information.* As discussed in Chapter Six, managers need to make sure that information about goals, priorities, and performance results is shared with teams. They need to make sure communication channels are formalized to enable multidirectional problem solving by those whose work is interdependent. They may also choose to foster the creation of forums where teams have the opportunity to interact directly with customers and with suppliers. Finally, managers must help team members feel free to give them feedback about how well they are supporting the team and what the team needs from them in order to perform better.

- *Resources.* Teams must have access to the resources they need to do their work—budget, space, computers, and so on. Resources are not unlimited, however, and priorities based on strategic objectives need to be determined. Team-based organizations must develop resource allocation systems that invite input from teams as well as managers and that are fair and understandable. As discussed in Chapter Eight, this is the responsibility of management teams at both the business-unit and corporate levels.

- *Authority.* Teams must have the authority to make decisions within their scope of activity (and that scope should be clearly defined). The team's authority needs to be broad enough so that the team makes decisions about both what it does and how it does it. The definition of scope of authority should occur when the team is chartered. When a team is considering issues that involve other teams, it cannot resolve those issues on its own; it must either obtain input from those teams or escalate the decision to a forum that has a broader scope (such as an integrating team, a cross-team, or a management team). In addition, it has the responsibility to contribute to decisions made at a higher systemic level. For example, the industry-specific teams at Netco regularly communicate information about customers' technical needs to the corporate technical center. These teams view their responsibility as both making decisions about their industry and contributing to the broader business.

Decision-making authority goes hand in hand with accountability. Managers need to hold teams accountable for the decisions they make; the members of a team should be jointly held responsible for the success or failure of that team. Even when team members have individual objectives (and most do), those objectives exist in the context of team objectives, and management communication about accountability should reflect this.

Issues in Capability Building

It takes time to develop the capabilities needed in the team-based organization, and capability-related difficulties inevitably emerge. Managers should view their role as both designing the team-based organization for capability and appropriately diagnosing and taking action to rectify capability-related problems. We provide examples of common symptoms of capability problems and potential solutions below.

• *Knowledge and skills.* A team that appears to be floundering may have a capability-related problem. Perhaps members lack critical technical knowledge, for example. If this is the problem, it can be addressed by adding new members, changing members, or providing training. On the other hand, the problem may have to do with the inability of members to transcend their specialized understanding and develop a common understanding. This can be diagnosed by asking different members about what the problem is and assessing the degree to which their interpretations reflect different and seemingly unbridgeable disciplinary thought-worlds. This problem can be addressed by creating interdisciplinary responsibility for events such as meetings with customers or customer focus groups and encouraging a dialogue focused on the customer. In addition, training can be developed to highlight the differences in disciplinary perspectives, and role playing can be used to allow individuals to practice voicing the perspectives from different disciplines. Longer-term solutions may include developing career systems that encourage lateral movement and job rotation.

• *Information.* A team that does not take active responsibility for monitoring its performance may lack the information it requires to do so. It is management's responsibility to make sure that the appropriate information systems and data bases are in place, and it is the team's responsibility to indicate if needed information is not available or too hard to obtain or to understand. For example, management needs to ensure that a team has access to data needed to develop performance measures. On the other hand, a team needs to request additional support if it receives feedback on financial performance but team members do not understand the financial measures. Perhaps the firm's financial officer might meet with the team to explain financial data or offer training in finance. A team should examine whether it has the information it needs to do performance monitoring; if information is missing, the team should alert management and others to the problem and help work to solve it.

Frequent communication slipups among teams reveal problems with information sharing. As discussed in Chapter Six, communication channels may need to be specified and formalized so that necessary communication takes place.

Information overload may be a problem if norms are not developed around what information should be shared. This is particularly true for organizations using electronic and voice mail systems. Information overload could be addressed by a task force charged with developing guidelines for information sharing. Another possible solution is technology that gives teams and individuals the capability to filter the messages they receive.

• *Resources*. Teams frequently complain that they do not understand how resource decisions are made. This illustrates the need for both a systematic process for determining how resources are allocated and communication channels that help teams understand the process and have fair access to it.

• *Authority*. A common problem that occurs in organizations is that teams do not understand the scope of their decision-making authority. They may assume far more authority than they have, or they may be reluctant to make decisions without checking with management even in areas that are within their scope. Clearly, managers need to explicitly define scope of authority when they charter teams, and then they need to clarify scope of authority as issues come up. For example, if a software team makes a decision that involves the systems architecture of the other teams, managers may need to intervene and make sure that this decision is checked with the appropriate integrating body. On the other hand, if a team refers too many decisions to managers, managers need to work with the team and encourage it to develop its own solutions.

Developing clear guidelines and norms for escalating issues helps. When chartering teams, management needs to specify its expectations regarding escalation. For example, one management team we studied developed the guideline that any decision on a product's critical path that the team could not resolve in five days should be escalated to the management team. Determining rules for escalation is not sufficient, however. Managers need to work with teams in an ongoing way, clarifying when escalation processes should and should not be used. As discussed in Chapter Six, escalation of an issue does not mean that the team gives up ownership of it. A management team can collaboratively work with the team to determine how difficult issues should be resolved.

It may be difficult for managers to learn the behaviors that strike an appropriate balance between control and abdication. Managers may find it difficult to let teams make decisions within their scope of authority, jumping in with their preferred solution even when the team's alternative solution is fine. Managers need to work on allowing teams to make the decisions they are responsible for. On the other hand, managers cannot abdicate. If a team is not able to solve a problem, or if its solution will not work, managers need to step in and work with the team to help it determine an appropriate solution. Dialogue with the team can help managers calibrate their own control or abdication tendencies.

Team Responsibility for Empowerment

So far in this chapter, we have stressed the management actions and organizational design elements that foster empowerment. But teams share responsibility for their empowerment; they are partners in an ongoing process. They cannot be empowered without their consent and participation. In this final section, we suggest the role teams must play in setting direction and building capabilities and comment briefly on some of the issues that arise with this role.

Teams have a key role in determining their goals and objectives, within the context of business goals and objectives and customer requirements. Team members "own" these goals and objectives; consequently, they share the responsibility and accountability for accomplishing them. Thus teams are partners in determining their direction.

Teams also share the responsibility for developing capability. They have a responsibility for self-diagnosing capability shortfalls and then taking corrective action. If a team lacks needed skills, it needs to approach management and request that the problem be addressed. A team might request that a particular engineer be assigned to them, for example, because he is the only person in the organization with the needed robotics skills. Similarly, a team whose progress is impeded by an inability to resolve conflicts needs to be proactive in requesting help. Perhaps it needs consultation from the human resource department or (if it is reluctant to escalate issues that are beyond its scope) direction from its managers. Another team might realize that it does not have sufficient information to develop a work plan and suggest to the information system department that it be given access to a data base to which it has not yet been connected. The general point is that teams need to be proactive in procuring the tools and resources they need to perform. Organizations can help teams in this by being responsive to their needs.

Teams may be reluctant to voice their needs to management. This reluctance may stem from a belief that nothing will happen when requests are made or that it is dangerous to admit problems. Management can reduce this reluctance by working as a partner with teams and encouraging joint dialogue about what supports are needed and what barriers need to be removed. If dialogue is followed up by corrective action, teams will learn that the organization is serious about addressing team problems and developing capability. In addition, managers should encourage teams to be proactive and should recognize teams for taking appropriate initiative. This encouragement and recognition help to build an organizational culture that supports proactive behavior.

Teams may be unaware of capability shortfalls or unwilling to admit problems. They may view asking for help as airing their dirty laundry and be unwilling to disclose their vulnerabilities. Again, management has to work as a partner with the teams it supports so that they receive necessary help. Managers need to initiate conversations with teams about problems, particularly if teams do not take the initiative. Managers need to communicate that it is not acceptable to ignore problems that prevent task accomplishment, and they need to work with teams on addressing these problems. What needs to be communicated is that managers care and will help solve problems without undue focus on blame.

Another frequent problem occurs when teams are expected to be self-managing. Teams whose may members view their role as simply performing their technical tasks may resist assuming responsibility for performing managerial functions; they may have no interest in developing a self-managing capacity. Managers need to be clear in communicating their expectations as part of the team chartering process. As discussed in Chapter Five, managers need to work with teams to specifically delineate what tasks the team will perform and what tasks management will perform. Responsibility charting may need to be done several times as team members learn how to handle managerial functions. Once agreement is reached about who will perform specific tasks, reviews should be scheduled to monitor how well work is going.

As we have repeatedly emphasized, empowerment takes time and work. Building an empowered organization occurs over time, as shared understanding of direction deepens and capability is developed. Just calling organizations or teams empowered does not make them so. Exhorting people to be empowered may not make them more willing to exert influence and take risks. Managers and teams are partners in the process of empowerment. They engage in dialogue that clarifies and deepens the understanding of shared direction. They work together to develop the capability that leads to team self-sufficiency. They understand that self-sufficiency has no meaning unless the team's scope of authority is clearly defined and understood. Managers and teams understand that empowerment implies accountability for results. Mistakes are made but learned from as managers and teams develop new ways of working with one another.

Key Issues

Key issues regarding empowerment in a team-based organization include the following:

1. The desire of organizations to dramatically improve their performance without having to make major changes has generated several myths about empowerment:

Empowerment is a business strategy.

Empowerment is an individual characteristic.

Empowerment is a substitute for organizational design.

Empowerment means complete autonomy.

Empowerment requires that management stand aside.

Empowerment is self-management.

Empowered teams are the same as effective teams.

2. Empowerment is defined as "the capability to make a difference in the attainment of individual, team, and organizational goals."

3. Many elements of the organization, including management, play a role in empowering teams by setting business direction and building team capability (that is, making sure team members have the knowledge and skills, information, resources, and power needed to accomplish performance objectives).

4. Teams share the responsibility for their empowerment by participating in determining their goals and being proactive about developing team capability.

5. Developing an empowered team-based organization takes time, work, and learning.

10

· ·

Developing Organizational
Support Systems

Organizational support systems are part of the organizational infrastructure that facilitates carrying out the processes necessary to do the work; to manage, control, coordinate, and improve it; and to manage the people who are doing it. These systems are frequently developed at the corporate level because of the investment and specialized expertise they require and their role in creating common ways of doing things that permit coordination, task integration, and a company identity. These systems must support the conduct of work in the organization and must fit with the way the organization is designed. As the design of an organization changes and as work is conducted in new ways, the support systems must change to fit the new logic. This chapter discusses support systems in the team-based organization. It briefly describes the key systems that are required, the challenges in designing support systems that fit the team-based environment, and the design and maintenance of these systems in the dynamic, lateral organization.

The core of this book is a five-step design model that includes structures and processes that are important to the functioning of team-based organizations. The basic transformation processes through which work is done—that is, the processes by which various inputs are converted to products or services that have value to the customer—are the underlying targets of the design sequence.

Integration processes (communication, decision making, and direction setting) and performance management processes (defining, developing, reviewing, and rewarding performance)—all addressed in the design sequence—enable the transformation processes. These three types of processes can take place in such an informal way that the people engaged in them are operating with tacit knowledge or even "flying by the seats of their pants." Alternatively, people can be guided by systematic procedures, steps, technologies, techniques, programs, and practices that have been formalized by the organization. Support systems are created by the organization with the intent of guiding the nature and the quality of the processes that take place. The more important organizational processes described in the design model should not be left to chance but require the establishment of systems that support their occurrence. Traditional systems, designed to support the hierarchical, work-breakdown mode of functioning, have to be fundamentally changed to support the team-based organization.

The Importance of Support Systems

Many of the organizations we studied had adopted a team-based design to allow better responsiveness to customers and to eliminate the bureaucratic logjam often caused by hierarchical and procedural control. While these organizations were flattening, dispersing staff groups, and creating empowered units, they often initiated major process improvement efforts to systematize the way work was done throughout the business. In addition, they reduced the extent to which control was vested in people—in managers and staff groups—and increased both the self-control of performing units and the control inherent in the systematic processes.

Systematic processes provide a basis for collaborative work, build in the steps to ensure high quality, and prevent employees from having to reinvent procedures repeatedly. This is consistent with the recommendations of process-reengineering advocates, who recommend organizing around processes (Hammer and Champy, 1993; Davenport, 1993). Processes are structured and measured sets of activities designed to produce an output of value to the customer (Davenport, 1993, p. 5). Organizing around processes emphasizes *how* things are done within an organization rather than *what* is done. Support systems are enablers of systematic processes.

In our research, we found the presence of systematic processes for decision making to have a strong and consistently positive impact on team performance. We measured, among other things, the degree to which there were rigorous tools for making trade-offs, the degree to which decisions were data-based, and the degree to which the costs and benefits of various alternatives were evaluated. When we investigated more closely, we found that these kinds of decision-making practices were sometimes the result of the informal influence of managers and team members, but most often they were the result of formal organizational systems and procedures by which decisions were expected to be made. The Alpha Program, for example, has a number of stages during the new product development process at which the teams are required to collect customer reactions to the product. Strict rules prescribe the type and level of customer reaction that have to be attained before teams can go on to the next developmental phase. These processes enable the resolution of contention between marketers (who are charged with ensuring that the product meets the needs and demands of the customers) and the engineers developing the product (who focus instead on the technical niceties of the product and the extent of reuse of technology).

An excellent example of the importance of systematic processes can be found in the pharmaceutical industry: there are systematic processes for generating data about the effects of a potential drug and for interpreting those data, and there are rules to determine under what conditions to proceed to the next step of development.

These systematic processes facilitate the resolution of disagreement and allow decisions to be made. In pharmaceutical companies, contributors bring different disciplines and orientations. Toxicologists are charged with finding toxicological impacts that might stop the development of the drug. Chemists and biologists are charged with finding efficacy. The systematic processes provide a guide to producing, displaying, and interpreting information that enables these various contributors to get beyond their thought-worlds and agree on a decision and course of action. Thus systematic processes enable the generation of divergent information, but they also provide a road map to help participants converge on a decision.

Much current writing emphasizes the importance of information technology in enabling and supporting new lateral ways of organizing (Galbraith, 1994; Allen and Scott Morton, 1994; Scott Morton, 1991). Computer systems are the most obvious tools that support modern knowledge work. Many of the systematic processes we discuss here are or can be facilitated by or embedded in computer systems. As teams have become a more prevalent reality in organizational life, computer-based tools have been developed to support their work: "groupware" is a category of systems designed explicitly to support group work (such as meetings or jointly written documents).

In our team-based organizations, we found that the higher the adequacy of information technology, the better the teams performed. Adequacy was measured in terms of the extent to which people were both electronically connected to the people with whom they had to work and shared common languages and data bases. Some of our organizations felt that their computer support badly lagged behind their new ways of doing work, but several others felt that the computer systems they had developed gave them a competitive advantage. Among the benefits they cited for computer systems were the ability to communicate within and between teams and with customers, suppliers, and partners via computer networks and the widespread or universal access to data bases. Access to common data was seen by these organizations as important in fostering the shared understanding necessary for lateral coordination and integration.

The importance of information systems for lateral linkage is underscored in organizations whose various parties are separated in time and location. These systems enable integration across different locations and time zones and are a repository for organizational memory that enables different people to work interactively with information generated anywhere in the organization (Scott Morton, 1991).

Key Systems and Processes

As we noted above, support systems provide the infrastructure for three kinds of organizational processes: transformation processes, organizational integration processes (which enable coordinated functioning of various subsystems of the organization in support of overall system performance), and performance management processes (which enable the performance of various units to be managed). All of these processes are performed differently in a team-based organization than in a traditional organization, and the systems that support them must change correspondingly.

The systems that constituted the infrastructure of the traditional, bureaucratic organization were painstakingly built and implemented over a period of decades. Components were added as environments changed, organizations grew, and specialized knowledge increased. Many organizations began the journey to become more lateral from a starting point of rigid, patchwork systems controlled by increasingly powerful staff groups whose careers rarely included experience in the operating aspects of the organization.

A revolution is now under way in how we think about these support systems, their technological capacity, and the way in which specialized expertise in these areas is being organized and applied (Galbraith and Lawler, 1993). The technological capacity to support the lateral organization and the increasing need to provide flexibility and increase employee involvement are driving these changes in support systems. The list below shows the major differences in support system orientation between the traditional organization and the team-based organization:

Traditional	Team-Based
Individually oriented chain-of-command systems	Collective performing systems
Manager-dependent systems	Dispersed, manager-independent systems
Hierarchically integrated systems	Laterally integrated systems
Management-controlled systems	Self-managed, dispersed-control systems
Systems promoting stability	Systems facilitating dynamic adjustment
Systems promoting uniformity	Systems promoting flexibility
Systems based on general discipline models	Systems based on enterprise-specific models

Historically, support systems adapted to the prevailing image of the organization as composed of individual performers arrayed along a chain of command. They treated the individual as the focus of the support, they were mediated by managers, and they assumed and supported organizational integration by hierarchical means. For example, information systems to support performance measurement in the traditional organization often measured individual behavior, aggregated those measurements over the several individuals working under one manager, and considered the aggregated measurements to be a "measure" of the manager's performance. Aggregated and individual data were returned to the manager, who was expected to mediate the use of the data. Phone companies, for instance, used hundreds of individually oriented measures, such as average time to answer a call or time for a call to go through, but they had no measures of performing units (how they were doing in terms of overall financial performance, for example, or how they were meeting the needs of the customers). In a team-based organization, on the other hand, support systems are designed to support teams and other collective performing units, to facilitate lateral interaction within and among teams, and to offer performers direct, unmediated access.

In their more advanced embodiment, hierarchically oriented support services were designed not to support managerial control but to actually manage and control managers. Staff groups were charged with developing systems that kept departments from delivering too much merit pay, having too much head count, and so forth. At the most extreme, staff groups were held accountable for these results, and managers adopted the stance of getting away with as much as possible. The support systems managed and controlled managers in much the same way directive supervisors managed people. The team-based organization, on the other hand, disperses control and requires increased self-management; support systems need to be designed to fit this new philosophy and mode of operation.

Support systems, which traditionally were bastions of stability and uniformity of practice, defined many aspects of the corporate culture. For example, pay systems defined what was equitable; career systems shaped attitudes regarding commitment and reinforced the segmentation of the organization; budgeting practices influenced attitudes toward investment and risk; measurement/appraisal systems told people what was really important. The existence of large, powerful staff groups in traditional organizations served as impediments to change and flexibility. Support systems in these traditional organizations were based on general discipline knowledge. Traditional performance appraisal practices, for example, were based on the learnings of generations of specialists about what would stand up in court and how to achieve reliable differentiation among employees. The goal was often to create objectified rating forms that yielded high interrater comparability. In a team-based situation, however, an organization may not be able to or want to differentiate between employees. Furthermore, dispersed control means that the views of quite different stakeholders are critical; objectifying works against the open-systems learning model of a team-based organization. Increasingly, systems are being developed based on the work and the organizational model of the enterprise. The underlying philosophy is to generate systems that are flexible enough to meet the needs of a variety of units within the organization.

We will now briefly discuss some examples of the various system reorientations required to support the transformation processes, integration processes, and performance management processes of team-based organizations.

Transformation Processes

In a manufacturing environment, transformation processes are those that transform the raw materials into the finished product. They are supported by tools and technologies that, when applied in certain sequences, will accomplish the transformation. A manufacturing plant or line is really a system of steps, tools, and technologies that support the transformation process. Comparable knowledge-work systems exist to support the processing of information and the creation and use of knowledge. When teams are the performing units, these systems must be developed and specified in terms of the team. They must support individuals with different knowledge bases and algorithms working concurrently, using common data sets, and jointly solving complex problems, designing products, and delivering services. When designed to function in this manner, the systems to support the conduct of work also support the integration of work, serving as tools for teams that are self-managing their technical integration within and between teams.

Integration Processes

Chapter Six makes the case for the importance of properly designing the related integration processes of communication, direction
setting, and decision making when work is being performed by a
constellation of interrelated teams. Since the conduct of knowledge
work frequently entails the integrated application of multiple
knowledge bases (estimating the cost of a system requires joint specification of the system by sales, service, and systems experts, for
example), the line between the systems that support the transformation processes and those that are organizational integrating supports is blurry (and sometimes even nonexistent).

The most obvious communication support systems are the myriad computer-based information technologies that exist. Local-area
networks, global networks, video-conferencing, electronic mail, and
common data bases are all part of the communication infrastructure. By now everyone is familiar with the problems of incompati-
bility that for so long have hampered the use of such networks. Even
though recent technologies are rapidly overcoming many of those
problems, it is still common for cross-functional teams to find themselves unable to communicate adequately. The required change in
mindset is illustrated by Analytico, which had a long heritage of
attracting and retaining top-notch engineers. Analytico's long-
standing pledge to supply each engineer with the tools the engineer
preferred clashed with the need to have concurrent, team-based task
execution and was gradually changed. Information technology has
become such an important knowledge-work tool that its support systems must be among the first established when creating a team-
based organization. As mentioned earlier, these information
technologies also provide the infrastructure for many of the other
needed support systems.

Team-based organizations will have to come to terms with the
ongoing tension between the potential use of technology for
increased monitoring and surveillance and its capacity to enable
self-management and decentralized decision making (Zuboff, 1984;

Walton, 1989). Consider computerized systems that extend human capability to keep track of and monitor performance. Call-center systems, for example, can keep track of the time spent on each customer call, the time that customers wait for a phone to be answered, and the number of sales that are made by phone. These data can be used by managers to closely monitor the performance of customer-service work teams and individuals. The data can also be used by work teams to figure out how they can improve their responsiveness to customers and their ability to effectively sell new products. Electronic mail, another valuable technology, can be used by work teams to get technical assistance from employees throughout the company. But electronic mail has another side as well: managers can covertly read electronic mail messages and keep track of who is communicating with whom. How the new information technology is used (and potentially abused) depends upon the company's philosophy and operating practices, but the resolution of this tension will help shape the limits of self-management.

Distributed information is required to support self-management and lateral decision making. To avoid overloading employees with information, much of which is irrelevant, organizations need to seek out applications that allow selection of relevant displays and reports. Perhaps the most important component of this issue of technology is the philosophy of broad ownership and access to data.

Systems that support direction-setting processes are among the most important integrating agents in a team-based organization. In firms transitioning to teams, existing goal-setting systems that solicit potential department goals, establish business goals based on corporate and business strategies, and cascade business goals back to departments can form a good basis for the new team-based direction-setting system. The goals must lend themselves to being expressed in terms of teams rather than departments, however, and provision must be made for teams to negotiate their goals laterally with other teams as well as with business-unit management.

Reward systems for managers in traditional organizations were often used to support corporate direction. Rewards for department managers, for instance, were often based on the degree to which the goals that they negotiated for their department were achieved. Underlying this practice were the old managerial role and the old assumption that the performance of a department was a function primarily of how well the manager managed the unit and negotiated unit goals. The difference in team-based organizations is that entire teams and business units are negotiating goals, directing their own performance, and managing aspects of their own performance. If reward systems are to be used to set direction in team-based settings, all the participants in the performing unit need to be rewarded for the unit's performance; a reward system consistent with nested goals would reward a team member for how well the team did, how well the business unit did, and how well the larger organization did. Rewards for individual performance may not be logically consistent with some team-based organizations, since teams are the core performing units and it is difficult to separate out each individual's impact.

Performance Management Processes

Because the essence of managing a business is managing the performance of its performing units, we will devote considerable attention to support system needs in this area. Chapter Seven enumerated the four basic processes that make up performance management: defining, developing, reviewing, and rewarding performance. These processes are potentially supported by a host of organizational systems.

• *Defining performance*. The systems just discussed that support direction setting (such as business planning, goal setting, and reward systems) also support the defining of performance. Organizations can help further guide the performance definition and performance planning process through the establishment of team-based performance management systems that follow the model described in

Chapter Seven. As we discussed in that chapter, performance planning in team-based settings requires input from all the stakeholders in the team's performance and should result in clear performance expectations for team members. Project scheduling and PERT-charting are systems that can drive project team planning. Among the performance definition and planning systems that were extremely efficacious in some of the new product development organizations we studied were quality functional deployment and the "house of quality" approach (Hauser and Clausing, 1988).

• *Developing performance*. The development process results in the creation of new capabilities. Team development should be supported by systems for organizational development and training. There can be no doubt that team-based organizations benefit to the extent that team and organizational development are supported by personnel (such as organizational effectiveness consultants or expert facilitators) who can apply development expertise and systems. As we have stressed throughout this book, team-based organizations are multilevel systems. The broadest level is the entire organization; the narrowest is the individual. Development support systems must be prepared to deal with all systemic levels. At the individual level, these systems must address team members' technical and organizational process capabilities. At the team level, they must address team capabilities by giving the team the necessary tools, organizing it appropriately, staffing it properly, and ensuring that team members determine appropriate strategies for accomplishing work. At the business-unit level, too, development systems address organizing, tooling, and staffing, but the domain is larger: organizing at the business-unit level (and higher), for example, requires designing an organization of teams. That, of course, has been the subject of this book. The organizational self-design model (Mohrman and Cummings, 1989; see Chapter One) can be the basis for systems that support team and organizational development processes.

Other support systems collaborate with development support systems in the development of teams and team organizations. Two that are fundamental are team-oriented information systems and human resource allocation (staffing) systems. We have been struck by the degree of variation that exists in the ability of organizations to keep track of their teams and the people in them. In some of the organizations we studied, our request for a list of teams and their members could not be complied with without a major organizational effort. These organizations continue to use their traditional human resource information systems (HRIS) and cannot easily answer simple questions such as, "To which team does John Doe belong?" or "Who is with the Beta Program?" Ascertaining more fundamental data for us (tracking performance numbers for various teams or determining the adequacy of skills represented by a team's members, for example) likewise necessitated major contortions in organizations whose information systems were developed for an individual-oriented, departmental organization. Team-based organizations often have to superimpose their own team-based information systems over those demanded for traditional corporate needs. Teams in several organizations we studied found that they had to operate with a dual accounting system—one that kept track of financial data by team for the local organization's purposes and simultaneously aggregated it by function for broader corporate purposes.

The change in mindset that is required is illustrated by one of the most frequently heard laments in team-based organizations: that managements frequently reassign a team member to a special project or to another team without attending to the detrimental effects that assignment can have on the team the individual was already working with. Unilaterally reassigning key members can significantly and adversely affect the team's performance; some depleted teams have been known to make no progress at all until the key member returned. One way to understand this phenomenon is that managers are allocating their human resources according to the logic of the traditional organization and using traditional informal processes. They think of each person as occupying a job that can be refilled or stand vacant for a while without interrupting the organization's work. But team members are part of a carefully balanced set of activities and interdependencies. In team-based organizations, human resource allocation is a process that must be coordinated both laterally and vertically. It is difficult to imagine that this kind of coordination can be adequately handled informally. Systems for human resource allocation are extremely important tools. Team-based organizations that lack such systems may be performing under their potential in ways they are not aware of because they are not able to see the systemic repercussions of moving people around.

Career opportunities and opportunities for growth are also different in team organizations; growth no longer means simply moving up. In team-based organizations, the opportunity for promotion to managerial roles is less than in more traditional organizations, for example, but the opportunity for development through wide-ranging experiences that both broaden and deepen task and leadership skills is greatly increased. Team-based organizations must set up systems that take advantage of these opportunities by building base-pay systems that acknowledge these competencies and encourage lateral movement by clearly delineating experiences that are prerequisite for various leadership opportunities. These opportunities are the stuff of which people fashion careers and by which they remain employable either in the host organization or in another organization (Waterman, Waterman, and Collard, 1994). This new concept of career will require fundamental reorientation by employees and underlines both the organization's and the individual's responsibility for planning experiences and roles in a way that affords continuous growth.

• *Reviewing performance.* The process of reviewing performance, like other performance management processes, demands support systems that operate at all systemic levels: individual, team, business unit, organization. In some cases, performing units have the kind of performance that can be tracked on a real-time basis and can be put into a data base accessible to those in the performing unit. In other cases, performance may need to be judged by those who are directly affected by it, such as customers. In the latter cases, systems need to be set up that periodically gather performance data from stakeholders and make those data available to members of the performing unit. For instance, many public utilities divide their customer base into geographical groups and assign a cross-functional team to each customer group. Each month a separate polling organization surveys a random sample of each customer group about the utility's performance and feeds the results back to the customer team for problem solving and planning for the next period. Internally, if shared services are to seriously view teams as their customers, a similar review process should be in place to enable customer teams to assess the services they receive.

• *Rewarding performance.* We have already described reward systems as mechanisms that should support the process of direction setting. Reward systems in team-based organizations must fit the logic of the organization in order for people to feel equitably rewarded. In light of this axiom, individuals could (and generally should) be rewarded for the performance of all the performing units to which they belong and contribute. This implies a multilevel reward system based on team performance, business-unit performance, and organizational performance and may imply recognition of multiple-team membership. Although such systems are complex, reluctance in many organizations stems not from the perceived difficulty of implementation but from a fundamental disconnect between espoused and actual beliefs of management. Many managers who use rhetoric extolling lateral organization and teamwork are products of a hierarchical, management-oriented system. Despite their rhetoric, they often continue to believe that good performance is primarily a function of superstars and reflects the skills of the manager.

The reward system in a team-based organization should reflect the fact that advancement in such an organization is more likely to involve lateral development than traditional "promotion." As we noted earlier, organizations should use base-pay systems that reward and encourage multiple competencies.

The Relationship Between Processes and Support Systems

Although our research indicates the importance of support systems for guiding processes necessary to team and organizational functioning, it is not the case that the presence of team-based support systems automatically results in good processes. Support systems in team-based organizations have some of the same potential problems as their counterparts in traditional organizations (and others that are more salient in the team-based model). These will be discussed below.

Bureaucratization of Support Systems

Because support systems are primarily formal, people have a tendency to "bureaucratize" them—to follow procedures rather blindly without fully appreciating the need for or intent of each system. In one firm we studied, for instance, new product development endeavors were required to follow a set of formal development stages, each of which was to be officially completed with the signature of each of the various functional representatives on a formal document; this document certified agreement with the product design at that stage and commitment to plans for the next stage. Such agreement, the organization knew, is pivotal to new product development success. Nevertheless, the procedure was gradually reduced to a bureaucratic exercise. When pressure grew to speed up the development process, teams sometimes signed off on stage-completion documents even though full agreement had not be reached. Lack of agreement on earlier stages invariably came back to haunt projects during later stages, forcing project participants to loop back to earlier issues in order to make progress. A system designed to ensure that convergence among the various contributors was achieved at each stage was being only mechanistically followed (and was therefore distorted). The result was to slow the development process.

Confusion Between Systems and Administration

Formalized support systems often come to be viewed as administrative burdens, and often they actually are. Some of the perception (and reality) of administrative burden comes from the fact that support systems are often developed and administered by people in staff functions. Performance appraisal systems, for instance, are traditionally designed and administered by human resource departments; these departments demand that appraisals be completed not for business reasons but for use in determining salary actions. When appraisals out of these departments are expanded to include goal setting and development planning, other departments often still consider them "exercises" that are imposed from without and that detract from the ability of the organization to get its work done. This perception may persist when performance management systems are developed for team-based settings. Even though successful management of team performance demands that considerable time be spent defining and reviewing performance with stakeholders and developing the team, when such processes are systematized, there is a strong tendency for people to see the time spent as an administrative burden, resent the burden, and only perfunctorily carry the processes out. They continue to see the purpose of performance management as delivering equitable rewards and to conduct performance management activities in a way that minimizes their value in managing performance.

Tension Between Managing the How and Managing the What

The traditional way to approach team self-management and corporate decentralization is to specify the direction of performance and the outcomes needed from the team or other performing unit (the "what" that it is to accomplish) and allow the team to determine the internal means that it uses to achieve the outcomes (for example,

Hackman, 1990). Unfortunately, the need for common processes across team-based organizations requires that this notion be amended. In one aerospace company we studied, an important organizational strategy, intended both to control costs and increase efficiency, was to maximize the use of common parts throughout the system's design. Parts procedures were created that constrained parts choices to those that the company had stipulated whenever possible, and the required percentage of common parts was built into the goals of each team. This requirement conflicted directly with the expectations of the engineers, who enjoyed being able to make decisions solely on the basis of maximizing the performance of the component for which their team had responsibility, and with the expectations of the teams, which wanted to determine for themselves how they met their goals.

Common processes across the organization are an asset in communication systems as well; communication, whether for local or organizational purposes, is facilitated by common conventions. These conventions vary all the way from usage of common terms to usage of common software. The earlier example of the Analytico engineers who expected to use their own individually preferred information technology tools is a case in point. The proliferation of tools and languages in that organization initially prevented the optimal introduction of concurrent engineering processes. Design engineers could not always work with each other's designs, let alone feed directly into the test manufacturers' computer applications.

In several of the organizations we studied, process redesign and optimization that relied on the development and implementation of common processes were viewed by the teams as inconsistent with the expressed empowerment philosophy. Teams expected to be told what their mission was but not how to accomplish it. To a great extent, this misunderstanding reflected the fact that these evolving organizations had not yet adequately clarified how teams would be linked to each other and to the larger organization. The freedom of all teams is constrained when it comes up against the needs of the larger organization (Hackman, 1990). More than that, teams are elements of the larger system, and team members have to understand their role as embedded subsystems.

Tension Between Local and Global Development Needs

The design of team-based organizations, as we have seen, is dictated largely by the nature of the corporate task and the organizational interdependencies inherent in the situation. Because of this, each organization is idiosyncratic in its structures and the interdependencies it chooses to organize around; therefore, its support system needs are idiosyncratic as well. At the very least, this means that corporate systems for team-based organizations have to be generic enough and flexible enough to fit with a wide variety of team-based structures. Since systems usually involve a lot of imbedded expertise, even the adaptation of generic systems to specific situations requires the involvement of systems experts as well as experts on the work processes and information needs of the local setting.

Because of local idiosyncrasies and needs, there will be a tendency for staff expertise to be developed locally. Performing units within almost all team-based organizations we studied had evolved their own expertise in information technology, human resource management, and financial management, often independently and sometimes without the knowledge of corporate groups. Local expertise is useful and necessary, but it can be dangerous if it ignores the multiple larger units in which teams are embedded; these larger units have strategic and performance needs that also must be met by support systems. In the traditional, hierarchical organization, on the other hand, the needs of these larger units often so dominated local needs that support systems did not support local processes. A balance must be achieved. To be widely useful, support systems must be designed so that they meet both local and larger-unit needs.

Local needs can also compete with each other. It is not uncommon to find teams within a business unit that are interdependent but are organized in very different ways and therefore have different support system needs. In this case, the design task is to meet local team needs as much as possible without getting in the way of between-team processes. If the multiple teams of a single business unit require different data bases and/or groupware, for instance, communication between the teams will be jeopardized unless care is taken to make sure that the differing systems used by the individual teams conform to standard practices.

Like the organization that uses them, team-based support systems have to balance interdependence among teams laterally and interdependence among systemic levels hierarchically. We have seen throughout this book that the existence of lateral and hierarchical interdependence leads to a constantly dynamic situation. Organizations and business units must continually respond reactively and proactively to developments in their competitive environments. These strategic developments can drive changes in support systems. For instance, financial planning models can change, demanding a change in behaviors at the local level during the budgeting and planning processes. Changes in the performance environment of teams can also necessitate adjustments in support systems. For instance, a team or business unit's primary customer might begin to demand certain information technology capabilities on the part of the team(s) servicing it. Such a local requirement can have profound impact on the information systems needed throughout the organization. Consequently, the reality facing support systems is the same as that facing team-based organizations in general: one of continual organizational change and accommodation to local and global sources of change. This means that there is continual pressure to redesign support systems.

The Currency of Systems in a Dynamic Context

Formalized systems need time to develop and require time and resources to change. These facts conflict with the just-cited reality in many team-based settings: that things are constantly changing, whether the change is driven by environmental developments or by organizational learning. Klein and Maurer (1994) describe a team-based organization that developed a skills register to keep track of the core competencies in the organization's employees. As people were assigned to various teams, gaining experience and developing new competencies, the skills register needed to be updated. The constant and extensive administration that it required outstripped management's ability to keep up. This support system was intended to be used as part of the process of allocating personnel to teams, which in this organization were frequently being formed around new projects. In actuality, however, the allocation process did not use the skills register but relied on managerial expertise in the staffing of teams. Although this approach was successful in getting teams with the skills and competencies they needed, its reliance on managers' knowledge about the competencies of employees and the staffing process failed to move the organization toward diminished dependence on the management hierarchy as integrator.

Dynamic environments only serve to highlight the tensions that always exist between the work process to be supported and the system that supports it. In becoming systematized, the process loses its essence and life. The system becomes detached from the process it is supposed to facilitate. As long as people use the system as a road map for carrying out the process, it serves its function. As soon as people let the system substitute for the process, the link is broken. When well constructed and implemented, the process and the system enjoy a mutually reinforcing relationship. The system can supply data and remind people about how best to carry out the process. Doing the process makes apparent the usefulness of the system; systematic data help resolve conflicts, and systematic procedures keep people from floundering in the process.

In order for support systems to work, they need to be perceived as helpful—that is, as adding value to the process—not as an administrative burden imposed for purposes of an external group. In team-based settings, the system must be consistent with and supportive of organizational logic. Since team situations are usually undergoing externally or internally initiated change, support systems must be able to adjust. And since each team is uniquely designed to accomplish its mission, support systems must be adjustable to local needs and idiosyncrasies. At the same time, it is through the consistency with which processes are carried out that support systems add value to the organization.

The remainder of this chapter is concerned with describing the process by which support systems can be designed and redesigned to deal with the issues raised in preceding pages.

The Design and Maintenance of Support Systems

Support systems embody considerable knowledge and expertise. In most corporations, staff groups have been created around the design and maintenance of support systems. Information system (IS) departments traditionally have housed the expertise for the hardware and software infrastructures that underlie many of the data bases and communication networks. Human resource (HR) departments have been responsible for a large number of corporate systems aimed at the management of people, such as compensation systems, performance management systems, selection systems, career management systems, and human resource planning systems. Finance and accounting departments have been responsible for developing and using various systems that budget, account for, and track the use of monetary resources and track the financial performance of organizational units. Because of the specialized knowledge associated with these various systems, the design and management of them has gravitated to these departments.

Because the predominant systems developed by these departments (and currently in use in most organizations) are based on assumptions grounded in the traditional organizational form, team-based organizations are generally not well served by them. At the very least, team-based organizations require systems that assume that the performing units are teams, that all resources (information, human, and financial) must be managed according to team structures, and that processes governing these resources must be self-managed by the teams as well as hierarchically managed by those responsible for the larger organization and laterally managed by others who have an interdependent stake in the team. Many staff departments have considerable expertise in the technical issues of systems but have little understanding of the organizational issues of team-based settings. Even after bodies of technical knowledge are developed about how to build systems for the team-based organization, staff experts will need to partner with those in the team-based organization to develop appropriate systems because of the idiosyncratic nature of each team-based organization.

In traditional organizations, staff specialists and the systems they create have tended to seek to control the processes they support (Galbraith, Lawler, and Associates, 1993). Their major client has been corporate management. In the team-based organization, staff specialists cannot be controlling but instead must be facilitative. They must facilitate the trade-offs between corporate and local considerations, the design and redesign processes, and the balance between their system expertise and the organizational expertise of the system users. Staff specialists in the team-based organization need to acquire facilitative skills. To encourage a facilitative approach, teams and business units, which are key clients, need to be involved in both the goal-setting and the review processes of the support specialists.

The major mechanism by which support systems achieve a balance between local and organizational needs and by which change and redesign can be continually accomplished is the structure of the design process itself. Each support system (or family of support systems) requires a process of design that is structured to incorporate all the key stakeholders. In most cases that we have experienced, this has meant a system design team at the organizational level that has members representing the cross section of teams affected, business-unit and executive management, and the expert staff group. As the design process takes place, this design team has the responsibility to forge an ongoing relationship with the user teams and business units and to actively link the organization's executive team to the ongoing process. The design needs to incorporate corporate needs for an integrated system that permits broad-scope use and provides a foundation for integrated work processes with flexibility for local applications.

The design of support systems is knowledge work, and the design team is a process improvement team. The process of self-design that should be followed is identical to the process used in transitioning to a team-based organization (and described in Chapter One). The self-design process (Mohrman and Cummings, 1989) consists of three major stages, you will recall. The first and most important stage is laying the foundation. At this stage in the design of a support system, staff and organizational expertise is shared so that a common knowledge base is built and diverse and potentially divergent perspectives about system needs are surfaced. This is also the stage at which agreement must be reached about the values to be furthered by the system. For an information system, these values might include providing maximum flexibility; for a career system, they might include providing multiple growth and development paths. Finally, knowledge and values should be combined at this stage to diagnose the organizational situation in an effort to ascertain its system needs. Systems are often designed to facilitate certain processes, so a good understanding of the processes that must be enabled is input required by the team. In organizations conducting process reengineering, the systems and processes will be simultaneously designed. The outcome of laying the foundation should be convergence on a set of criteria to guide the next stage: the actual design.

The design stage entails the rather technical task of generating a system design that meets the criteria arrived at in the first stage. Several alternative approaches should be generated and judged by the degree to which they meet the design criteria. This design phase proceeds at various levels of specificity, starting with very broad parameters and proceeding to specific features and applications. At each level, the task is to converge on an approach that keeps as much flexibility in the system as possible. In developing a performance management system, for example, it is not uncommon to see design teams generate a toolkit of approaches that fit different work settings.

The final stage is that of implementation, assessment, and iteration: as soon as the support system is implemented, assessment begins; and as results of the assessment are fed back into the design process, a new design iteration can begin. Systems are quickly elaborated on as local and global factors push for ongoing change or new work processes yield new system requirements. Maintenance of systems is an ongoing organizational need, and it is best performed by a representative council with that function. After initial design efforts have resulted in a usable system, the original design team can be reconstituted into a council to oversee system usefulness and to redesign it over time (whether the redesign is initiated for corporate or local reasons). In this way, the dual needs of local flexibility and global connectivity can be addressed.

This organizational approach to support system development puts staff groups in a position of providing highly specialized expertise that must be merged with business expertise at the local and global levels. Because they operate through representative design teams, these expert staff groups may be very small. In the language of the team-based organization, they are "shared services"; their job is to support task and effectiveness needs at all systemic levels. These shared services are not the owners of the systems. They may, however, have accountability for seeing that they are developed and maintained to meet business needs. Part of their expertise, therefore, lies in change facilitation.

Key Issues

Key issues related to developing organizational support systems include the following:

1. Support systems provide an infrastructure to support the conduct of systematic transformation, integration, and performance management processes.

2. These systems have different orientations in a team-based organization than in a traditional organization. They are more oriented to collective performing, supportive of self-management and dispersed control, lateral, dynamic, flexible, and enterprise-specific.

3. Key issues in the design of these systems include the following:

   Preventing them from becoming bureaucratic exercises or administrative procedures separate from the work and management of the business

   Resolving tension between the desire for empowerment and the need for uniformity of process by making appropriate trade-offs, if necessary, between local needs for flexibility and global needs for commonalty

   Developing systems that can be changed and adapted through time because of local or global forces for change

4. Staff expertise and local and global business and organizational knowledge must be incorporated in support systems.

5. Responsibility for the design and maintenance of these systems should be executed by a multistakeholder council.

6. Information technology systems are components of the other systems as well as enablers of most organizational processes.

11

. . . .

Making the Transition
to Team-Based Design

Earlier chapters of this book described the team-based organization in some detail. They presented a new image of the organization as a system of embedded performing units, proposed a design model and sequence, and discussed some of the overarching issues that cut across the organization. The implementation of the team-based organization drives a related but different set of issues and must itself be planned. The design issues have to do with imaging the what and how of the new organization. What will it look like, and how will it function? The implementation issues revolve around the problem of getting from here to there.

This chapter deals with the implementation of team organizations. It builds on the model of large-scale change—that is, organizational redesign—as a learning process of self-design (as presented in the first chapter). It also addresses key transition challenges in moving to teams and suggests a sequence for introducing the changes. Finally, a high-level road map of the transition process is provided.

The Nature of the Transition

Implementation of a team organization is a large-scale organizational transition. It involves fundamental changes to the character of the organization in order to alter and/or improve its performance capabilities (Mohrman and Associates, 1989). Transitions of this sort have been found to be particularly challenging because of three characteristics:

- *They are pervasive.* They involve changes to almost all aspects of the organization. In discussing the design sequence in earlier chapters, we described how the structure, processes, and systems of the organization all need to change to accommodate and foster team performance.

- *They involve the whole organization.* Installing work teams, for example, does not change simply the frontline operating structure. It changes the processes and roles in the support components at all levels in the organization. Large-scale change cannot be contained in particular units of the organization.

- *They are deep.* The transition to teams requires fundamental changes in assumptions, beliefs, and even values about how organizations function best. It challenges the pronounced individualism that characterizes the traditional design of organizations and the values that have been both espoused and enacted by most organizational members. The process of empowering teams requires a redefinition of organizational control that calls into question the orientation of middle managers who have existed in an organizational design that required and rewarded hierarchical control; and the process of lateral integration requires that team members overcome fragmentation of the worldviews of different disciplines and eliminate the "caste system" that results when different groups have unequal status, power, and privilege.

Large-scale transitions of this nature are not quick fixes. For a business unit to implement a team design and work through the start-up tasks takes months. Becoming proficient at working in this new context and institutionalizing the new approach to doing work may require several years.

The transition to teams entails a technical design process and a social change process, both of which necessitate organizational learning. The technical design process (addressed in Part Two) involves conceptualizing and producing the new organizational design, while the social change process involves activities and interventions geared to helping organizational members accept and embrace changes and learn how to perform effectively in the altered context. The technical and social change processes are not separate phenomena; rather, they work in tandem to bring about total cultural change.

Most large, established organizations have a culture that is manifest in unconscious behaviors and deeply held assumptions and beliefs. The organizational context determines what is necessary for "success," and success shapes and reinforces the organizational culture—beliefs and assumptions about what is the best way to operate in the organization. In most traditional organizations, the culture is manifest in behavioral norms, symbols, and expressions that emphasize the vertical, hierarchical, and individualistic nature of the system.

Changing the culture is a painful and frustrating endeavor, partially because the beliefs and values of the old culture have become part of the self-concept of organizational members. Perhaps the main reason that culture change is difficult, however, is that culture cannot be operated on directly. We mentioned earlier that the facilitators of performance effectiveness in teams—timely decision making, integration, and efficacy—cannot be simply willed into the organization; they—along with almost all other aspects of organizational culture—must be designed for. In the traditional organization, hierarchical behavior, for example, stems from an organization that vests control in many levels of hierarchy, while vertical decision making is natural in an organization whose information systems stress the aggregation of knowledge, information, and skills at the top of the organization rather than at the operating level.

An organization moving to a team model will do well to think about the organizational features that hold the existing culture in place. Some of these will be addressed through organizational redesign. Others are symbols of the old way of operating. Symbols that differentiate among employees, such as size of office, assigned parking places, and executive dining rooms, send a message that the work and decisions of those at the top are most central to the organization's success. Even less obvious symbols communicate corporate culture: companies that have employee numbers on badges, for example, may be unwittingly both celebrating loyalty and sending a message that seniority carries with it a special influence. And one organization we studied found that meeting behavior changed when the firm stopped using different color badges to convey information about seniority. Such symbols work against the creation of a culture where people of mixed level and seniority can come together in a team and make decisions based on expertise. But organizational symbols can be changed to facilitate new behaviors and attitudes. Simply putting new design features and symbols in place will not automatically change the culture, of course. An extensive learning process is required.

Self-Design and the Organizational Learning Process

In Chapter One, we introduced a self-design model to guide the learning process by which an organization redesigns itself. We have repeatedly argued that such a process is required because each organization must tailor its own configuration and because, in a dynamic world, the constellation of performing units keeps changing, necessitating ongoing self-design.

An elaborated version of the self-design model is presented in Figure 11.1. It can be thought of as a high-level road map of the transition to a team-based organization. The first two stages of the design process have been discussed at length in earlier chapters: the organization lays the foundation through values clarification, learning, and diagnosis and defines criteria; then, following the sequence outlined in Part Two, the design team generates the overall design

Figure 11.1. Amplified Self-Design Model.

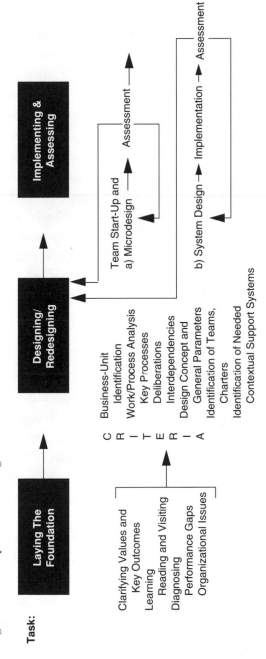

concept and the general parameters of the team-based organization, specifies the teams and their charters, and identifies broad parameters of the support systems that need to be developed. This chapter focuses on the third stage: implementation and assessment.

Initial implementation sets the work teams up and provides them assistance in determining how to go about enacting their new roles. Process design teams may be called for right away as well, to develop the necessary support systems. Implementation does not imply a finished design. On the contrary, ongoing design activities are part of the implementation: each team must design itself, and the systems must be designed.

Learning occurs throughout all three stages of an organization's self-design. It takes place as the organization lays a foundation for change. At that initial stage, it occurs best when there is reflection that is guided by specification of the desired organizational outcomes—that is, the design criteria (Shaw and Perkins, 1992). Further learning occurs as the actual design unfolds. Implementation, our focus here, is an ongoing learning process energized in large part by assessment, which leads to changes in design and implementation. Implementation also entails training and development, dialogue and reflection, and interpersonal feedback.

The learning is often spearheaded by a design team; however, that design team works interactively with the rest of the organization to involve other members, take advantage of their perspectives, and educate the organization about what to expect. The organization must go through the process of developing a shared understanding of what it is trying to accomplish and how the new organization is going to function. This requires extensive opportunities for dialogue among organizational members about the new organization and opportunities for multidirectional influence about how it needs to be shaped for successful goal accomplishment. Shared understanding includes the development, through time and dialogue, of behavioral agreement about the meaning of the words being bandied around. For example, what does it mean to "empower" a team? What does it mean for managers to "coach" a team? How do these concepts translate into a person's actual behavior?

The social change process begins even before the technical design process occurs, during the period in which the foundation for the design process is laid, and it continues through the design and implementation stages. Through participation in the design activities, key stakeholders develop a deep understanding of what the organization is trying to accomplish and how the design is believed to be able to promote those accomplishments. By involving others in the valuing, learning, and diagnostic processes, the design team can expand the number of those who share understanding and help organizational members begin to internalize the logic of the new organization.

Because implementation is necessarily a learning process, the design team can minimally specify the new design, leaving a number of design decisions to be made by the teams themselves and to be generated through the assessment process. When the experiences of the teams themselves influence the direction that the design takes, team members can feel more involvement in the success of the new organization.

Considerable local design is both inevitable and desirable (to achieve ownership and fit). However, carried too far, it can actually work against learning. Because locally idiosyncratic design leads to specific, local understandings, teams come to develop their own language for perceiving and describing their work situation and the team processes and designs they are using. This can result eventually in teams that are no longer able to communicate with each other about how they are going about things. An inability to understand design and process choices across teams can inhibit the ability of the organization to function as a larger performing system. It can remove the possibility of teams' learning from one another and limit the ability of the organization to reconfigure teams without having to go through major change efforts (since people changing teams encounter new social systems and new work conventions).

This problem underscores the importance for the organization of having systems supporting the design and redesign of teams by teams.

The Manager's Role in the Learning Process

The challenge facing managers in this transition is to help the people in the organization develop a new and common understanding of their organization and of their roles within it. Reorganizing into teams carries with it many implications for how people enact their roles, some of which are not self-evident at the beginning of the transition; rather, they are discovered in the process. Managers have to model and lead the organization in learning activities that contribute to a shared understanding of the processes and norms of the new organization. At the beginning of the transition to teams, it is not readily apparent to organizational members that the organization and its managers will truly value and reward the espoused new ways of operating. Thus managers have to continually reinforce the new behaviors and the learning that occur along the way.

Leadership in the learning process needs to be exerted by the management of the business unit and the executive management team. A design team can play a key operational role in planning and implementing the action-learning sequence, in which the organization introduces change, collects data, and continues to make refinements based on what it learns. Introducing ongoing changes involving additional design features and committing the organization to additional implementation activities require management input into the allocation of resources. Furthermore, changes in management behavior and more active management leadership will almost certainly be specified by the design team as needed elements during the initial learning cycle.

Organizational learning at both the design and the implementation stages should be based on specific assessment data. Managers need to grapple with those data to internalize the changes required in their own behavior. In our study, the organizations that were moving most rapidly to an effective team design were those that built in assessment at regular intervals. Data were generated from all stakeholders to reveal what was working and not working in the approaches being used and to suggest midcourse corrections in design or implementation. The management teams in these organizations were centrally involved in interpreting data and working with each other and with the teams to determine steps to address what they had learned. In some cases, management teams dedicated as much as half a day per week to this learning process.

The assessment component of organizational redesign need not be divorced from the operating flow of the teams themselves. Figure 11.2 illustrates how the performance management of teams fits neatly into an action-learning framework. Management in some of the organizations we studied did quarterly reviews of all teams. As part of the review process, each team was asked to generate a list of the barriers and facilitators to their effectiveness. These data were then used to identify areas that called for redesign and/or more implementation support. In several organizations, the data collected during the review process made managers aware that the teams did not have the correct composition, sparking a participative process to reconfigure the team structure.

The action-learning cycle requires norms that are in many cases far different from those that prevailed in the traditional organization. For example, learning requires the willingness to surface bad news and act on it. This norm will not emerge unless past norms of negatively evaluating the messengers of bad news are changed. Action learning also requires receptivity to multidirectional influence—that is, the willingness of people to learn from others who have different perspectives. Managers must be willing to learn from the experiences of the teams. The action-learning sequence will be interrupted if the organization does not establish the norm of taking time out to examine how the organization is working. Norms

Figure 11.2. Team Performance Management and Action Learning.

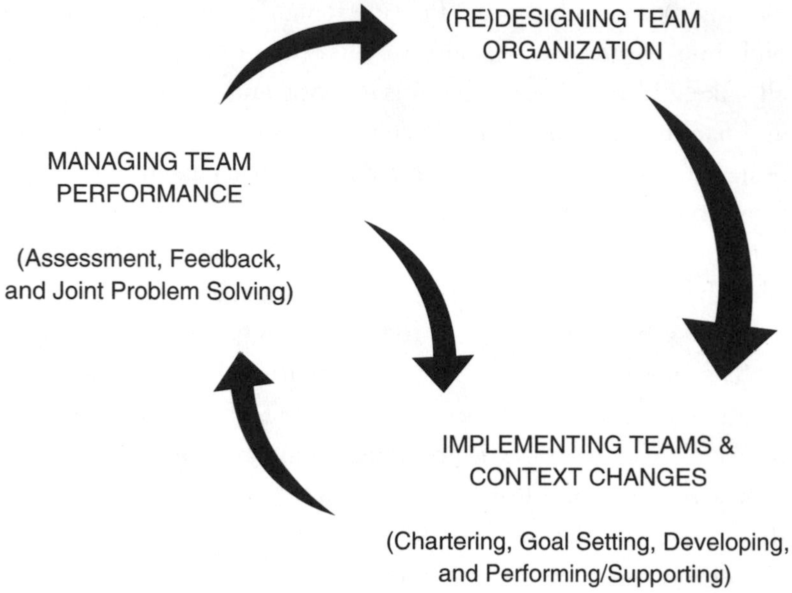

(RE)DESIGNING TEAM ORGANIZATION

MANAGING TEAM PERFORMANCE

(Assessment, Feedback, and Joint Problem Solving)

IMPLEMENTING TEAMS & CONTEXT CHANGES

(Chartering, Goal Setting, Developing, and Performing/Supporting)

do not simply happen; they must be created. They emanate from the top—from the managers who are the model for what is expected, acceptable, and rewarded behavior in the organization.

Iterations of Change

As with all learning processes, the action-learning process described above leads not only to the development of shared understanding but also to an evolution of the depth of understanding by organizational members of what they are trying to accomplish. Figure 11.3 illustrates the progression that occurred in two of the companies we studied in the understanding of what members meant when they said they were moving to a team organization. They started out with a relatively simple conceptualization: that they would establish teams to integrate the work of various contributors whose tasks were interrelated. After an early assessment, they realized that they had

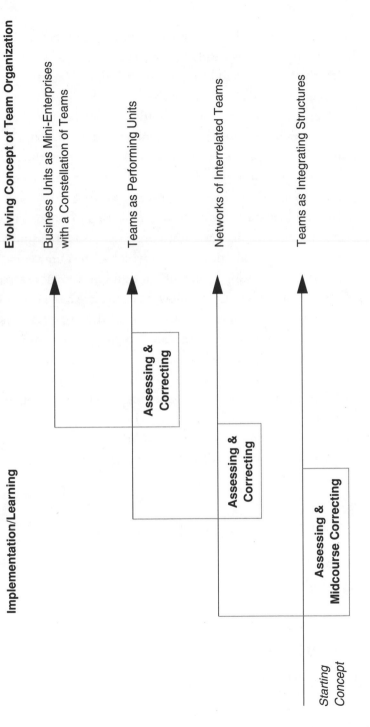

Figure 11.3. An Iterative Progression of the Team Concept.

not planned for dealing with interdependencies *between* teams. Because what they had really created was a network of interrelated teams, they designed additional integrating mechanisms. A later assessment yielded the learning that individuals were not always fully supporting the teams on which they served, because their functional bosses were treating team involvement as an "extra" part of their job. The organizations then seriously dealt with the meaning of "teams as performing units" and developed performance management tools to give this concept teeth.

In a third iteration, the organizations started to move to the clustering of related teams into mini-enterprises (small business units within a larger organization, each of which is measurable as a little business), then developed measures for and moved more resources into these mini-enterprises to allow them to have more control over their own destiny. For example, in one of the organizations—an aerospace firm—marketers were placed in program teams in an effort to make each program a self-sufficient business.

When these two organizations embarked on their journey to teams, they did not picture mini-enterprises as their destination; but as they learned more and more about what this transition was about, their understanding evolved. Their evolution occurred through periodic assessments and broad dialogue and learning among organizational members.

Typical Problems in the Transition to Teams

Organizations making the transition to teams often face problems in the following areas:

- Designing teams

  Work fit

  Charters

  Ownership

- Embedding teams in the organization

  Link to other teams

  Link to management

  Empowerment

- Developing team and management capabilities

  Training

  Development

- Aligning the context

  Information sharing

  Performance management

  Communication

  Decision making

If the organization does not get everything quite right in its first pass through (and few do), issues in these areas often are identified as barriers to effective team performance during assessments. Let us take a closer look.

- *Designing teams.* Most organizations we studied had to make at least minor (and often fairly major) changes to their team configuration in order to get it to fit with the work requirements. In some organizations, key stakeholders were omitted from certain teams for political reasons. In others, teams included members who, though they were in a supporting role, were so peripheral that the agenda of the many team meetings they sat through was largely irrelevant to them. In still others, the design team misjudged the most important interdependencies, requiring a relatively complete rejuggling of teams.

In many of our subject organizations, the redesign of the team configuration occurred at the behest of the teams themselves. Teams that were reconfigured based on employee input were more likely to be "owned" by the members, who understood the logic of the team boundaries because they had had input into their determination.

A related transition issue pertains to the charter of the teams. Organizations often make the error of establishing teams but failing to provide them with a clear sense of purpose or an explicit charter. Alternatively, organizations discover that they provided their teams with unrealistic charters and have to retrench a bit. For example, one aerospace firm we studied chartered a cross-functional team to manage and maintain the relationship with a major customer, when in fact as many as eight other teams had built-in interfaces with that customer (and many of those teams were more important than the cross-functional team in shaping customer relations). Once the teams were implemented, it became clear that their charters had to be changed to provide a forum for integrating the knowledge of the various teams that dealt with the customer. Furthermore, the composition of each team had to be expanded to include linchpin members from the other teams.

• *Embedding teams in the larger organization.* A common problem early in the transition to teams in many organizations is that teams are established for a particular purpose and then left to "float" without a clear sense of how their mission relates to the rest of the organization and to the accountability and review processes. Team members (and managers) often have no idea to whom the team is accountable, and they sometimes develop very unrealistic expectations regarding the amount of autonomy and authority they have. If management makes its expectations clear only later, when it reviews and evaluates the work of the team (and perhaps even reverses that work, if it feels the team has not met expectations), tension is inevitable. This need to clarify the accountability of the team—for what and to whom—is frequently learned the hard way in the early stages of teaming.

A related issue pertains to the links among teams. Because of myriad task interdependencies, many teams need to involve other teams in decisions rather than making them unilaterally. Other teams need to coordinate because they share resources. Cross-team teams and shared goal-setting and planning mechanisms often result from the identification of these issues in an organization.

Embedding the team properly in the organization is central to the notion of empowering the team. Clearly, the need to coordinate on key dimensions with other teams and to be accountable to a body that has a broader scope of responsibility can be interpreted as limiting what organizations perceive as empowerment. This is particularly true in the early stages of team implementation, when a relatively shallow understanding of the term *empowerment* can lead to unrealistic expectations for autonomy. On the other hand, managers may in fact be enacting their roles in a manner that unnecessarily constrains and consequently disempowers teams. In either case, the result is often conflict that erodes trust if not dealt with. Part of the learning that frequently occurs during the transition to teams addresses the meaning of and practical constraints on empowerment.

• *Developing team and management capabilities.* Organizations transitioning to teams often underestimate the amount of help that team members and managers in team settings will require to learn new behaviors. This is particularly likely in highly specialized knowledge work because of the mistaken belief that people who are highly educated have the basic skills to work effectively in team settings. In fact, highly specialized individuals, steeped in their own knowledge bases, find it especially difficult to be effective in settings that demand exchange across worldviews. They are often used to working as individuals and may lack some of the basic interpersonal skills that underpin collaboration. Furthermore, because they often apply their technical knowledge implicitly, it may no longer be salient to them that their work depends on highly structured and systematic approaches. Consequently, they may resist structured team processes, finding them constraining or believing that they do not need them.

When early assessments reveal that skills are inadequate, firms often provide classroom training for team members, sometimes jointly but frequently individually. What is generally missing in such an approach is the development of team capabilities—development that is best accomplished by treating the team as a whole and by applying the training as the team performs its actual tasks. In this way, the value of the training is established in the context of the work that the team has to do.

Assessments are also likely to yield a finding that many managers are having trouble adopting their new role and abandoning their old role. It is hard to overestimate the difference between managing teams and managing individuals. On top of that, managers sometimes find themselves part of management teams that are collectively managing business units and teams; in other words, their management role must be enacted for teams within teams. The change is so extreme that some organizations use personal coaches and other intense feedback approaches to aid in the transition. It should be stressed that we found, in our research, many cases where even managers who were strong advocates of the team organization required a great deal of assistance in making the required transition in management style.

• *Aligning the context.* The early stages of the transition to teams are generally fraught with inconsistencies between the new team logic and the traditional, hierarchical logic. At the beginning, most aspects of the organization remain unchanged; those that were designed to fit the old logic are still in place. As a result, teams are constantly running into barriers or experiencing tension with the old organization. Some examples: A team member may encounter a traditional manager in a customer organization who is unwilling to make decisions with someone who is not a manager. Teams may not have timely or adequate access to the performance measures they need to be self-improving. The communication system may be designed to systematically get information only as far as the second-level managers, so teams have to rely on those managers to informally share key information. The reward system may reward the second-level managers and above for the performance of the business unit but not the team members who are being asked to assume responsibility for achieving requisite integration for business-unit effectiveness. And so forth.

Although in concept it would be nice to be able to modify all aspects of the organizational system right away to support the new way of functioning, this is not realistic for several reasons. First, this may imply more simultaneous change than the organization is able to plan and support. Second, since the transition to teams involves learning as the organization goes through it, the organization needs some experience with teams before it fully realizes what needs to change (and how). Third, a number of features, such as team rewards, can work well only if the organization has the right teams in place, which, as we discussed above, often takes a number of iterations of the learning cycle.

Contextual inconsistencies become both increasingly salient as the organization gains experience with teams and increasingly likely to surface in assessments as barriers to effective performance. At the local level and in the short term, management needs to respond by jerry-rigging approaches to the performance of these key processes and in so doing create a local context for team effectiveness. For example, our discussion of performance management (Chapter Seven) outlines approaches that managers in a team setting can take while awaiting overhaul of corporate practices. Nevertheless, the corporate context will ultimately have to change if the team organization is to become the new status quo. This two-pronged strategy of making local modifications while awaiting contextual change will be further explicated in the section below, which deals with sequencing the change process.

Sequencing the Transition

We have repeatedly argued in these pages that a gradual transition to teams may be required. Most organizations are not in the enviable position of a start-up, designing a team organization from scratch. Rather, they are in the awkward position of redesigning an existing organization at the same time they are carrying out its work;

the transition unfolds through a sequence of redesign efforts that gradually put in place the elements of a system to support a more lateral way of functioning. Determining how to sequence such a transition is an important aspect of change management.

A number of different factors contribute to the decision whether (and how) to break up the transition. One of these factors is the extent to which relevant management skills already exist in the organization. Responsibilities may be gradually transferred from managers to teams, for example. A potential evolutionary path might be from a model that includes one first-line supervisor for each team to a model that eliminates the first level of supervision altogether as first-line supervisory responsibilities are gradually moved into the team. This sort of gradual transfer of responsibilities is one response to the reality that, if management skills are not at first present in the teams, they will have to be developed.

Another factor that plays into the decision about whether and how to stage the transition is the pragmatic situation faced by the organization. If an organization has a surplus of highly skilled supervisors, for example, it may prefer to lose them by attrition and promotion rather than by eliminating their positions and either laying off the supervisors or risking losing them through demotions. In other words, it may eliminate positions opportunistically. Another strategy used by some organizations is to create team leader positions and help supervisors "retool" to fit such positions. These strategies carry some risk, however. The presence of too many supervisors with unclear roles may ultimately lead to redundancy of responsibility as teams become more self-sufficient. In addition, these supervisors may not be motivated to help the teams develop self-management capabilities (and thereby work themselves out of a job). Furthermore, there is no guarantee that a supervisor can readily adopt an internal, nonhierarchical leadership role as a team leader.

Other companies face a different pragmatic situation: they may be forced, for financial reasons, to eliminate layers and make teams more self-managing quickly. If they cannot afford to maintain the first-line supervisory role, they may "cut teams loose" at once and allow them to learn through the school of hard knocks. This approach obviously carries with it its own set of dangers, which revolve around the fact that teams may flounder for a long period without sufficient development. Development opportunities and help in the form of support systems may be a long time arriving. In this situation, it would help to establish connections between teams so that they can learn from one another.

The culture of the organization may also limit the speed of the transition. Members of an extremely hierarchical organization, for example, may take longer to adapt to the lateral logic. Because of this, a very traditional organization may choose to move more slowly in removing the trappings of hierarchy. This approach is dangerous, however, as it may take an inordinate amount of time to implement a critical mass of organizational features supporting the new way of doing business. If momentum is lost, the transition may peter out. It is best to proceed as quickly as possible; the organization must at some point "bite the bullet" and create a consistent design. One organization we studied discovered that it could not take a gradual approach to changing management roles. Assessment data revealed that as long as teams had managers, they simply did not become self-managing. This company then eliminated two-thirds of the management structure and found that self-management emerged quickly. We are not arguing that radical change is always best; an organization can process only so much change at once, and learning takes time. However, iterative change requires assessment processes that continually correct and refine. The management team must juggle these factors and proceed with full intent and enough change to maintain momentum.

All of these factors will vary from organization to organization, of course; each organization has unique needs and characteristics. Nevertheless, we can draw some generalizations about sequencing the transition to teams. Figure 11.4—an amplified version of the star model introduced in Chapter One—suggests a rough sequencing for the

Figure 11.4. Amplified Star Model of an Organization.

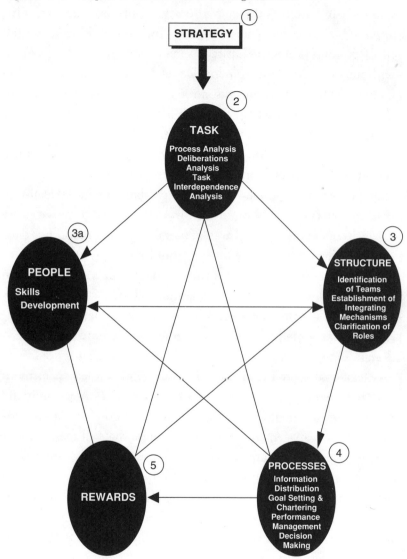

Source: Adapted from Galbraith, 1994.

design implementation. It presents the major elements of the organization that eventually need to be modified to create a team organization. An order is implied by the positioning of the elements. At the top is the strategy of the organization. What is the organization trying to accomplish in its environment, and how is the team design expected to facilitate that accomplishment? This is the first question an organization must ask, for the answer then becomes part of the foundation for the redesign process.

Working downward in the star model, we come to the organizational task: What task (or tasks) does the organization have to carry out to accomplish its strategy? The newly emerging reengineering movement stresses that the organization should eliminate work that does not add value. This advice also applies to designing teams. The organization should design teams to accomplish value-added work, not simply to replicate all work that has previously been done. Consequently, process analysis, deliberations analysis, and task interdependence analysis (see Chapter Three) are important not only because they contribute to an understanding of what teams should be created but also because they help the design team identify what work needs to be done and the most effective processes by which to do it.

Continuing down the star model, the organizational structural design and the beginning of the development of people can proceed somewhat in tandem. The strategic and task analyses provide a foundation for both, addressing what work has to be performed and what skills and capabilities will be important. As the structure begins to be clarified, a forward-looking organization can start to identify the skills and capabilities that its members will have to demonstrate and provide the necessary development opportunities. It can start to expose people to other disciplines, for example, or introduce a basic group-communications course. It does not have to wait until the new structure is actually in place for such efforts, although some development experiences happen best within the team.

The team organization structure, which includes the work teams, other integrating mechanisms, and the management and leadership roles of the organization, provides the basis upon which to design the integration and performance management processes of the organization—the fourth point in the star model. The implementation of teams will not be successful if, for example, the requisite information systems are not in place to provide the teams with the information required to perform their mission and to monitor their effectiveness. It may be possible to jerry-rig these information systems in the short term, but setting up teams without providing them with needed information is a recipe for failure. The process of goal setting, including chartering teams and establishing their local goals, is another process that can be carried out in tandem with the establishment of the teams (although again, management can jerry-rig a useful goal-setting process while a more systematic organizational process is being developed). The rest of the performance management processes, including review and feedback, can also be jerry-rigged during the first months of team functioning, particularly since this is a period of fundamental learning. However, because these processes are pivotal in determining whether a team can improve its functioning and in determining the relationship of the individual to the team, they should not be overlooked for long. Systematic decision-making processes, also crucial, are best taught in the team setting and should be introduced to the team during its first months of existence.

The reward component is the last piece to be put in place—the fifth point on the star—for two reasons. First, team rewards are difficult to develop and have to be tailored to the particular organizational configuration. They should be implemented once the organization is comfortable that it has a relatively stable design and knows the kinds of teams and units that can and should be rewarded. Second, the effectiveness of these rewards is dependent on team-based definitional and review processes. As early short-term steps, however, organizations can introduce teamwork and team success as central criteria in each individual's review and experiment with multidirectional review. There is a reason why organizational members fixate early on the reward system as a barrier to teamwork: individuals use the reward system to confirm what behaviors will get them ahead, and their behavior is consciously or unconsciously (through modeling, for example) shaped by it. So managers should take early steps to neutralize elements of a reward system that work against the behaviors needed for successful team performance and to clarify the kinds of behaviors that they will be looking for in the future.

Although Figure 11.4 reflects only a commonsense and very rough sequence, it also suggests the iterative nature of design by stressing the two-way feedback loops. The development of processes, for example, will have implications for the development of people, because individuals must learn how to carry out the new processes.

In summary, large-scale organizational redesign requires leadership, resources, and support; the implementation of a team-based design is a radical undertaking. Figure 11.5 portrays a global road map of this undertaking, outlining who does what when, and with what support. It also incorporates the design accountability that lies at the corporate level as well as with each business unit.

It would be elegant and even parsimonious if corporate designing could be done first, to provide a support context within which the business units could design and implement teams. In fact, however, designing generally goes on simultaneously at all levels. This fits with the observation of Beer, Eisenstat, and Spector (1990) that corporate renewal often begins in operating business units. In many of the organizations we studied, redesign processes began at the level of the business unit, where changes in strategy provided the "push" that enabled executive management to see the need for redesigning elements of the corporate context to add value in new ways. Corporate design often includes the creation of a cross-functional approach at the corporate level.

The bottom lines of Figure 11.5 list the kind of change support needed for each of the stages of transition. Process facilitation is helpful at all stages, because the transition involves both social

Figure 11.5. A Global Perspective on the Transition.

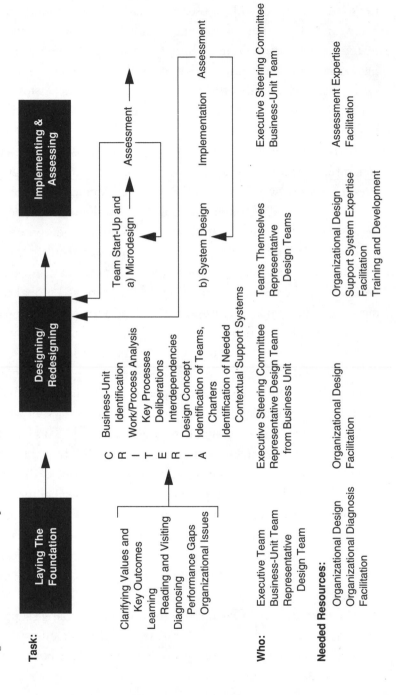

Task:

Laying The Foundation	Designing/ Redesigning	Implementing & Assessing

Clarifying Values and
Key Outcomes
Learning
  Reading and Visiting
Diagnosing
  Performance Gaps
  Organizational Issues

C
R   Business-Unit
I   Identification
T   Work/Process Analysis
E   Key Processes
R   Deliberations
I   Interdependencies
A   Design Concept
    Identification of Teams,
      Charters
    Identification of Needed
      Contextual Support Systems

Team Start-Up and
a) Microdesign → Assessment

b) System Design   Implementation   Assessment

Who:

Executive Team
Business-Unit Team
  Representative
  Design Team

Executive Steering Committee
Representative Design Team
  from Business Unit

Teams Themselves
Representative
  Design Teams

Executive Steering Committee
Business-Unit Team

Needed Resources:

Organizational Design
Organizational Diagnosis
Facilitation

Organizational Design
Facilitation

Organizational Design
Support System Expertise
Facilitation
Training and Development

Assessment Expertise
Facilitation

and technical change processes, and various technical expertise is needed at different stages. For example, organizational design expertise is needed at all of the design stages, and expertise in the development of particular support systems, such as rewards and information systems, is required during the period when these systems are being redesigned. Often this expert help must come from outside the organization, because internal experts are likely to be steeped in the logic of the old organization. Chapter Eight addressed the extensive skill development required to support the team-based organization. Most companies we studied said that they had radically underestimated the importance of developmental support.

This chapter has described the large-scale change process involved in the transition to teams and presented a road map to guide the journey. It has raised issues and provided guidance particularly relevant to the transition to a team-based organization.

Key Issues

Key issues facing those attempting implementation of a team-based organizational design include the following:

1. The transition to teams entails change that pervades all aspects of organizational functioning and fundamentally alters how people understand the organization and their role in it.

2. The transition to teams is a learning process, and management must take the lead.

3. The transition involves technical design aspects and social change dynamics.

4. The transition requires that a foundation be laid for informed change that is guided by agreed upon valued outcomes and a knowledge base about team organizations.

5. The design that is first implemented will not be complete; the

implementation and assessment process will guide ongoing iterations and improvements.

6. There are a number of predictable issues that arise in a team transition; learning processes must be in place to address these issues.

7. All organizational changes cannot be made simultaneously. Organizations need to determine how to stage the transition (as illustrated in the road map and sequence proposed).

12

. . . .

Facing the Challenges Ahead

The team-based organization that we have described in this book requires a whole new way of operating. Moving from the traditional, hierarchical organization of yesterday to the team-based organization of tomorrow is a large-scale transition that requires fundamental changes in how people think about and behave in organizations. Some people find this transition more difficult than others. For some, the new organization provides exhilarating opportunities and satisfactions. For others, it presents a threatening and unsettling set of challenges. Currently, organizations are in the midst of this long and difficult transition, and no organization has emerged on the other side. Some organizations may retreat, deciding that the changes are too difficult and too complex. Most will continue on the journey, learning and adapting as they go.

As organizations implement team-based designs, their very nature changes. New organizational forms develop, new systems need to be implemented, and difficult issues emerge. In this chapter, we will describe a few of the many implications of implementing the team-based organization, identify the fundamental changes that people need to make for successful implementation, and discuss what needs to be learned to better support and create the conditions for success.

Implications of the Team-Based Organization

Each of the following characteristics of the team-based organization has implications for organizational structure and behavior.

• *The team-based organization changes the whole notion of organizational boundaries.* The boundaries between organizations become fuzzy as companies develop various types of cross-organizational partnerships and alliances. Increasingly, work teams have external customers and suppliers as members. The voice of the customer is more directly heard as work teams develop products and services for specific customers, receiving on-line information about customer requirements from shared data bases that connect the customer and supplier organizations. Similarly, external suppliers are members of work teams with increasing frequency, integrating the development of their subcontracted components with the components developed by the work teams. In addition, joint ventures, strategic alliances, and other partnering arrangements continue to be formed in record numbers. These networks of interrelated companies will increasingly compete with other networks in an industry field (Galbraith, 1993). Teamwork will increasingly occur across organizational boundaries, strengthening the connectedness and cooperation among groups of companies that are competing against other groups of companies. These partnership arrangements make organizational boundaries far more permeable.

• *The team-based organization is a learning organization.* It is not enough to say that learning is necessary for teams to be effective in the team-based organization. Learning is the *essence* of the team-based organization. The team-based organization is a multilayered, dynamic open system composed of interrelated and interdependent performing and integrating subunits. Multidirectional learning is required within and across systemic levels. When people from different perspectives come together in a work team to design products or deliver services, they combine specialized knowledge bases and produce new shared knowledge. This lateral learning occurs through dialogue and collaboration, and integration cannot occur without it. Vertical learning is also required between work teams and integrating teams at the business-unit and corporate levels. Knowledge must be shared across systemic levels and new learnings produced in order for teams to rapidly respond to changing environmental and strategic demands (Mohrman, Mohrman, and Cohen, forthcoming).

The dynamic nature of the team-based organization generates learnings about the process of doing work. Organizations continually charter new teams to perform new projects. These teams evolve into new forms in response to changing circumstances, and different integrating structures are designed to fit local preferences and requirements. Even organizations that mandate a particular team design soon discover that variations evolve in response to different situational demands, and learning can occur from reflecting on that variation. Some designs are effective; others are not. Local learning and innovation occur from trial and error. Broader learning depends upon whether organizations establish mechanisms for reflecting upon and capturing learnings from a variety of experiences. Organizations that encourage norms of experimentation and innovation and set up mechanisms for shared reflection can capitalize on this learning potential.

Teams can be the explicit mechanisms by which organizational learning about the process and content of work occurs. They can be assigned the responsibility for reflecting upon the variation in organizational forms and making recommendations about how to improve team design, and they can be assigned various process improvement or quality improvement functions. Teams can also be defined as the repository of specialized content information. Technical councils can be given the mandate of ensuring that employees stay at the cutting edge of their fields. Product councils can be assigned the responsibility for ensuring that product competitive intelligence is widely shared. Organizations that strategically use teams to capture and disseminate organizational learnings can achieve competitive advantage over companies that do not explic-itly manage the learning process. The strategic use of teams for orga-nizational learning will become a competitive necessity as more organizations explicitly engage in a learning process.

• *The team-based organization demands high levels of formalization and informal cooperation simultaneously.* The coordination challenges of the team-based organization are formidable. Team members inter-act with many other employees to get work done in their teams and across teams, systemic levels, functional areas, business units, and sometimes organizations. If structures and processes have not been formalized, coordination slippage and rework are the inevitable result. Defining work teams and integrating teams and providing teams with charters that delineate mission, goals, and authority help to create a shared understanding of what is to be accomplished and the mechanisms to accomplish it. Clarifying communication chan-nels and decision-making accountability helps to clarify ex-pectations about how work will be integrated as well. Thus the formalization of structures and processes provides a foundation for the team-based organization.

At the same time, the team-based organization depends upon informal cooperation and voluntary processes, particularly across organizational boundaries. It is neither possible nor desirable to specify all necessary organizational connections at the outset. Say, for example, that a robotics issue comes up on a work team for which the answer resides in the robotics technical council. The lack of a formal relationship between the work team and this technical council does not stop a work team member from volunteering to contact the technical council and get the needed information. These voluntary acts of coordination happen all the time, and the team-based organization cannot survive without them.

The relationship between formal and informal processes is reci-procal; formal processes shape informal connections, and informal connections shape what needs to be formalized. People tend to walk on paved paths. People also naturally pursue paths on the grass, however: they create new paths if they need to. These new paths are often later paved, if there is enough demand and functionality. Co-locating people in teams, connecting the teams through information technology, and defining expectations for communication and decision making powerfully shape the informal interactions that occur. These voluntary interactions enable the work of multiple contributors to be integrated and the task objectives to be met. Over time, though, the needs and experiences of those involved in voluntary interactions may suggest formalizing what has been informal, solidifying learnings that have emerged from practice. For example, suppose that the work team discussed above frequently needs information from the robotics council; then it makes sense to formalize the connection between these two teams.

• *Extensive systems development efforts are required to support the team-based organization.* The team-based organization relies on people across organizational boundaries being able to communicate electronically, integrate their own data and tools with those of the people with whom they work, and collaborate with others despite their location or choice of hardware or software. Given the current fragmented state of technology design and the existence of "technology islands"—systems that cannot communicate with one another—extensive investment and development efforts are required to ensure that connection. Both building systems that connect and expand access to functional islands and designing new, interconnected data sets are massive undertakings. In addition, the team-based organization calls for new information tools. Human resource information systems that keep track of people, skills, and assignments can be enormously helpful in selecting people for teams across the organization and facilitating voluntary contacts. Electronic performance appraisal systems can expedite the collection and aggregation of performance data from multiple sources: customers, peers, and managers. Developing new information systems to support the team-based organization is an ongoing process; technology changes continually, enabling new capabilities to be developed, and emergent needs are defined in the process of doing collaborative work.

• *The demands generated by the team-based organization challenge the capabilities of organizational participants.* The technical demands are considerable in many knowledge-work settings; people need to be able to apply state-of-the-art specialty knowledge to their projects. In addition to this in-depth knowledge of a specialty, however, much broader knowledge is also required. People need to have the cognitive ability to develop an understanding of ideas and frameworks different than their own in order to successfully work with people from different disciplines. Furthermore, people need to be able to understand the requirements for performance at multiple systemic levels and to deal with constant change. People need to take action to coordinate their activities with those of others in their team and to make sure that their team's efforts are integrated with those of other teams. This necessitates the ability to understand and deal with complex trade-offs. Finally, team members need to be able to handle the emotional challenge presented by dependence on others and by the inevitable conflicts that occur when work is done in teams. These diverse demands often occur in a broader context of extreme performance pressure and ongoing downsizing. The combined impact of all these pressures tests the capabilities of organizations and participants. The good news is that many people in the organizations we studied faced these challenges with enthusiasm, in large part because the new team designs provided more fulfilling jobs and new ways to have influence in the organization. Most team members felt that performing in teams made sense (although they were less sanguine that their organizations were willing to make the transition completely). For others, the transition was rough, and some were having serious difficulties adjusting to the new organization.

• *Managers are designers in the team-based organization.* A key responsibility of management teams is to ensure that the configuration of performing units is optimal for the work that needs to get done. Managers assess whether there are too many teams and consequently too many conflicting priorities. They determine when teams are required and when individual contributor roles are appropriate. They make sure the information, communication, and performance management processes support the team-based organizational unit. For many managers, this is a new role, and one in which they need training and expert support.

Fundamental Changes Required for Success

The changes that people need to make to be successful in the team-based organization are fundamental. The team-based organization demands basic changes in how people experience their work, their relationships with others, and their relationship to the organization. It requires a new mindset about who we are and what we do at work. Most people have internalized the old hierarchical logic, in which their organizational position determined what they did, who they related to, and how they were treated. The key relationship in the traditional organization was with a manager, who spoke for the organization in managing the performance of his subordinates and was responsible for coordinating efforts among the people in his department. People were accountable for their individual performance and viewed this as fair and equitable (Mohrman and Cohen, forthcoming). The logic of the team-based organization challenges the assumptions of the traditional organization. People need to make deep changes in their basic assumptions, values, beliefs, and behaviors to adapt to the new team-based setting. Several components of this change are discussed below.

• *Change in the definition of a job.* In the traditional, hierarchical organization, individuals were placed in a position and were responsible for performing the duties listed in that position's job description. In the team-based organization, job descriptions may not exist. Instead, a person's job may be applying a set of competencies to a variety of problems in a changing set of teams. Doing one's job means working with others across functions and across systemic levels and being able to make trade-offs that consider the divergent perspectives at all levels. It means negotiating priorities with those who have some stake in one's performance. Dealing with ambiguity, uncertainty, and continual change is not an exception but is a routine part of one's job; there is no steady state. A company moving to a team-based design must ask whether its employees will accept this notion of a job. Do they have the cognitive abilities to deal with the complexity that must be managed? Do they have the adaptability to cope with constant change?

• *Change in working relationships.* In the hierarchical organization, the manager mediated the relationships among co-workers. In the team-based organization, people work directly with those with whom they are interdependent. Rather than depending upon a job description and direction from the manager, people work jointly with co-workers to determine what they do. Co-workers are likely to come from different functions and backgrounds and thus are likely to have different values, expectations, and priorities. Because personal success is dependent upon collective success, the fate of an individual is tied to co-workers who may not share the same assumptions about how things should be done. For some, this situation offers opportunities to expand horizons and skills and knowledge: working closely with co-workers and producing something together can create meaning and be emotionally satisfying; feelings of mutual trust and partnership may engender effective collaboration. This dependence on co-workers is difficult for certain individuals to accept or manage, however. What if co-workers are not dependable? What if self-interest rather than collective interest guides behaviors? What if feelings of anger, competitiveness, and powerlessness get in the way of effective collaboration? The organization transitioning to teams needs to determine what will help its people develop the collaborative relationships required in the team-based setting.

• *Change in the basic role and function of management.* What management is and does fundamentally changes in the team-based organization. In the hierarchical organization, managers provided direction and supervised the performance of the individuals who reported to them. Authority went hand in hand with rank. In the team-based organization, multiple reporting relationships are common, managers may belong to management teams that are collectively responsible for setting direction, nonmanagers may belong to integrating teams that are collectively responsible for integrating the work of their peers, managers may serve on teams as equal members with nonmanagers, and nonmanagers may be assigned to team leadership roles. In the team-based organization, scope of authority is separate from hierarchical rank. This is a sea change that challenges basic assumptions about the legitimacy of authority. What gives peers the right to set parameters that constrain the activity of peers? Why should someone who is the head of a function accept the recommendations of a cross-functional team composed of members lower in the hierarchy? If position does not bestow authority, what should be its source? The complexity of the multiplicity of roles is also difficult to deal with. Who are the leaders? Who are the led? Both managers and employees in the team-based organization need to be able to adjust to this dramatic shift in the managerial role.

• *Change in performance requirements.* In the traditional, hierarchical organization, individuals were concerned with their own performance. If they met their objectives, they succeeded (even if business objectives were not met). In the team-based organization, people are responsible for collective performance at multiple systemic levels. Individuals are part of teams that need to be concerned with the business unit's performance, the team's performance, and their own performance. Optimizing performance at any one level may hurt performance at another level. The trade-offs may not be obvious, however; the link between behavior and performance at one level may be uncertain and at multiple levels indeterminate. Considering the impact of different approaches to a problem on performance at multiple levels is cognitively challenging. So is negotiating with teammates and others about the trade-offs that should be considered. Teammates are likely to view the required trade-offs from very different perspectives. Will the cognitive complexity of trying to optimize performance at multiple systemic levels outstrip many people's capacity to process and integrate information? Can people develop the interpersonal skills required to collectively make good decisions under these conditions?

• *Change in the basis of accountability.* In the traditional organization, people were held accountable for individual performance. In the team-based organization, accountability is broadened: people are held accountable for collective results. These results can be at the level of the business unit or the team. Individuals are still held accountable, but it is in the context of achieving collective results. Reconceiving accountability so that collective accountability makes sense and is viewed as fair is a dramatic shift. The bureaucratic logic of thinking about accountability only in terms of individuals is ingrained in many organizational participants. They may not be able to picture what it means to hold a collection of people accountable. If a team performs well, how do you reward the team? What do you do if some team members fail to do their share of the work? If a team performs poorly, how do you punish the team? At the extreme, can you fire a team?

Part of the difficulty in viewing collective accountability as fair has to do with feelings of control. Individuals have more control over their own behavior than the behavior of others. Especially in the early stages of the team transition, team members may not view themselves as having sufficient control over team performance. If they feel that they cannot sufficiently influence the other members of the team, they may be concerned that they will be hurt by others' poor performance. These feelings may exist even if a team is relatively self-managing and members plan how they will work together to achieve performance goals. A second obstacle to viewing collective accountability as equitable is the human need to know where we stand. People are concerned that they will not get adequate feedback on how they are performing when the focus is on collective performance. This concern is sometimes reality-based; in work that is highly interdependent, it is not possible to differentiate separate contributions. Ironically, under these conditions, basing accountability on individual performance is less fair than basing it on team performance. A third issue is pervasive cultural values. In an individualistic culture such as the United States (and in the traditional corporate culture), people value individual responsibility and individual achievement. It may take time and experience in a team-based organization for people to adjust their notions of fairness and equity to include collective accountability.

• *Change in the levels of commitment.* In the traditional organization, employees were paid for doing their jobs and were not expected to do more. The team-based organization demands high commitment to both work and co-workers (Mohrman and Cohen, forthcoming). The performance demands and the requirements for integration in the team-based organization mean that people need to take the initiative to solve complex problems and work through difficult lateral transactions. People are collectively responsible for doing what is necessary to achieve performance goals. Because people must rely on one another and often must work very closely together in order to achieve collective goals, the team-based organization also requires high levels of commitment to co-workers. This commitment implies that relationships tap both professional and personal elements and that an emotional bond exists (Kahn, 1990).

This requirement for high levels of commitment to work and to co-workers runs counter to other trends occurring in the team-based organization. Many work relationships are temporary; teams form and disband when their projects are concluded, and many projects are short-term. In addition, people may work on teams that are not co-located but whose interactions are computer-mediated. Many organizations even have "virtual teams"—groups of people who are linked electronically but are not formally constituted as teams.

Finally, companies have redefined the employment contract. No longer can an employee expect a lifetime career with the same company. Years of downsizing have communicated to employees that companies are not committed to them.

Thus, on the one hand, the team-based organization is calling for high levels of commitment to work and to co-workers. On the other hand, work relationships are temporary and mediated by computer, and employment stability no longer exists. Are the requirements for commitment in the team-based organization unreasonably inconsistent with the temporary nature of the work and relationships? Can companies expect employees to be committed to their work and teammates when they cannot promise employment stability? Will people be willing to invest themselves in their work and do whatever is required to succeed?

In general, the psychological contract between employer and employee has been fundamentally altered. The past understandings about jobs, work relationships, management, performance, accountability, and commitment are no longer applicable. The new contract is in the process of being written; it is emerging as people work together in new ways. It has been suggested, for example, that organizations have a responsibility to provide their employees with opportunities to develop "career resiliency"—that is, to develop skills and experiences for employability in the future (Waterman, Waterman, and Collard, 1994). Team-based organizations would appear to be an ideal place for employees to have such diverse experiences and gain varied skills, but the cognitive and emotional demands are high.

Some companies have already moved a significant way along the path toward teams, and they have achieved some successes. They are experiencing considerable performance improvement, and many of their managers and employees are enthusiastic about the new ways of doing things. They enjoy working in teams, having the opportunity for growth, development, change, and challenge, and being part of collective efforts. They appreciate the opportunity to manage themselves and deal with significant issues. The experiences of these companies provide evidence that the team-based organization can operate effectively.

Suggested Future Research Areas

The organizations that have begun the transition to teams are pioneers. Much will be learned from their experiences. These organizations are identifying the problems that this transition entails and developing approaches and tools for dealing with them. Academic researchers are joining the practitioners in generating knowledge that can be useful for those attempting to survive and even thrive on this frontier. In this section, we will speculate about further knowledge that needs to be developed to better understand the conditions for success in the team-based organization.

Coping with Complexity

The crux of many of the issues discussed above is the ability to cope with complexity. How well can organizational participants cope with the cognitive and social complexity involved in making decisions in a network of people across functions and across systemic levels, for example, or with the complexity created by constant change? What can be done to help people deal with the complexity created by the team-based organization?

Basic research on cognition can help. First, we need to have a better idea of the cognitive capacities and limits of individual human beings. Is the cognitive ability required to make good decisions that take into account multiple and changing dimensions a matter of general intelligence? Are there specialized abilities that are needed? What are they?

Second, group-level research on human cognition is needed. What can groups do to improve the collective ability of their members to process complex information? Are groups more or less than the sum of their parts? Cognitive and organizational researchers working together could provide leverage on all these questions.

A related issue addresses whether organizations can select for the ability to deal with cognitive and social complexity. Should team-based organizations assess prospective employees' cognitive ability to deal with complex decision making under conditions of extreme uncertainty, for example? This is a dubious proposition: we are not confident that valid selection tests could even be developed. Previous experience working in teams may be the best predictor of someone's ability to deal with social and cognitive complexity. However, perhaps assessment simulations could be designed to provide realistic job previews and elicit information about a person's capacity and inclination to deal with decision making in a team situation. Given that we know that human cognitive limits are surpassed in most organizations (Cyert and March, 1963; Simon, 1957), the best approach may be to provide tools to help individuals and teams process information and make decisions.

The development of tools to support collaborative decision making is the most promising arena. In our study, as we have discussed throughout the book, we found systematic decision-making processes of various kinds to be strongly related to team and business-unit effectiveness. Organizations could develop a decision-making process that specified the steps to be taken in evaluating cross-functional and systemic trade-offs, for example; this process could help the team decide who needed to be involved in the decision, the steps that needed to be followed, and the data that needed to be considered, and it could provide methods for evaluating alternatives and trade-offs at both the team level and the business-unit level.

Systematic decision-making processes are cognitive tools. Electronic group-decision support systems that expedite these decision-making processes are tools of a more tangible nature. Although the concept of group-decision support systems has been around for about twenty years (Johansen, 1988), few commercial products have been developed, and their use has been limited. However, we expect to see rapid expansion in the development of these tools.

Finally, organizations that explicitly manage their learning processes can help people enhance their capacity to deal with decision-making complexity. By institutionalizing forums for reflection and dialogue about decisions reached and alternatives considered (and not considered), organizations can help participants refine their thinking. In the process, organizations can expand their ability to deal with complexity.

Dealing with Changing Relationships at Work

As discussed above, the nature of relationships with co-workers and with managers has changed in the team-based organization. The required dependence upon co-workers can bring up difficult emotional issues, while the need to relate to a complex array of bosses, some with and some without hierarchical authority, can tap complex and personal feelings about authority. These changing relationships suggest two major issues: What can be learned to help people adapt to the new affective demands, and what new conceptual underpinnings regarding the legitimacy of authority need to be developed?

Although many people respond positively to team settings, we know there are some managers and employees who have great difficulty adjusting. Basing their work on clinical, psychological research (Bowlby, 1980; Freud, 1936), Kahn and Kram (1994) postulate that people have an internal model of authority formed early in life that they bring to their work relationships with peers and bosses. Clearly, for some individuals, the emotional demands triggered by being dependent on peers, relating to multiple bosses, and dealing with a changing configuration of relationships can create the kind of insecurity that generates dysfunctional behaviors. For others, being free of the monolithic boss-subordinate relationship is experienced as liberating. How important are individual differences? Are there particular team dynamics that stimulate either appropriate or inappropriate behavioral responses?

We need to learn how to help people cope with the demands of these new relationships. Therapeutic insights suggest that change comes from becoming aware of defense strategies and inappropriate patterns of behaviors and thoughts and developing new ways of relating to others. Awareness of patterns usually occurs through feedback about the effectiveness of behaviors from those with whom significant relationships exist. This sort of feedback can be problematic in a work relationship, though. Is it appropriate for people at work to give each other this type of personal feedback? Most organizational participants do not have the therapeutic skills (or the time) required to guide co-workers through a process of personal change. Organizations may be able to expand their personal assistance programs to provide support that enables people to reflect upon the difficulties they are experiencing in their work relationships and what could be done to better manage them.

New concepts that define legitimate authority need to be developed. If authority no longer stems from position, what should be its base? Perhaps legitimate authority can be redefined as being derived from principle, mandate, and expertise. We have argued in this book that no team has the decision-making authority to resolve issues that go beyond its bounds and that the appropriate forum for a broader issue involves representatives of the various units that will be affected. By this standard, then, scope of authority depends upon systemic level. This can be the principle underlying a new concept of legitimacy.

When teams are chartered, their scope of authority needs to be explicitly defined. To ensure an organizational mandate, that charter then needs to be shared with all stakeholders, along with a specification of the roles, responsibilities, and authority of team leaders and managers. The mandate serves the purpose of creating and formalizing shared agreement to specific descriptions of scope of authority.

Expertise is another basis for legitimate authority. People are more likely to recognize authority in those who have the expertise (including both technical competence and interpersonal skills) to get things done. Expertise is an attribute of the person rather than of the person's role. Viewing personal attributes rather than position as a basis for legitimacy is beginning to have some currency, and it certainly fits the requirements of the team-based organization.

Developing New Underpinnings for Performance Management and Accountability

We have argued that the new performance management processes and collective accountability entail a change in people's definitions of equity. The new performance management processes include review systems that collect input from multiple stakeholders about performance at multiple levels and reward systems (such as gain-sharing and team bonuses) that recognize performance at multiple levels. These new systems require people to accept that different stakeholders have the right to evaluate performance and that holding people accountable for collective results is equitable. They raise the question of what the conceptual underpinnings for the new performance management systems should be.

We need additional research on performance management, accountability, and equity in team-based settings. This new research has to be guided by the assumptions of the team-based organization. Unfortunately, most research and consulting on appraisal systems has been based on the traditional, hierarchical assumption of the manager-subordinate reporting relationship. This research has proceeded on the related assumptions that the manager is the appropriate evaluator of the subordinate's performance, that individual performance is what should be measured, and that it is possible to design a system that accurately and objectively measures performance. These assumptions are inconsistent with the logic of the team-based organization. As already discussed, there are multiple appropriate evaluators of performance—customers, peers, and managers—and each is likely to view performance from a unique, subjective perspective. These stakeholders will give feedback in both overlapping and unique performance domains. For example, only customers can say how satisfied or dissatisfied they are. On the other hand, both customers and managers can give input as to how responsive the team has been their requests (although their experiences may differ). The balance among the various perspectives is important.

The new research will need to take these different assumptions into account and develop new conceptual underpinnings for its activities. One possible underpinning is the concept of consensual validity. If different stakeholders have their own unique perspective on performance, then any particular viewpoint is subjective, reflecting a particular experience with the focal performing unit. The viewpoints in total, generally containing areas of both agreement and disagreement, reflect how the performing unit satisfied the needs of its multiple stakeholders. Once those viewpoints have been aired, the focal unit needs to engage in a process of dialogue with its stakeholders to make sense of the performance information it receives—a process that is the basis of consensual validity. That sense-making process might take place with the focal unit's management (which may have also received input from all stakeholders) or with representatives of the stakeholder groups. Together, they can work to reach agreement about how well the focal unit is performing and about areas that need improvement. Consensual validity is achieved by developing shared agreement about performance that takes into consideration the relevant multiple viewpoints.

New definitions of equity need to be developed that take into consideration collective responsibility for success. Traditional views of equity have been shaped by the traditional, hierarchical model: individuals compare their compensation and their performance and capabilities with those of others and determine whether they have been fairly treated. The new definitions of equity will consider that the assessment of performance and the distribution of rewards need to occur, at least in part, at the collective level, because it is teams and networks of contributors that collectively are responsible for results. These new definitions will often be buttressed by the fact that objective measures of results may exist only at the collective level. These definitions are likely to evolve from experiences in the lateral organization. Feelings about equity are very personal and are likely to be shaped by experience. We see evidence that, as people work in team-based settings and discover how much they mutually have to rely on one another, their beliefs change; they want to be assessed at least in part based on how well their team performs.

In general, organizational practice precedes theory. Organizations making the transition to teams are propelled by forces so powerful that the organizations cannot wait for academic theory and research to catch up; they are changing before academic theory and research can provide the underpinnings for sound practices. The changes involved in this transition are so fundamental that academic researchers will have to spend time finding out how much existing theory and research still applies and how much new theory needs to be developed to understand, explain, and predict behavior in team-based settings. These changing organizations provide exhilarating opportunities for the development of new knowledge. The development of sound organizational practices and systems depends upon replacing the old bureaucratic paradigm with a new one. That new paradigm is being developed as more is learned about this dynamic organizational form.

References

Allen, T. J., and Scott Morton, M. S. (eds.). *Information Technology and the Corporation of the 1990's: Research Studies*. New York: Oxford University Press, 1994.

Ancona, D. G., and Caldwell, D. F. "Bridging the Boundary: External Activity and Performance in Organizational Teams." *Administrative Science Quarterly*, 1992, *37*, 634–665.

Beekun, R. I. "Assessing the Effectiveness of Sociotechnical Interventions: Antidote or Fad?" *Human Resources*, 1989, *47*(10), 877–897.

Beer, M., Eisenstat, R. A., and Spector, B. *The Critical Path to Corporate Renewal*. Cambridge, Mass.: Harvard Business School Press, 1990.

Bennis, W., and Nanus, B. *Leaders: The Strategies for Taking Charge*. New York: HarperCollins, 1985.

Block, P. *The Empowered Manager: Positive Political Skills at Work*. San Francisco: Jossey-Bass, 1987.

Block, P. *Stewardship: Choosing Service over Self-Interest*. San Francisco: Berrett-Koehler, 1993.

Bowlby, J. *Attachment and Loss: Loss, Sadness, and Depression*. Vol. 3. New York: Basic Books, 1980.

Burns, J. M. *Leadership*. New York: HarperCollins, 1978.

Cohen, S. G. "Designing Effective Self-Managing Work Teams." In M. Beyerlein (ed.), *Advances in Interdisciplinary Studies of Work Teams*. Vol. 1: *Self-Managed Work Teams*. Greenwich, Conn.: JAI Press, 1994.

Cummings, T. G. "Self-Regulating Work Groups: A Socio-Technical Synthesis." *Academy of Management Review*, 1978, *3*, 625–634.

Cyert, R., and March, J. *The Behavioral Theory of the Firm*. Englewood Cliffs, N.J.: Prentice-Hall, 1963.

Davenport, T. H. *Process Innovation: Re-engineering Work Through Information Technology*. Cambridge, Mass.: Harvard Business School Press, 1993.

Deming, W. E. *Out of the Crisis*. Cambridge, Mass.: Center for Advanced Engineering Study, Massachusetts Institute of Technology, 1986.

Donnellon, A. *The Paradoxes and Contradictions of Team Work*. Cambridge, Mass.: Harvard Business School Press, forthcoming.

Dougherty, D. "Interpretive Barriers to Successful Product Innovation in Large Firms." *Organizational Science*, 1992, 3(2), 179–202.

Dyer, W. G. *Team Building: Issues and Alternatives*. (2nd ed.) Reading, Mass.: Addison-Wesley, 1987.

Fisher, K. *Leading Self-Directing Work Teams: A Guide to Developing New Team Leadership Skills*. New York: McGraw-Hill, 1993.

Freud, A. *The Ego and the Mechanisms of Defense*. Madison, Conn.: International · Universities Press, 1936.

Galbraith, J. R. *Designing Complex Organizations*. Reading, Mass.: Addison-Wesley, 1973.

Galbraith, J. R. "The Business Unit of the Future." In J. R. Galbraith, E. E. Lawler III, and Associates, *Organizing for the Future: The New Logic for Managing Complex Organizations*. San Francisco: Jossey-Bass, 1993.

Galbraith, J. R. *Competing with Flexible Lateral Organizations*. (2nd ed.) Reading, Mass.: Addison-Wesley, 1994.

Galbraith, J. R., and Kazanjian, R. K. *Strategy Implementation: Structure, Systems, and Process*. (2nd ed.) St. Paul, Minn.: West, 1986.

Galbraith, J. R., and Lawler, E. E., III. "New Roles for the Staff Function: Strategic Support and Services." In J. R. Galbraith, E. E. Lawler III, and Associates, *Organizing for the Future: The New Logic for Managing Complex Organizations*. San Francisco: Jossey-Bass, 1993.

Galbraith, J. R., Lawler, E. E., III, and Associates. *Organizing for the Future: The New Logic for Managing Complex Organizations*. San Francisco: Jossey-Bass, 1993.

Glaser, B. G., and Strauss, A. L. *The Discovery of Grounded Theory*. Hawthorne, N.Y.: Aldine, 1967.

Goodman, P. S., Devadas, R., and Hughson, T. L. "Groups and Productivity: Analyzing the Effectiveness of Self-Managing Teams." In J. P. Campbell, R. J. Campbell, and Associates, *Productivity in Organizations: New Perspectives from Industrial and Organizational Psychology*. San Francisco: Jossey-Bass, 1988.

Hackman, J. R. "The Psychology of Self-Management in Organizations." In M. S. Pallak and R. O. Perloff (eds.), *Psychology and Work: Productivity,*

Change, and Employment. Washington, D.C.: American Psychological Association, 1986.

Hackman, J. R. "The Design of Work Teams." In J. W. Lorsch (ed.), *Handbook of Organizational Behavior.* Englewood Cliffs, N.J.: Prentice-Hall, 1987.

Hackman, J. R. (ed.). *Groups That Work (and Those That Don't): Creating Conditions for Effective Teamwork.* San Francisco: Jossey-Bass, 1990.

Hackman, J. R., and Oldham, G. R. "Motivation Through the Design of Work: Test of a Theory." *Organizational Behavior and Human Performance,* 1976, *16,* 250–279.

Hackman, J. R., and Oldham, G. R. *Work Redesign.* Reading, Mass.: Addison-Wesley, 1980.

Hammer, M., and Champy, J. *Reengineering the Corporation.* New York: Harper Business Press, 1993.

Hauser, J. R., and Clausing, D. "The House of Quality." *Harvard Business Review,* May-June 1988, pp. 63–73.

Johansen, R. *Groupware: Computer Support for Business Teams.* New York: Free Press, 1988.

Juran, J. M. *Juran on Leadership for Quality.* New York: Free Press, 1989.

Kahn, W. A. "Psychological Conditions of Personal Engagement and Disengagement at Work." *Academy of Management Journal,* 1990, *33*(4), 692–724.

Kahn, W. A., and Kram, K. E. "Authority at Work: Internal Models and Their Organizational Consequences." *Academy of Management Review,* 1994, *19*(1), 17–50.

Kanter, R. M. *The Change Masters.* New York: Simon & Schuster, 1983.

Katzenbach, J. R., and Smith, D. K. *The Wisdom of Teams: Creating the High-Performance Organization.* Cambridge, Mass.: Harvard Business School Press, 1993.

Klein, J., and Maurer, P. "Integrators, not Generalists, Needed: A Case Study of IPD Teams at Textron Defense Systems." Case Study—Lean 94–01, Massachusetts Institute of Technology, January 17, 1994.

Lawler, E. E., III. *High-Involvement Management: Participative Strategies for Improving Organizational Performance.* San Francisco: Jossey-Bass, 1986.

Lawler, E. E., III. *The Ultimate Advantage: Creating the High-Involvement Organization.* San Francisco: Jossey-Bass, 1992.

Lawler, E. E., III, and Mohrman, S. A. "Quality Circles After the Fad." *Harvard Business Review,* Jan.-Feb. 1985, pp. 64–71.

Lawler, E. E., III, and Mohrman, S. A. "Quality Circles: After the Honeymoon." *Organizational Dynamics,* Spring 1987, pp. 42–55.

Lawler, E. E., III, and Mohrman, S. A. "With HR Help, All Managers Can Practice High-Involvement Management." *Personnel,* Apr. 1989, pp. 26–31.

Lawler, E. E., III, Mohrman, S. A., and Ledford, G. E., Jr. *Employee Involvement and Total Quality Management: Practices and Results in Fortune 1000 Companies*. San Francisco: Jossey-Bass, 1992.

Lawrence, P. R., and Lorsch, J. W. *Organization and Environment*. Homewood, Ill.: Irwin, 1969.

Ledford, G. E., Jr., Lawler, E. E., III, and Mohrman, S. A. "The Quality Circle and Its Variations." In J. P. Campbell, R. J. Campbell, and Associates, *Productivity in Organizations: New Perspectives from Industrial and Organizational Psychology*. San Francisco: Jossey-Bass, 1988.

Ledford, G. E., Jr., Mohrman, S. A., Mohrman, A. M., Jr., and Lawler, E. E., III. "The Phenomenon of Large-Scale Organizational Change." In A. M. Mohrman, Jr., and Associates, *Large-Scale Organizational Change*. San Francisco: Jossey-Bass, 1989.

Lewin, K. *Field Theory in Social Science*. New York: HarperCollins, 1951.

Likert, R. *New Patterns of Management*. New York: McGraw-Hill, 1961.

Lubinski, D., and Dawis, R. "Aptitudes, Skills, and Proficiencies." In M. D. Dunnette and L. M. Hough (eds.), *Handbook of Industrial and Organizational Psychology*. Vol. 3. (2nd ed.) Palo Alto, Calif.: Consulting Psychologists Press, 1992.

Macy, B. A., Bliese, P. D., and Norton, J. J. "Organizational Change and Work Innovation: A Meta-Analysis of 131 North American Field Experiments—1961–1990." Paper presented at the National Academy of Management meeting, Miami, Aug. 1991.

Manz, C. C., and Sims, H. P. *Superleadership: Leading Others to Lead Themselves*. Englewood Cliffs, N.J.: Prentice-Hall, 1989.

McGregor, D. *The Human Side of Enterprise*. New York: McGraw-Hill, 1960.

Melcher, R. "Roles and Relationships: Clarifying the Manager's Job." *Personnel*, May-June 1967.

Mohrman, A. M., Jr., and Associates. *Large-Scale Organizational Change*. San Francisco: Jossey-Bass, 1989.

Mohrman, A. M., Jr., Mohrman, S. A., and Lawler, E. E., III. "The Performance Management of Teams." In W. Bruns (ed.), *Performance Measurement, Evaluation, and Incentives*. Cambridge, Mass.: Harvard Business School Press, 1992.

Mohrman, A. M., Jr., Mohrman, S. A., and Worley, C. G. "High-Technology Performance Management." In M. A. Von Glinow and S. A. Mohrman (eds.), *Managing Complexity in High-Technology Organizations*. New York: Oxford University Press, 1990.

Mohrman, S. A. "Empowerment: There's More to It Than Meets the Eye."

Tapping the Network: Journal of the Quality and Productivity Management Association, 1993 4(1), 14–17.

Mohrman, S. A., and Cohen, S. G. "When People Get Out of the Box: New Attachments to Co-Workers." In A. Howard (ed.), *The Changing Nature of Work*. San Francisco: Jossey-Bass, forthcoming.

Mohrman, S. A., and Cummings, T. G. *Self-Designing Organizations: Learning How to Create High Performance*. Reading, Mass.: Addison-Wesley, 1989.

Mohrman, S. A., and Ledford, G. E., Jr. "The Design of Employee Participation Groups: Guidelines Based on Empirical Research." *Human Resources Management*, 1985, 24(3).

Mohrman, S. A., and Mohrman, A. M., Jr. "Organizational Change and Learning." In J. Galbraith, E. E. Lawler III, and Associates, *Organizing for the Future: The New Logic for Managing Complex Organizations*. San Francisco: Jossey-Bass, 1993.

Mohrman, S. A., Mohrman, A. M., Jr., and Cohen, S. G. "Organizing Knowledge Work Systems." In M. Beyerlein (ed.), *Knowledge-Workers in Teams*. Greenwich, Conn.: JAI Press, forthcoming.

Myer, C. *Fast Cycle Time: How to Align Purpose, Strategy, and Structure for Speed*. New York: Free Press, 1993.

Nadler, D. A., Gerstein, M. S., Shaw, R. B., and Associates. *Organizational Architecture: Designs for Changing Organizations*. San Francisco: Jossey-Bass, 1992.

Pasmore, W. A. *Designing Effective Organizations: The Sociotechnical Systems Perspective*. New York: Wiley, 1988.

Pava, C. *Managing New Office Technology: An Organizational Strategy*. New York: Free Press, 1983.

Pinchot, G., III. *Intrapreneuring*. New York: HarperCollins, 1985.

Savage, C. *5th Generation Management: Integrating Enterprises Through Human Networking*. Digital Press, 1990.

Scott Morton, M. S. *The Corporation of the 1990's: Information Technology and Organizational Transformation*. New York: Oxford University Press, 1991.

Senge, P. *The Fifth Discipline: The Art and Practice of the Learning Organization*. New York: Doubleday Currency, 1990.

Shaw, R. S., and Perkins, D. T. "Teaching Organizations to Learn: The Power of Productive Failures." In D. A. Nadler, M. S. Gerstein, R. B. Shaw, and Associates, *Organizational Architecture: Designs for Changing Organizations*. San Francisco: Jossey-Bass, 1992.

Simon, H. A. *Models of Man*. New York: Wiley, 1957.

Stalk, G., Jr., and Hout, T. M. *Competing Against Time*. New York: Free Press, 1990.

Stein, B. A., and Kanter, R. M. "Building the Parallel Organization: Creating Mechanisms for Permanent Quality of Work Life." *Journal of Applied Behavior Science*, 1980, *16*, 371–386.

Thompson, J. D. *Organizations in Action*. New York: McGraw-Hill, 1967.

Thompson, J. D., and Tuden, A. "Strategies, Structures, and Processes of Organizational Decision." In J. D. Thompson and others (eds.), *Comparative Studies in Administration*. Pittsburgh: University of Pittsburgh Press, 1959.

Trist, E. *The Evolution of Sociotechnical Systems*. Paper no. 2. Toronto: Quality of Working Life Center, 1981.

Trist, E., and Bamforth, K. "Some Social and Psychological Consequences of the Longwall Method of Coal-Getting." *Human Relations*, 1951, *1*, 3–38.

Van Berkholm, M., and Tsovold, D. "The Effects of Social Context on Engaging in Controversy." *Journal of Psychology*, 1981, *107*, 141–145.

Von Glinow, M. S. *The New Professionals*. New York: Ballinger, 1988.

Walton, R. E. *Up and Running: Integrating Information Technology and the Organization*. Cambridge, Mass.: Harvard Business School Press, 1989.

Waterman, R. H., Waterman, J. A., and Collard, B. A. "Toward a Career-Resilient Workforce." *Harvard Business Review*, July-Aug. 1994, pp. 87–95.

Wellins, R. S., Byham, W. C., and Wilson, J. M. *Empowered Teams: Creating Self-Directed Work Groups That Improve Quality, Productivity, and Participation*. San Francisco: Jossey-Bass, 1991.

Wheelwright, S. C., and Clark, K. B. *Revolutionizing New Product Development*. New York: Free Press, 1992.

Zand, D. "Collateral Organizations: A New Change Strategy." *Journal of Applied Behavior Science*, 1974, *10*, 63–89.

Zuboff, S. *In the Age of the Smart Machine: The Future of Work and Power*. New York: Basic Books, 1984.

Index

Jon Werner